T0244508

THE
Teaching Office
IN THE
Reformed Tradition

THE
Teaching Office
IN THE
Reformed Tradition

A History of the Doctoral Ministry

ROBERT W. HENDERSON

WIPF & STOCK · Eugene, Oregon

Wipf and Stock Publishers
199 W 8th Ave, Suite 3
Eugene, OR 97401

The Teaching Office in the Reformed Tradition
A History of the Doctoral Ministry
By Henderson, Robert W.
ISBN 13: 948-1-62564-581-4
Publication date 1/10/2014
Previously published by Westminster Press, 1962

*In love and gratitude
to my parents*

Contents

vii

Preface

At a time when one of the major American communions of a Calvinistic heritage is engaged in an extensive and intensive restudy of the " Nature of the Ministry," at a time when the whole matter of the church's relation to education, particularly to higher education, and the relation of the " Christian " college to the church is under extensive and intensive discussion, it would appear that a historical inquiry into the background and practice of a particular teaching office of the church in the academic arena is not without some peculiar value. The present text, although extensively revised, originally took shape as a dissertation under the direction of Prof. George Huntston Williams at Harvard Divinity School. To Dr. Williams and to Profs. John T. McNeill, Heiko A. Oberman, and Dean Douglas Horton, I owe a great deal more than I can express in this limited space. Particularly, am I indebted to them for their recognition of the current value of the subject matter for the contemporary church and the advisability of continuing the discussion beyond bounds ordinarily set for a dissertation project.

Every author who has arrived at the point of looking back must recognize how impossible would have been the task except for the gracious and efficient co-operation of many others. In this connection my appreciation goes to Mr. and Mrs. Walter Grossman and Mr. Herbert Kleist,

2 PREFACE

of the Harvard University Libraries; to Mr. Guy Klett, of
the Presbyterian Historical Society; to Rev. Calvin
Schmitt, at McCormick Theological Seminary Library;
and in a special measure to Rev. James Tanis, librarian of
Andover-Harvard Theological Library. I count among the
willing co-workers Mrs. Jane Reuf, Mrs. Norma Lou
Bridges, and Mrs. Marylee Gulliksen, who have typed all
or part of the manuscript in its various stages of preparation.

And yet, when all appreciation is duly noted and expressed, there remains the undoubted fact that without the
support, encouragement, and understanding of my wife,
June, and our children this study would never have been
completed. By their love, I am humbled and sustained.

R.W.H.

The University of Tulsa
Tulsa, Oklahoma

Frequently Used Abbreviations

Aymon	*Tous les synodes nationaux des églises réformées.*
B.U.K.	*Acts and Proceedings of the Kirk of Scotland, 1560–1616.*
CO	*Joannis Calvini opera quae supersunt omnia.*
Fasti	*Fasti Ecclesiae Scoticanae.*
Genevan Order	*Forms of Prayers and Ministration of the Sacraments used in the English Congregation at Geneva.*
Haag-1	*La France protestante* (1846–1858).
Haag-2	*La France protestante* (1877–1888).
Inst.	*The Institutes of the Christian Religion* (Calvin)
Pardovan	*Collections and Observations Concerning the Worship, Discipline, and Government of the Church of Scotland.*
Post-Acta	*De Post-Acta of Nahandelingen van de Nationale Synode van Dordrecht.*

3

Quick	*Synodicon in Gallia Reformata*
Reitsma en van Veen	*Acta der Provinciale en Particuliere Synoden, gehouden . . . gedurende de jaren 1572–1620.*
Sewall	"A Brief Survey of the Congregational Churches and Ministers in the County of Middlesex, and in Chelsea in the County of Suffolk."
Acta Syn. S. Holl.	*Acta der . . . synoden van Zuid-Holland, 1621–1700.*
WAD *Min.*	"Minutes of the Sessions," Westminster Assembly of Divines, on microfilm from original manuscripts and transcriptions.

I

Introduction

THE EDUCATIONAL TASK, or " ministry," of Protestantism has been undergoing a protracted scrutiny during the past two or three decades. It is not yet altogether clear what this scrutiny will produce, motivated as it is by so many divergent factors. The " high priests " of religious education have had their day, and now the churches know that they " must teach or die." [1]

Because of a combination of historical circumstances, the re-evaluation of the church's teaching ministry is currently being carried on most resolutely in relation to two apparently disassociated arenas of its organizational life: the congregational church (Sunday) school, and the church's involvement with the collegiate campus. In the case of the former, I refer the reader to Wesner Fallaw's *Church Education for Tomorrow* (The Westminster Press, 1960), and for the situation on the campus, I believe that some of the roots of the problem have been admirably stated by John S. Duley in his provocative article, " The Work of the Church in the University " (*The Christian Scholar*, September, 1959).[2] The fact that the discus-

[1] The slogan with which the *Christian Faith and Life* curriculum was ushered into the congregations of the then Presbyterian Church in the U.S.A.

[2] Vol. XLII/3, pp. 201–214. The comments of Pastor Henry Horn, of the Cambridge (Mass.) University Lutheran Church, should be read in connection with this; *ibid.*, Vol. XLIII/1 (March 1960), pp. 8–10.

sion is being carried on in apparently disparate areas must not blind us to the fact that the problems are essentially similar, that the questions being raised are mutually inclusive.

It is not my purpose here to pay attention to all the questions, important as they are, that obtrude in the current re-evaluation of the traditional educational patterns within the contemporary church, but rather to confine my perspective to the problem of the office and function of the teacher. The " teaching ministry" remains an abstraction until it takes on flesh and blood in the form of persons. This truism is not intended to degrade or call in question the didactic function of the corporate institution; rather, it is intended to underscore the fact that the *magistral* function always is exercised by particular members of the one body at any given time, in any given place. This is highlighted when we note that both Fallaw and Duley raise a basic question in relation to whom the specific ministry of teaching *within* the church shall be committed. Fallaw wishes to call the clerical leader of the parish " pastor-teacher," and Duley is concerned to style the accepted function of university pastor by the term " teaching elder." I do not believe that either author is motivated by a desire to play a game of semantic chess, to substitute one title for another that has been outgrown or tainted by evil association. Rather, I suspect that both are motivated by the purest of reasons, the realization that there is a didactic function within the church which devolves on some of its members in a way that it does not on others, just as there is a pastoral function that devolves on some and not on others, or a governing function that is the lot of some and not of others. Furthermore, this didactic function places the individual to whom it has been committed in a peculiar relationship with the whole body which appears to necessitate a kind of recognition (" office," if you like) that is not, willy-nilly, the recognition of all Christians.

Ironically, such an attempt to reidentify the church's teaching with a particular office comes exactly at a time when the nature of the whole "public ministry" of the church is undergoing rather drastic reassessment, with the result that a sharp and definite "image" of what the "public ministry" consists is extremely difficult to present with any kind of clarity.

It would appear that one of the weaknesses of certain features of the re-evaluation of both the total public ministry of the church and the particular teaching ministry is the absence of a dependable body of historical data on which to hypothesize, evaluate, criticize, and extrapolate. Thus, in the study carried out for the American Association of Theological Schools (1954–1956), under the direction of Prof. H. Richard Niebuhr, regarding the educative process associated with the preparation for the American Protestant parish ministry, the need for a volume devoted to the historical development of the ministerial office was regarded as an extremely desirable project, even though its subject matter lay outside of the field of the inquiry (H. Richard Niebuhr and Daniel D. Williams, eds., *The Ministry in Historical Perspectives;* Harper & Brothers, 1956).

That contemporary Protestantism must pause momentarily to reassess the role, character, and function of its "public ministry" is not necessarily a sign of weakness or of lack of vitality, although there are those both on the ecclesiological "right" and eschatological "left" who will draw such conclusions. Rather, this venture of internal analysis may very well argue that the Protestant tradition is simply being itself when it seeks to "reform" a part of its total life in terms that will more adequately allow it to be an effective instrument for the purposes God has laid upon it.

However, current reform cut off from any anchor in tradition runs the risk of repeating the same errors that have plagued previous generations. I do not mean to imply that tradition, as such, is sacrosanct or that attention to it is insurance against contemporary error. I do mean that in a particular sense the controversy that God has had with his people, and the responses men have made to God, are the very stuff of history and tradition. As such, they convey a " revelation " of the divine in the human scene, and are to be given both positive and negative weight.

One of the side effects of the ecumenical movement of the mid-twentieth century has been a renaissance of confessionalism, a resurgence of traditional family loyalties. In some quarters this resurgence has been frankly obscurantist. But there are many issues up for restudy simply because Christians of various traditions are aware, as they have not been for some generations, that they need to know the roots of their own tradition and practice of the faith when they attempt to come to grips with what other equally sincere and dedicated Christians believe and practice. Because of the thorny questions that obtrude both in theory and in practice from the life of any Christian communion in relation to other Christian groups in regard to the nature of the " public ministry," there does not seem to be any point where a restudy of origins is more in demand than in the area of the nature of the " public ministry," that part of the church to whom are committed certain acts and responsibilities which are exercised for the whole.

A clear statement of the need and desirability of such a restudy of the traditional roles, functions, authorities, and responsibilities of the various offices of the ministry has been provided by Daniel T. Jenkins (*The Gift of Ministry;* Faber, London, 1947) . However, Jenkins points out a further factor that complicates the proceedings. The contemporary church is hampered, at least in part, because the church at large is so ill equipped with fruitful study of the interrelatedness of the offices by which it has sought to fulfill its total ministry in the past.

Thus, current studies based on the available sources of the history of the various offices of the "public ministry" would seem to be real desiderata within the life of the contemporary church. This is particularly true of the teaching ministry, partly because of the current temper of faultfinding, partly because in the attempt at reconstruction there are certain points to which the historian may speak with authority and say "this" and not that, or "that" and not this, are the facts, and partly because the Christian church needs to be reminded of its teaching officers. Nowhere is such reminder needed more than in relation to the Reformation office of the doctor.[3]

There is indeed an air of mystery about the disappearance (perhaps "atrophication" would be more exact) from the ecclesiology of one of the main currents of Reformation tradition of a separate, peculiar, yet integral teaching office. Perhaps the student or reader who has tried to cope with the doctrine of the "public ministry" as it is presented in John Calvin's great systematic work[4] has asked: "Who is Calvin's doctor? What is his function? Why did the church abandon what seems to have been a very special part of its ministerial function?" The reader of these places in the Institutes is familiar with the offices of pastor, elder, and deacon. He can point to individuals within the Christian community who are set apart and function as such, but the only "doctors" with whom he is acquainted are practitioners of some kind of medical art, or he may recognize the title as being associated with aca-

[3] The title "doctor" will be used generally throughout rather than the term "teacher," except where "teacher" appears in English documentary sources. Calvin used the term in a technical sense in 1539 (Reply to Sadolet, CO V:386).

[4] Calvin: Institutes of the Christian Religion, edited by John T. McNeill, translated and indexed by Ford Lewis Battles, in 2 vols. (The Westminster Press, 1960), Book IV; hereafter referred to as Inst. by book, chapter, section.

demic and research circles. But little of this has the slightest relation to the church, the Word of God, or the gospel. And yet Calvin, who has been commended by friend and foe alike for penetrating insight and clear exposition, regarded the office of doctor as sufficiently important to be included in his magnum opus of systematic theology as well as in the working constitution of the Church of Geneva. The *Ordonnances Ecclésiastiques* [5] were written and adopted in 1541, while the final Latin edition of the *Institutes* was not completed until 1559, yet both are equally explicit regarding the existence of the doctoral office as part of the church's ministry.

In brief, our problem would seem to be, How can we account for the place and importance attached to an office of the " public ministry " at a seminal stage in the church's life, yet also account for its demise or atrophication four centuries later if, as Prof. Wilhelm Pauck assures us, the Calvinian ecclesiological structure was built on the idea of the divine prescription of the " four ministerial offices "? [6] The idea of a " divine prescription " only evokes a deeper mystery, for there is certainly no unanimity among the heritors of Calvin as to the actual existence of such an office in the church. Heinrich Heppe has documented a lack of unanimity among the Continental Reformed commentators of the seventeenth and eighteenth centuries, [7] and expresses himself in such general language that the

[5] Text used is found in *CO* Xa:15, *Project d'Ordonnance Ecclésiastique*, 20 November 1541.

[6] " The Ministry in the Time of the Continental Reformation," in H. Richard Niebuhr and Daniel D. Williams (eds.), *op. cit.*, pp. 129–131.

[7] Heinrich Heppe, *Reformed Dogmatics* (London, 1950), pp. 676, 679–680, where the views of Gulielmus Bucanus (*Institutiones Theologicae*, Geneva, 1609), Johannes Wollebius (*Christianae Theologiae Compend.*, Basel, 1626), Samuelis Maresius (*Collegium Theologicum*, Geneva, 1662), Johannes Braunius (*Doctrina Foederum*, Amsterdam, 1688), J. H. Heideggerus (*Medulla Theologiae*, Zurich, 1696), and Petrus van Mastricht (Utrecht, 1714) are brought to bear on the question.

reader is not sure what his own opinions might be. Indeed, there is no doubt in some Reformed circles that the answer has been given unequivocally in the negative; Herman Bavinck states categorically that the doctoral office, especially when identified with the professorate of theology, does not relate to the church because it is " not of apostolic institution." [8]

However, it is necessary to point out that Heppe adduced the testimony of a comparatively select few of the commentators and that Bavinck was scarcely more catholic in the selection of his evidence; witness the spirited rejoinder of Ds. G. Doekes in the wake of what was evidently a rather extended newspaper controversy.[9] More recently, the question has been allowed to lie fallow, save for slighting references from time to time expressing doubts that the church ever really experienced the doctoral office as a ministry; a recent study concerning the nature of the Reformed ministry in the Reformation and post-Reformation period went so far as to disallow the whole question by demoting the doctor qua doctor from the ranks of the ministry altogether.[10]

In the face of all this negative and ambiguous evidence, the question naturally arises: Why flog a dead horse? Why spend any more time with an office of the ministry that has not stood the test of the church's life? The simple answer to this is that although the churches of the Reformation may have allowed one formal teaching office to atrophy, they have not thereby been able to exorcise the " memory " of such an office from their midst. Further-

[8] Cf. Herman Bavinck, *Gereformeerde Dogmatiek* (4 dln., 3d ed., J. H. Kok, Kampen, 1918), 4:423 and a published lecture on the subject, *Doctorenambt* (J. H. Kok, Kampen, 1899).

[9] Ds. G. Doekes, *Het kerkelijk Doctorenambt* (J. H. Kok, Kampen, 1917), especially pp. 74–102.

[10] James L. Ainslie, *The Doctrine of Ministerial Order in the Reformed Churches of the Sixteenth and Seventeenth Centuries* (T. & T. Clark, Edinburgh, 1940), p. 91.

more, this "memory" has insistently recrudesced in several interesting ways: (1) the long history of formal statements regarding a special doctoral status in the church in constitutional, liturgical, and doctrinal symbols; (2) the Puritan, especially the Independent Puritan, insistence and practice that every congregation ought to have a teacher as well as a pastor; (3) the special concerns that have marked certain phases of the church's involvement in "higher" education and in ministerial training; (4) the various movements of Christian nurture that began outside the church, partly because the church did not know how to deal with them, that having finally been accepted by the church, still create problems for the church in terms of personnel; (5) the current movement in a number of communions to provide training *and* status for a special educator's office, a movement that is not confined to communions maintaining a strong tie to the Calvinian tradition. And not least of all is (6) the current re-evaluation of the total nurturing ministry of the church that has caused some thinkers and writers to question the traditional, i.e., current, structure of the public ministry and to call for a reshaping if the task of the church is to be fulfilled.[11] Thus we are forced to conclude that the horse is not dead, that the need if not the realization remains as great today as it ever did, and that historical experience of the church in this matter may well speak to us today.

Because of the air of mystery, the forgotten but insistent "memory" that continues to obtrude, our task in this study will be anything but simple, yet we can proceed in a relatively simple way. First of all, we shall try to discover what John Calvin had in mind when he postulated a doctor as the second order of the public ministry of the

[11] That this is not confined to the English-speaking scene ought to guarantee the true catholicity of the quest; cf. *Foi et Vie*, No. 5 (September–October, 1957) as well as the more recent Conference on the Ministry at Bossey in 1960–1961.

church; next, we shall gather the available evidence showing that the Reformed churches recognized this office as
an integral part of the ministry of the church. By presenting evidence that the doctoral office was not only a formal
principle but a functioning principle in the exercise of the
public ministry of the churches, we shall lay the ground for
a description of the final developments in relation to the
atrophication of the office both on the Continent and in
America.

In collecting this evidence, we shall rely particularly on
the Church Orders of several Reformed communions as a
demonstration of what the " formal " mind of the church
was during a particular period. We shall supplement such
formal evidence, wherever possible, with material from
the active proceedings of judicatories, for these records
help demonstrate the practice in the ongoing life of the
church. This will necessitate a survey, not only of Strasbourg, Lausanne, and Geneva, but of the Reformed communions in France, the Netherlands, and the Rhine Valley,
the Presbyterian Church of Scotland, and, not insignif-
icantly, the Puritan synthesis of Elizabethan and Stuart
England. The material will be handled in a chronological
fashion, so that the debates on the doctoral office that took
place in November of 1643 in the Assembly of Divines at
Westminster will come as a capstone to the account.

Westminster and the middle of the seventeenth century
provide effective and intelligible terminal points for the
discussion of the office as regards the Continental and English developments. However, we shall trace the idea of the
doctorate to date in a concluding section by reference to
the existing situation in the Church of Scotland and by a
short account of what some of the American churches have
done in regard to their practice in recognizing or rejecting
the doctorate as an integral ministry of the church.

Because of the ambiguity that has marked so much of the
thinking about the doctoral office, it would be well if cer-

tain presumptions of the author were quite well defined. One of the stumbling blocks of this study as a historical exercise is the absence of criteria that are acceptable to all who would judge the evidence. Take, for instance, the terms " minister " and " ministry." To many, these are synonymous with " pastor " and " pastorate." However, such an equation presents a terrific terminological ambiguity, so we shall reserve the term " ministry" as an inclusive designation for the various offices to which individual Christians are called and set apart within the fabric of the whole ministry of the whole church; or to paraphrase a debater in the Westminster Assembly, " what I may do by right and not another." It is fairly easy to identify the offices of the public ministry when they are mentioned in documentary sources; not so easy is the attempt to provide conclusive evidence that certain persons did or did not exercise a particular office at a particular time. However, in so far as we are able to do so, the designation of doctoral status will be reserved for persons who cannot otherwise be identified as having been pastors, yet who are acknowledged by their contemporaries (explicitly or implicitly) as exercising a public ministry of the word of God within the structure of the church. This distinction occurred very early in certain of the Reformation communities and thus provides us with a recognizable yardstick.

Before it will be profitable to assess Calvin's thought in this matter, it will be of value to review the nature of instruction at the onset of the Reformation.

II

Historical and Theoretical Background for a Teaching Office in the Church

CERTAIN DEVELOPMENTS should be outlined in order to give a sense of the relationship of the teaching office to the church in particular and to society in general as they existed in the opening years of the sixteenth century.

There seems to be no doubt that a peculiar teaching ministry existed in the primitive church alongside of, and even at times in competition with, the established local ministry of bishops, elders, and deacons.[1] Certainly as late as the first quarter of the third century there still existed within the Egyptian Church an order of teachers (*doctores ecclesiae*) alongside of the cultic and administrative ministry. Their function was clearly didactic, for their area of endeavor was by this time confined largely to the catechetical school.[2] But, as in the case of Origen,[3] their function was not totally confined to the school, and they were free, even expected, to preach and teach within the liturgi-

[1] Cf. The Didache 10:7; 15:1-2.

[2] Carl Vernon Harris, "Origen of Alexandria's Interpretation of the Teacher's Function in the Early Christian Hierarchy and Community" (unpublished dissertation, Duke University, 1952), pp. 233, 211.

[3] Cf. E. G. Weltin, "Origen's Church," in G. E. Mylonis and Doris Raymond (eds.), *Studies Presented to David M. Robinson*, 2 vols. (St. Louis, 1953), II:1014–1022; Origen cited as defending the prerogatives of "lay" teachers *after* his ordination as a presbyter in *Hom. in Gen.* 14, *Hom. in Num.* 2, and *Hom. in Lev.* 6:6.

cal life of the church.[4] During the course of the third century, the office was both suppressed and clericalized as the doctors were thrust out of the church (that is, out of the liturgical service), with the further possibility that some of them may have been inducted into the office of reader — an order and office which originally had been charismatic but which had come early under episcopal jurisdiction.[5]

The connection of these catechetical schools, and the teaching ministry associated with them, with the subsequent development of educational institutions in Western Christendom is very tenuous, to say the least. Bavinck insisted that the catechetical school was an "extraordinary" institution, and when its purpose had been fulfilled in bringing an adult catechumenate into full stature in the church, it ceased to exist. He further maintained that the establishment of the prototype of the cathedral and convent schools of a later age could be located in the practice by bishops in the sixth and seventh centuries of taking candidates for the clergy and even the clergy themselves into their own households for training — the creation of a *monasterium* of sorts.[6]

THE TEACHING OFFICE AT THE DAYBREAK OF THE REFORMATION

The history of education in Western Europe cannot be told apart from the involvement of the ecclesiastical structure and ecclesiastical personnel in the process. This was as true of the development of secondary instruction as it was of the rise of the medieval university. From the twelfth century onward, it is necessary to keep these two levels of

---

[4] Harris, *op cit.*, p. 249, cites Eusebius, *H. E.* VI:xxvii, as stating that Origen began regular preaching Wednesdays and Fridays in the Church of Caesarea *before* his ordination as a presbyter.

[5] A. Harnack, *Sources of the Apostolic Canons* (London, 1895), pp. 54–95.

[6] Bavinck, *Doctorenambt*, pp. 20–21.

instruction separate, but both found their common ancestry in the convent or cathedral school of the earlier period.[7] The complex factors that brought about the development of certain of these centers of clerical instruction into centers of general studies are too long to detail here, and not every one of the universities had such a point of origin.[8] However, for our purposes, education of a nonecclesiastical origin is of secondary concern. The fact remains that in the transalpine church and the transalpine school a close relationship is quite evident.

In all probability, one of the earliest permanent officers of the cathedral chapter was the *magister scholarum*. In the beginning, this *magister* was the instructor, but as a school became popular and attracted other instructors and students, as Paris did under William of Champeaux, the duties of the *magister* became increasingly administrative, and his office developed into that of chancellor. As chancellor, he became the bishop's alter ego in relation to a growing corps of teachers and to the students. The original ecclesiastical character of the university as an outgrowth of the cathedral or monastery school had not been completely dissipated at the outset of the Reformation, although the content of its ecclesiastical character had been largely recast.

From the first, as soon as a school began to expand and draw to it a number of teachers, it had been the duty of the *magister scholarum*, or *scholasticus*, to license in the name of the bishop those who were allowed to exercise the teaching office in the city or diocese. In the course of time, those individuals possessing such a license organized them-

---

[7] Hastings Rashdall, *The Universities of Europe in the Middle Ages*, new ed. in 3 vols., edited by F. M. Powicke and A. B. Emden (London, 1936), I:26–28; and Auguste Vallet de Viriville, *Histoire l'instruction publique en Europe* (Paris, 1849), p. 197.

[8] Rashdall, *op. cit.*, I:90–109.

selves, to safeguard and enhance their working conditions, into associations or craft guilds, which were well-recognized forms of medieval life. The guilds of masters (*magistri* or *doctores*) came to exercise the predominating influence in the granting of the *licentia docendi,* which had originally been the prerogative of the *scholasticus.* Even though a latter-day chancellor (as happened at Paris) might seek to assert his authority independently of the guilds, his independent exercise of authority was impeded by papal intervention in a series of enactments that shifted the ecclesiastical basis of the school from the local diocese to the Bishop of Rome.[9]

It is too much to say that the *licentia docendi* elevated its holders as an order of the church's " divinely commissioned ministry to the side of bishops and presbyters." [10] Yet the fact remains that as a result of the efforts in the fifteenth century to reduce the scandal of multiple claimants to the throne of Peter, no real opposition developed to the suggestion by the University of Paris that its representatives sit on the General Council of the church alongside of the assuredly clerical representatives.

The titles *magister* and *doctor* originated as designations of those who held the *licentia,* but by the mid-fourteenth century these titles were well on their way to being recognized as academic degrees as well.[11] Eventually the term " regent " came to designate those masters or doctors who actually engaged in the academic exercise of their func-

---

[9] *Ibid.,* pp. 308–310, 401. The action in 1292 by Nicholas IV, conferring the *ius ubique docendi* on licentiates of the University of Paris, may well have been a *de jure* sanction of a *de facto* condition, but the fact remains that subsequent to that date the chancellor of Paris conferred the license in the name of the pope rather than the bishop.

[10] Rashdall, I:574.

[11] *Ibid.,* p. 287; as the recipient of the chancellor's authorization, the candidate was a " licentiate "; but only as he was accepted by his peers in the guild was he regarded as having become in the fullest sense entitled to the grade of " master," or " doctor."

tion.[12] Bavinck's desire to limit the teaching office in the church to the episcopate [13] passes too quickly over the fact that the holder of the *licentia* did so initially from the hand of the bishop and subsequently from the hand of the pope. Furthermore, when he maintains that the doctorate of the medieval university was not an office (*ambt*) with a call, but a gift,[14] he is neglecting the obligations at regenting implicit in the initial concept of the doctorate and the fact that regents of a later period were all required to possess the doctoral degree.[15]

The ecclesiastical, if not the clerical, status of the faculties of the medieval universities is open to some misconception as well as a good deal of uncertainty. Some evidence would tend to demonstrate that both faculties and students in the medieval university enjoyed a special status

[12] Rashdall, I:439, 409–410. When this had been firmly established, mere possession of the degree did not confer active teaching office, although holders of the degree were still entitled and expected to participate in certain legislative activities of their particular faculties.

[13] Bavinck, *Doctorenambt*, p. 19; upheld by Yves M. J. Congar, O. P., *Lay People in the Church: A Study for a Theology of the Laity*, tr. by Donald Attwater (Westminster, Maryland, 1957), pp. 258–260, 266, 281, who sympathizes with Calvin's re-emphasis on Christ's triple office (priest, king, prophet) in the church, but backs off from accepting its implications for "a structural ecclesiological principle."

[14] Bavinck, *Doctorenambt*, pp. 25, 45.

[15] Rashdall, I:286–287, 460–462, notes the close resemblance in form and terminology of the "inception," or formal entry, into the magistral office, to entry into ecclesiastical order. The immediate entry of the newly admitted *magister* into the *cathedra* to propound two theses for disputation is linked to the concept in Roman law that investiture with an office was not complete until the essentials of that office have been performed. Thus, the giving of the insignia of various minor orders in the ancient and the medieval church comprised the whole of ordination; the deacon read the gospel, and the new priest was concelebrant with the bishop of the Mass. A vestigial remnant, even in the Free Churches, may be found in the practice (which, if not "canonical," is *de rigueur*) of having a newly ordained or installed pastor mount the pulpit to give the benediction.

in the eyes of the church that did not apply to nonacademic Christendom. This special status may be comprehended in the term *clericus*, but we are warned against equating this term with either major or minor orders.[16] Actually, holy orders were required only for the members of the faculty of theology, although some schools required that recipients of the doctorate be priests. However, initial association with the clergy and subsequent identification with ecclesiastical foundations as a source of income while undergoing training had so conditioned the whole framework of academic life that in terms of medieval life many of the privileges and responsibilities of those in clerical orders were attributed to the academics, and especially to the faculties.[17]

A further extension of this peculiar position of learning within the hierarchy of the church may be seen in the title *doctores ecclesiae* attributed to some of the ecclesiastical writers of an earlier era.[18] The first action of the church toward formalizing this as a title occurred in 1298 when Boniface VIII on the basis of current usage among the scholastics referred to Gregory the Great, Ambrose, Augustine, and Jerome as such. The conditions for naming an individual to this dignity were " eminent teaching, evidence of a sanctified life, and the pronouncement of the Church." A later pope, Benedict XIV, explained that the pronouncement by the church could be accomplished only by a "supreme pontiff or by a general council." Actually, the title *doctor ecclesiae* has never been bestowed by itself,

16 Rashdall, *op. cit.*, III:394–395.
17 *Ibid.*, p. 396; cf. also George H. Williams, " An Excursus," in *The Harvard Divinity School* (Beacon Press, Boston, 1954), for a demonstration of the theological rationale of the medieval university based on a study of the major themes associated with that institution in the work of medieval writers.
18 *Catholic Encyclopedia* (New York, 1909), V:75, art. " Doctors of the Church." Cf. also F. L. Cross (ed.), *The Oxford Dictionary of the Christian Church* (London, 1957), p. 410, art. " Doctors of the Church."

but the title *doctor* has been appended to the name of a scholar or teacher of the church in the same action by which the Congregation of the Sacred Rites, with papal approval, allows the church to honor him by including him in the " office and Mass of a saint." Practice has reserved the use of this title, generally, for graduates in canon law and theology.

Some of the weight of this practice undoubtedly affected the use of the term by the Reformers, especially Calvin, who made frequent reference to the false doctors of Rome.[19] It was Calvin's conviction, we think, that the doctorate of the medieval church represented a legitimate and fruitful ministry that had been corrupted, which caused him to include it as an integral office of the public ministry of the church in its Reformed estate.

However, before entering into a discussion of the doctrinal foundation upon which Calvin sought to ground the second order of the church's ministry, we should pause briefly to consider another aspect of the educational spectrum. Generally speaking, two different types of secondary schools existed in northern Europe in the late fifteenth and early sixteenth centuries. On the one hand were numerous institutions that had been born and prospered under various types of ecclesiastical control; on the other hand, there were an increasing number of schools that had either developed under lay initiative or in fact had become institutions related to the authority of the community or city rather than the church. Again, in a general way, we are able to point out that a pattern may be observed in relation to the reform of the church and the reform of the school. In those areas where declericalization had gained considerable headway, the school as an institution underwent less noticeable alteration at the onset of the Reformation than was true of schools in areas where ecclesiastical control was the norm rather than the exception.

[19] Cf. *CO* 27:244; 44:345; 50:124.

The latter situation prevailed most obviously in Scotland and France.[20] Although a number of the French secondary institutions were of recent foundation or had managed to achieve a certain amount of community control, the greater part were still closely associated with either the university complexes or with cathedral chapters in more important towns. The situation was not appreciably different in Scotland. A few municipalities had managed to establish limited prerogatives in relation to a local school, but the personnel in all schools were regarded as related to the hierarchy of the church.

The situation in the Rhine Valley, from Switzerland to the Low Countries, presented another stage of development. Without denying that the prototype of secondary education in these areas was closely dependent on the cathedral or convent school, and never forgetting that a goodly number of these institutions continued to function within their original framework, it becomes apparent that a type of schooling had been developed that looked to the political and economic community rather than to the ecclesiastical for its rationale, its curriculum, its finances, and for basic authority over the teaching personnel. This development can be documented for the Low Countries, the regions of the Rhine Valley, and for German-speaking Switzerland.[21]

This chain of events need not be demonstrated in its entirety here, but it may be valuable to review the particular sequence that took place in Geneva, recognizing that this sequence was part of a larger development and that certain basic presuppositions were shared by a rather extensive European community.

The institutional involvement of the medieval church in

[20] Cf. Vallet de Viriville, *op. cit.*, pp. 197–201, and James Grant, *History of the Burgh Schools of Scotland* (Glasgow, 1876), p. 29.
[21] Cf. J. Müller (ed.), *Vor- und frühreformatische Schulordnungen und Schulverträge*, 2 Abt. in 1 Bd. (Zschopau, 1885–1886).

instruction in Geneva dates at least to the early years of the thirteenth century, with the establishment of a cathedral school on an avowedly gratuitous basis.[22] During the fourteenth century, an attempt to erect a university foundation came to naught because of political involvements. Instruction in the cathedral school suffered under inept, and perhaps corrupt, administration, and the whole of instruction was reduced to cathedral supervision over private grammar masters.[23]

In the first part of the fifteenth century, the General Council of the city tried to fill this educational vacuum, but actual realization of the Council's pious dream was the work of a foundation established by a wealthy merchant, François de Versonnex, who bequeathed both his fortune and his name to an institution that by the standards of the day was never regarded as anything more than a secondary establishment, regardless of how grandiose may have been the intentions and dreams of its benefactor.[24] In addition to a statutory curriculum in " grammar, logic, and the other liberal arts," the charter provided that the students were to pray each morning for the souls of their benefactor and his parents, that the instruction was to be absolutely free, that the buildings were to be the property of the city of Geneva, and that the rector and the masters were to take oath to the syndics of the city for the performance of these conditions.

Over the years the rector of the Collège de Versonnex was granted additional supervisory functions in regard to the masters of private schools.[25] This seems to have been

---

[22] J. B. Gabarel, *Histoire de l'Église de Genève*, 3 tomes (Genève 1858), I:493.

[23] Cf. Charles Borgeaud, *Histoire de l'Université de Genève:* Tome I, " L'Academie de Calvin, 1559–1798 " (Genève, 1900), p. 6, and Jules Vuy, " Notes historiques sur le collège de Versonnex," in *Mémoires de l'Institut National Genevois,* XII (Genève, 1869), p. 4.

[24] Vuy, *op. cit.,* pp. 8–9, and Borgeaud, *op. cit.,* p. 14.

[25] Vuy, *op. cit.,* pp. 18–19.

directed to two ends, standardization of instruction and performance of certain religious obligations. For example, the rector of the *collège* was held responsible that all students in the city were in attendance at church services. There is evidence that the Council backed up the rector in these matters against offending schoolmasters and recalcitrant parents.[26] In addition, it was the rector's responsibility to read to the students passages from the New Testament and from the lives of the saints on days dedicated to their honor.

By the third decade of the sixteenth century, in Geneva, and in Switzerland generally, the institutions of secondary education were firmly in the hands of civic authorities, the status of the teaching force was dependent upon its relationship to that authority rather than to ecclesiastical institutions, and religious instruction by the school was but one of the avowed goals of "good manners, virtue, and knowledge."[27] This, then, was the educational tradition and institutional history that existed when Calvin came to Geneva. This was the "stuff" with which he had to work in terms of the local situation.

CALVIN'S ESTIMATE OF THE THEOLOGICAL FOUNDATION OF THE CHURCH'S TEACHING OFFICE

Jansen has noted the frequency with which the interpretations of Christ's offices as either priest-king or prophet-priest-king occur in the major Christian writers prior to Calvin.[28] His work suggests that a co-ordinate understanding of the prophetic office has had difficulty maintaining a foothold in Christian thinking, and that the tendency has been to subsume the prophetic office in the priestly. How-

[26] Gabarel, *op. cit.*, pp. 496–497.
[27] Vuy, *op. cit.*, p. 18.
[28] J. F. Jansen, *Calvin's Doctrine of the Work of Christ* (London, 1956), pp. 26–38.

ever, that Calvin made a connection between the prophetic office of Christ and the doctoral office in the church, and that he did this in the realm of the work of Christ, is very evident. He regarded the prophetic succession as continual, conceived its given purpose as that of never leaving God's people " without useful doctrine," and referred to Christ's use of prophetic language as his participation in the teaching office, "for he is distinguished from other teachers [i.e., prophets under the law] with a similar office. [And] . . . we must note this: he received anointing, not only for himself that he might carry out the office of teaching, but for his whole body that the . . . Spirit might be present in the continuing preaching of the gospel." [29]

The first mention by Calvin in the *Institutes* of the *munus triplex* of Christ as prophet, priest, and king came in the 1539 edition.[30] The triple anointing involves not only Christ but also his people,[31] among whom some are specially designated to carry on the particular functions implied in the offices involved in Christ's own commissioning.[32] However, it is one thing to recognize this in the abstract; it is another to construct it into a self-contained system with the minimum of internal tensions.

In a general way, we are bound to ask, How far can the prophetic role of Christ be used to support or give substance to a theology of instruction? In view of the radical change that the work of Christ has wrought on the temporal function that the priest and king had under the law,

---

[29] *Inst.* II.xv.1–2.

[30] *CO* I:LIII, "Synopsis Editionum Institutionis Calvinianae " and also *CO* I:513–515. No mention is found of this in the 1536 edition.

[31] *CO* I:513. Christ's people share in his anointing " not in an external or ceremonial way but in a spiritual manner."

[32] *Ibid.* The *prophet* is recognized because " he is an expounder of God to men," the *priest* because he " is an Angel of the Lord," and the *king* because he " bears the reflection of divine majesty on the earth." These anointings are " not foolish symbols, but a *sacramentum* of that true and singular anointing [of Christ]."

does the same radical shift occur in the temporal function of the prophetic office? In the fullness of time, Christ fulfilled the priesthood of the Old Covenant and became the supreme sacrifice as well as the supreme sacrificer (Heb. chs. 5 to 9), with all his people sharing in this unction and estate.[33] Thus, under the New Covenant, what remained of the priestly function under the Old Covenant was transferred to the apostolic office of messenger or herald, or as we have already seen, " the Angel of the Lord." Also, in the fullness of time, Christ fulfilled the regal expectations of the Davidic line, but shifts the scene from the temporal to the eternal, from the material to the spiritual,[34] so that under the Christ, the king (magistrate) but " bears the reflection of the divine majesty "; he is *not* divine in himself or in his office. In the same way we are brought to consider in what manner Calvin can utilize the prophetic ministry under the law and Christ's prophetic role to substantiate a prophetic (doctoral) ministry under the gospel, when Christ has likewise by his work wrought a radical change in it and " made an end to all prophecies." [35] That Calvin does so utilize it is obvious, for his parallel structure is without equivocation: " Our teachers correspond to the ancient prophets, [as] do our pastors to the apostles." [36]

Calvin's conception of Biblical prophets is interesting and crucial in this connection. Essentially, he conceived the role of the Old Testament prophet as being twofold: first and foremost, they were seen as guides,[37] expounders

---

[33] *Inst.* II.xv.6.

[34] *Inst.* II.xv.3–5.

[35] *Inst.* II.xv.2. Christ is: " the chief and captain of the prophets," " Sermon I on Luke 1:1-4," *CO* XLVI:2.

[36] *Inst.* IV.iii.5; cf. *CO* II:780. This parallel construction is a word-for-word quotation from the 1543 edition, *CO* I:564c.

[37] John Calvin, *Commentaries*, various translators and editors, printed for the Calvin Translation Society, Edinburgh, various dates. Hereafter referred to as *Comm. on* [name of canonical book], vol. and/or page (exact text ref.) with *CO* reference. *Comm. on Harm. of Gospels* III:359–360 (Luke 24:27), *CO* XLV:806–807: " no other

of the law,[38] sowers (but not reapers) of the doctrine of the gospel,[39] teachers whose *docendi forma* sets forth Christ; [40] in other words, they perform a didactic office and their doctrine is based on the teachings of Moses,[41] whom Calvin calls the chief teacher (*summus doctor*).[42] Only secondarily and as a kind of textual necessity did Calvin consider the prophetic role of " foreteller " of future events (*quibus res futuras praedicere*)[43] and he repeatedly pushed this interpretation of the prophetic function into the background, acknowledging that it could be substantiated, but concerned with it only in so far as it served to give substance to doctrinal foreshadowing [44] of the Christ.[45] Calvin granted that as a foreteller of his own posterity David was a prophet,[46] but with that statement the matter was allowed to rest and no doctrine was erected on it. Moreover, Calvin interpreted the fact that the function of foretelling had ceased sometime prior to the advent of the Messiah as a result of a definite plan on the part of God. In this way, the prophetic message of the Christ would make a greater impact.[47] And although the function of prediction had been in abeyance, that of expounding

office assigned to them than to renew a remembrance of the covenant, to point out more clearly the spiritual worship of God, to found on the Mediator the hope of salvation, and to show more clearly the method of reconciliation."

[38] *Ibid.;* also *Comm. on Acts* I:284 (Acts 7:37), *CO* XLVIII:149–150.

[39] *Comm. on John* I:173 (John 4:36), *CO* XLVII:94.

[40] *Comm. on Acts* I:451 (Acts 10:43), *CO* XLVIII:250.

[41] *Comm. on Harm.* III:361 (Luke 24:27), " The prophets . . . derived their earliest acquaintance with [the Mediator] from Moses."

[42] *Comm. on Acts* I:154–155 (Acts 3:22), *CO* XLVIII:73.

[43] *Comm. on Acts* II:83 (Acts 15:32), *CO* XLVIII:365.

[44] *Comm. on Harm.* III:360: " at a distance Moses may exhibit Christ in shadows."

[45] *Comm. on Rom.*, pp. 457–462 (Rom. 12:6-8), where he grants that some do consider prophecy the gift of prediction, but as for him he prefers something " wider." *CO* XLVIII:45–46.

[46] *Comm. on Acts* I:108 (Acts 2:30), *CO* XLIX:238–240.

[47] *Ibid.*, II:271 (Acts 21:9-10), *CO* XLVIII:477–478.

the law had not, and Calvin had no hesitation in applying the term *doctor* [48] to the Jewish scribe, and even the title *ecclesiae doctores* to those who were the " public teachers," whom he further identified as scribes. The fact that the scribes misused their calling or corrupted their teaching did not invalidate the fact that they had a lawful call " to sit in the chair of Moses," which, as Calvin put it, meant simply " to teach."

As for John the Baptist, he presented something of a special case. Calvin said that the law has been fulfilled in the Advent of Christ, so that in effect the prophetic role under the Old Covenant had no more validity under the gospel, for " to think that Prophets were ministers of the Gospel as were the Apostles [is a common confusion, for we have] the commencement of the Gospel with the preaching of John." [49] The distinction John made between himself as a " voice crying in the wilderness " and a prophet (O.T.) is to be sought in the difference between one who is " merely a subordinate minister " preparing the way for another *magister,* and one who is the bearer of an independent revelation " as was usually the case with the prophets." [50] Even if John was not a prophet (O.T.), yet he had the essential qualification of a *doctor ecclesiae,* for he was sent from God, thus his *docendi auctoritas* was " founded . . . on God alone." [51]

Although it is true that Calvin considered Christ's principal office to be the " Lamb of God," [52] thus highlighting the sacerdotal role, this was not done at the expense of either the regal or the prophetic. For example, when Christ cleansed the Temple at the beginning of his public

[48] *Comm. on Harm.* III:70–81 (Matt. 23:1-12; Mark 12:38-39; Luke 11:45-46), *CO* XLV:619–620.
[49] " Argument " . . . *Sermons sur l'Harmonie des Trois Evangel, CO* XLVI:v.
[50] *Comm. on John* I:57-58 (John 1:19), *CO* XLVII:22.
[51] *Ibid.,* I:36 (John 1:9), *CO* XLVII:7–8.
[52] *Ibid.,* I:63 (John 1:29).

ministry (as the Johannine account has it), Calvin said that he thereby made " himself known as *doctor* and *propheta.*" [53] Repeatedly, Calvin used these titles in connection with the work of Christ, and in such a way as to emphasize the didactic and critical office that Christ performed.[54] Christ brought with him " the full perfection of wisdom *(sapientia)* " and as such acted as " chief master " for all, as well as in his prophetic role being ordained by God to be the *magister* of the Jews.[55]

It was when Calvin dealt with Rom. 12:6-8 that he brought all this together, recognizing that in Christ and his gospel " all the ancient prophecies and all the oracles of God have been completed," being, as it were, subsumed in the work of Christ, and that the title of prophet under the gospel economy ought to be restricted to those who, from a " peculiar gift of revelation[,] . . . perform the office *(munus)* of an interpreter, explaining the will of God." [56] In the same passage, he commented that a " *doctor* is one who forms *(format)* and builds *(instituit)* the Church by the word of truth." Thus the prophet and the act of prophesying in the New Testament were both closely iden-

[53] *Comm. on Harm.* III:10–11 (Matt. 21:10-22; Mark 11:11-24; Luke 19:39 ff.), *CO* XLV:580.
[54] *Comm. on Harm.* III:359–360 (Luke 24:27) : " never more able or skillful *doctor* than our Lord "; III:42 (Matt. 22:16; Mark 12:14; Luke 20:21) : words applied to Christ are " a definition of a good and faithful *doctor* "; III:79: Christ asserts that the honor of being *magister, rabbi,* and *doctor* " does not belong to any except himself." This is literally true only during his earthly sojourn, for he himself " appoints and ordains *magistros* for us "; II:145–147: Christ has been appointed by the Father to be a *doctor. Comm. on John* 1:70 (John 1:38) : the people consider Christ a " *propheta ac doctor,* which is the first step toward teachableness "; I:311 (John 7:40) : the multitude calls Christ " prophet " — Calvin said they approved of the *doctor. Comm. on Acts* I:32 (Acts I:1) : because Christ " was a prophet," he stands as the example for " good and proper *doctores.*"
[55] *Comm. on Acts* I:284 (Acts 7:37), *CO* XLVIII:149–150; I:154–155 (Acts 3:22), *CO* XLVIII:73–74.
[56] *Comm. on Rom.,* p. 410, *CO* XLIX:239.

tified with the didactic and critical functions.[57] Dealing specifically with those places in the New Testament where an office of prophet or a function of prophesying was mentioned, Calvin again rejected the primacy of the predictive note, underlining in plain language the didactic role of the gospel prophet.[58]

Agabus and the four daughters of Philip presented a special problem in this connection, for the text is rather definite that these did predict events as a consequence of their prophetic gifts. However, Calvin got around this by postulating the predictive element as a special dispensation of God by which the church in its new state was glorified.[59] The problem of the false prophets and unstable charismatics of the early church was recognized in this connection, and Calvin hazarded the opinion that the " forwardness " of the " brain-sick fellows . . . may be the [reason] the Church was deprived of this gift." [60]

The office of doctor and the office of prophet under the gospel were closely linked; Calvin never succeeded in drawing a completely clear line of distinction between them. That there was a difference in his mind is apparent.[61] What distinction he did draw between prophets and doctors would seem to lie in the area of the intensity of the exercise of their didactic function and in the fact that he

[57] " Sermon I on Luke 1:1-4," where Luke is identified as *maistre et docteur* and the *docteurs* are identified as those who " never allow the introduction of false metal, false alloy, nor false money in either form or substance." *CO* XLVI:10, *Comm. on Acts* I:353 (Acts 8:22). The evangelist Philip was spoken of variously as interpreter and *magister* and also interpreter and *doctor* in the " school of God." *CO* XLVIII:191.

[58] *Comm. on Acts* I:497 (Acts 13:1); II:83 (ch. 15:32); II:271 (ch. 21:9-10).

[59] *Comm. on Rom.,* p. 460 (Rom. 12:7).

[60] *Comm. on Acts* (Acts 21:9-10).

[61] *Ibid.,* I:497 (Acts 13:1): " in the Church that was at Antioch certain prophets and teachers." Calvin refers the reader to his commentary on Eph. 4:11 and I Cor. 12:28: " for there is a difference (in my judgment) between doctors and prophets."

seemed to give to the gospel prophet a slightly wider range of responsibility, in that he is to make known " the will of God by applying with dexterity and skill prophecies, threatenings, promises and the whole doctrine of the scripture, to the present use of the Church"; while the office of doctors (doctorum munus) " consists in taking care that sound doctrine be maintained and propagated, in order that the purity of religion may be kept in the Church." [62]

Thus for Calvin, the prophetic-doctoral ministry under the gospel was not to be confused with the apostolic-pastoral office. It rested squarely on the prophetic-doctoral office of Christ himself, and performed functions that are essentially didactic and critical in contradistinction to the liturgical, shepherding, and governing competence of the apostolic-pastoral office. It is true, all pastors ought to be doctors, but functionally and by office all doctors are not pastors. [63]

[62] Comm. on Corinth. I:413–417 (I Cor. 12:28), CO XLIX:505–508.

[63] Comm. on Gal. and Eph., p. 279 (Eph. 4:11) : " no objection to [pastors] receiving the name of doctores, as long as we know there is a distinct class of teachers (alterum esse doctorum genus) who preside in the education of pastors, and in the instruction of the whole church."

III

The Genevan Reform in School and Church

CITATION OF THREE DOCUMENTS will exemplify the ecclesiastical structure of the Genevan Church throughout Calvin's ministry. The first, *Articles concernant l'organization de l'Église et du Culte à Genève*,[1] was in reality
a loosely composed " tract " under four major headings:
The Holy Supper, Public Worship, Instruction of Youth,
and Reform of Marriage Laws. Although only one office of
the public ministry, " ministers of the word," was mentioned as such by the *Articles*, it is possible, in the light of
subsequent developments, to find adumbrated *les anciens*
and *les docteurs* although the diaconate failed completely
of recognition.

Following the Strasbourg sojourn (1538–1541), Calvin
and his colleagues presented a scheme of ecclesiastical organization to the city council for ratification. Here, for the
first time, the fourfold public ministry of the Reformed
churches was set forth in its classical formulation. " There
are four orders of officers which our Lord has instituted for
the government of his Church. [First] pastors, then the doctors, next the elders, fourthly the deacons." [2] By its acceptance and ratification this document became known as
the *Ordonnances Ecclésiastiques*, and its text stood until
May, 1561, when it was extensively revised.[3]

[1] *CO* Xa:5–13, 16 January 1537.
[2] *CO* Xa:15 ff., presented 20 November 1541.
[3] *CO* Xa:91 ff.

As might be expected, the office of pastor was given the most attention as to its functions, duties, and the conditions surrounding admission of new members to its ranks. The admission of a pastor consisted of three main parts: examination, institution, and induction. Of these, each in turn was made the subject of specific regulations.

Examination was designed to test both the doctrine and the life of the candidate as well as his academic proficiency, and was administered by an unnamed authority. The problem of who was competent to conduct the examination of the candidate for the gospel ministry became the subject of controversy in several of the Reformed communions (cf. Pays du Vaud, the Dutch Church, and the Scots Church, which had the added complication of royal intervention). A tradition in the Genevan community of examination in the *school* was already in vogue, but because of the close relationship of the ministry with the academic personnel, it is not desirable to place too much emphasis on this. The doctrinal part of the examination was primarily a test of the breadth and depth of Scriptural knowledge, and also of the ability of the candidate to communicate this knowledge to the " edification of the people." [4] The examination was concluded by an inquiry into the life and conduct of the candidate, " whether or not he always conducts himself without reproach."

Institution was a distinct act and was the process by which the church, in the persons of its ministers, nominated a specific candidate for a specific vacancy. Naturally, one who had failed to satisfy his examiners on life or doctrine would not be chosen, but by the same token not everyone qualified by examination could be nominated to a position. As a part of institution, the nominee of the ministers must be presented to the city council for its approbation and presumably was required to take an oath of allegiance " to uphold the honor and primacy of the magis-

[4] *CO* Xa:17.

tracy and city " [5] at this point. Only then was the new pastor presented to the congregation for induction.

Induction, as it appeared in the form submitted by Calvin and his colleagues, was to be by laying on of hands, following presentation to the congregation. The congregation might object, in which case a new selection was necessary. However, the text was altered in the definitive edition to allow induction by simple proclamation of that fact (by a minister) accompanied with prayers and supplications " to the end that the Lord would grant to him [the ordinand] the grace to do it." [6]

The second order, or the *docteur*, was charged with the duty of " teaching the faithful in wholesome doctrine " that the church might never lack *pasteurs et ministres* and that youth might be prepared to participate in the *gouvernement civil*. Interwoven with the enumeration of these functions was a recognition that this office would be exercised in the school. Indeed, both the documents of 1541 and 1561 identify the term *lordre de escolles* (*l'ordre des*

---

[5] The requirement of the oath was not mentioned in the text until *after* the act of induction, but the logical time for the administration of the oath would be at the time the candidate was presented to the council. (*Ibid.*, col. 18.) The actual text of the oath was included in the text of the edition of 1561, and obligated the candidate to (1) faithfully fulfill his pastoral functions, (2) uphold the Ecclesiastical Ordinances and exercise their holy discipline, (3) act in loyalty and good faith toward the civil government, and (4) bear himself as a law-abiding citizen, except in so far as the freedom of witnessing for truth against error was laid upon him by his office. (*Ibid.*, col. 95.)

[6] In the matter of laying on of hands, the original draft (1541) called for it on the basis of apostolic example and practice, as long as it was done " *sans superstition et sans offense*," but conceded that it probably would be misinterpreted due to " *l'infirmite du temps.*" The article, as finally accepted, called for one of the ministers to make " *une declaration en remonstrance de loffice auquel on lordonne puis quon fasse priers et oraisons affin que le seigneur luy fasse la grace de seu acquiter.*"

escoles) as the common term for the doctoral office.[7] In the 1541 edition a rather sketchy outline was made of the status and duties of all who were engaged in *l'ordre des escoles.* These were explicitly divided into " a rank close to the ministry," engaged in superior theological training, and a class who were to be engaged in secondary training in the " languages and humaine sciences " of the male youth.[8] The appointment of both classes of instructors was by nomination and approval of the *ministres,* following a successful examination at which two of the syndics of the *petit conseil* were present, and was contingent upon taking the oath to the syndics. Both classes — the lecturers in theology and the masters or undermasters with the title *bachelier* — were decreed to be subject to ecclesiastical discipline in the same way in which the ministers were, indicative of a close parallelism of their functions in the minds of the framers. Thus the body of instructors was regarded as responsible to the ecclesiastical organization rather than to the civil, although the interest of the magistracy was accommodated.

The enactment of 1561 repeated verbatim the previous language regarding the two classes of instructors, which established in general that the *docteur* was to be regarded

---

[7] *Ibid.,* col. 21. *" Le degre plus prochain au ministers et plus conjoinct [adjoingt] au gouvernment de leglise est la lecture de theologie, dont il sera bon quil yet ait au vieil et nouveau testament."*

[8] This class of instructors was not given a title in the text comparable to the " *lecture de théologie* " cited above, but there can be little doubt that the masters of the Collège de Rive were in the minds of the authors. The language of the enactment gives some evidence that at this particular moment the *collège* was not functioning well, if at all, for it was stated that " *il fauldra dresser college pour instruyre les enfans."* *Ibid.*

That there had been some provision for the education of females prior to this time seems evident (" *les filles avent leur escolles a part, comme il a este faict par cydevant."*) but it was rudimentary, at best, for such instruction was classed together with that of " *les petit enfans."*

as an order of the ecclesiastical ministry. It also provided that instruction was to be carried on at two levels, and then referred the reader to " The Book of the School Order " for a more detailed account of the exercise of the teaching profession in Geneva.[9] Thus our attention is naturally directed to a more detailed consideration of *Leges Academia Genevensis* of 1559.[10]

But before getting into an extended discussion of this enactment, which was to climax Calvin's educational concern, we shall: (1) survey those influences prior to 1541 which may have shaped Calvin's thinking; (2) review the educational system and situation in Geneva during the years of Calvin's ministry prior to the successful establishment of the Academy in 1559, and (3) comment upon Calvin's thought in regard to the practice of the academic doctoral office as it may be traced in his writings.

THE INFLUENCE OF STRASBOURG ON CALVIN

Certainly there is no evidence that Calvin considered the *docteur* a separate ecclesiastical officer prior to his sojourn in Strasbourg, where he was first pastor of the French refugee congregation and then lecturer in the Strasbourg school.[11] We have noted his concern for the religious instruction of children in the *Articles* (1537), but even there he did not envisage a corps of ecclesiastical catechists. Rather, the responsibility for religious instruction was placed on parents and the schools.[12] Two things lead us to

[9] *Ibid.*, p. 100. " *De la facon d'y proceder elle se trouvera au livre de l'Ordre des Escoles.*"

[10] Cf. *CO* Xa:66 ff., with French text of 1561 and 1562 as well.

[11] Cf. Jacques Pannier, *Calvin à Strasbourg* (Paris, 1925), and François Wendel, *Calvin: sources et évolution de sa pensée religieuse* (Paris, 1950).

[12] Cf. *CO* Xa:12. The device of a catechism for religious instruction was contemplated, but no provision for its use was projected, which leaves us to assume that the institutions involved would be those which had functioned heretofore in this matter — the family and the school. However, mention of the school immediately raises the

believe that the influence of Strasbourg may have been decisive in his conception of the nature of the public ministry of the church: first, the fact that he did not elaborate a corporate, or collegiate, ministry until his return from Strasbourg; and second, prior to Calvin's sojourn in Strasbourg that church had begun to practice, tentatively to be sure, a fourfold ministry, exactly mirrored in the Genevan *Ordonnances* of 1541 drawn up by Calvin on his return. The Strasbourg synthesis has been elucidated by Prof. François Wendel in his detailed study of the documents prior to and during the Strasbourg Synod of 1533.[13] It will be sufficient here to recapitulate the evidence he presents.

There was a system of schools with no over-all orientation in the city prior to the Synod of 1533 whose existence had been recognized by the city ordinance of 30 October 1531.[14] The system was capped by two Latin grammar schools — one under the mastership of Jean Sapidus, who, prior to 1528, had been director of the rather famous Latin school at Schlettstadt, the other under Otto Brunfels — and by a kind of superior instruction including courses in Hebrew, law, classical languages, mathematics, and theology. This instruction was given by some of the pastors and several members of the Chapter of St. Thomas, which had a reputation as a center of learning even prior to the Reformation. Capito, as a canon, gave courses in the Old Testament, Bucer, in the New Testament, and Hedio dealt with history and theology; George Casélius taught Hebrew, and Chrétien Herlin instructed in mathematics, geography, and rhetoric. These courses were given in the convent of

---

question of the status of its staff as agents, or ministers, of the religious establishment. As we shall show, there was at this period some understanding of the teaching staff of the school in Geneva as standing next in line to, or partaking of, clerical status.

[13] François Wendel, *L'Église de Strasbourg: sa constitution et son organisation 1532–1535* (Paris, 1942).

[14] *Ibid.*, pp. 27, 47; cf. Karl Schmidt, *La Vie et les traveaux de Jean Sturm* (Strasbourg, 1855), p. 30.

the Dominicans prior to 1528, and after that date were transferred to the chapter house of St. Thomas. In addition to those mentioned, Jacques Bédrot taught Greek and dialectic, Nicolas Gerbel taught Latin, and Michel Délius had succeeded on the death of Casélius in 1528 to the chair of Hebrew. It was the intention of Bucer and his pastoral colleagues that individuals involved in both the superior and secondary process were to be regarded as exercising a public ministry within the church, " for schoolmasters ought to teach, in addition to writing and the liberal arts, Christian discipline and the fear of God." [15]

The plans for the Synod to be convened on 3 June 1533, envisaged that the lecturers in languages (Misner and Bedrotus) and liberal arts (Herlin and Bittelbronn), as well as the masters of schools and regents,[16] were to attend as constituent members. On 5 June, when the Synod exercised its function of ecclesiastical censorship over the ministry, the schoolmasters took their turn with the pastors and vicars in appearing before the assembled *Kirchenpfleger* and synodical presidents (the four representatives from

[15] Quoted in Wendel, *L'Église de Strasbourg*, p. 54, from the request for a synod dated 30 November 1532. Of the seven items mentioned by the pastors as needing discussion by a church synod, two were directly concerned with some part of the educative process, and two had to do with the nature of church government and the nature of the church's ministry.

The request was turned over to a committee of the magistracy that subsequently reported that masters and regents had been instructed to conduct their students to worship, and that visitation of the school would be conducted on a quarterly basis with monthly examinations for students on city scholarships. In addition, this committee proposed the creation of a post of " superintendent " for public instruction and agreed to the desirability of calling a synod, provided that prior to the general convocation, a presynod of city pastors and elders be held (pp. 58–59).

[16] By the time of the Synod, Brunfels had left town and been replaced by Pierre Dasypode from Frauenfeld in Switzerland, the Latin school at St. Pierre the Elder was under the charge of Jean Schwebel, and the school at the Dominican Convent was under the direction of Jean Sapidus (Schmidt, *op. cit.*, p. 28).

the magistracy) to undergo an examination on life and manners and to make complaints about their colleagues or their jobs. The first round of synodical meetings did not produce a finished *Kirchenordnung*, although a commission was appointed to take up the matter. The magistracy called a second session (23 October 1533) to deal with the work of the commission,[17] and again the schoolmen are included among those to be summoned. The propositions submitted by the commission projected the inclusion of the lecturers, schoolmasters, and regents as a part of the Ecclesiastical Assembly,[18] as well as some or all of the *Kirchenpfleger*.[19] The magistracy resisted this action, although they did concede that the members of the teaching body might be called to meet with the ecclesiastics as the occasion might warrant.[20]

Thus by 1538 when Calvin arrived at Strasbourg and became involved in its ecclesiastical and educational affairs the collegiate character of the Reformed ministry had been formulated,[21] the Reformed doctorate had been postulated,

[17] Wendel, *L'Église de Strasbourg*, p. 100, the call had been issued ten days previously to the *Kirchenpfleger*, pastors, vicars, masters, and regents, and to the deacon of the poor.
[18] The article entitled "Conventus ecclesiastique"; cf. *ibid.*, p. 102.
[19] The projected *Kirchenordnung* called for the attendance of at least three *Kirchenpfleger* at the *Conventus Eccles.*, but the discussion revealed that some wished the attendance of all twenty-one of these officers. No mention was made of the frequency of the meetings of the *conventus* but under another item a weekly meeting of the pastors and *Kirchenpfleger* of each parish was contemplated. (*Ibid.*, p. 104.)
[20] *Ibid.*, p. 117 and p. 192, where Wendel takes the position that Bucer regarded the lecturers, masters, and regents of the schools as the doctors of the church, a position that was resisted by the magistracy, who only agreed that "*so es auch die notturfft erforderet mögen sie die ordinarios Lectores Schül unn leermeyster sampt und sonder wie sie das für nutz und gut ansihet zu ihnen berüffen.*"
[21] Henri Strohl, "La théorie et pratique des quatre ministères à Strasbourg avant l'arrivée de Calvin" (*Bulletin*, Soc. Hist. Prot. Fr., LXXXIV), pp. 123 ff., takes the position that Bucer had picked up

and the rudiments of an educational system affiliated with the work of the church had been established.[22]

Jean Sturm had been called from Paris in 1537 to head up the educational program of the Alsatian city, and had organized public education at three general levels: elementary reading and writing in the vulgar tongue;[23] secondary classical education, where a study of things followed a study of words;[24] and a system of superior courses to pre-

---

this idea from Oecolampadius in October of 1530 in connection with the Basel experiment with lay assistants for the parish pastors. Wendel, *L'Église de Strasbourg*, pp. 189–191, points out that a multiplicity of ministerial function was recognized in chap. xv of the Tetrapolitan Confession, that the Fourth Article of Ulm (1531) enumerated a number of different *diener* of the church, and that the call issued for the Synod of 1533 was addressed specifically to " *das v. g. h. die presidenten uffs fürderlichest die kirchenpfleger, pfarren und helffer, leser und schulmeyster, sampt dem dicon der armen,*" which parallels exactly the four offices Calvin subsequently projected for the Genevan Church.

Also, in the same vein, Strohl, p. 124, cites the fact that Bucer's commentary on Rom., ch. 12 was in its 3d edition in 1536, and had been translated into French by 1540, and that in speaking of the power of the keys, Bucer had said, " the public ministers of the Church, the doctors, the pastors, the governors, and the deacons, all persons who serve in an economy of place to the Christian community." The same order and distinction appeared in Bucer's Commentary on the Gospels.

[22] Bucer's first official position in Strasbourg had been that of lecturer, to which he had been inducted with a salary and assistants in December, 1523. During the same year the chapter schools had ceased to function and for a time what instruction was carried on in the city was done by the lecturers and preachers; Hastings Eells, *Martin Bucer* (New Haven, 1931), pp. 46–49. From 1524 on, the preachers had urged the magistracy to take action on public instruction, but the progress had been slow: in 1526, the city council had asked Melanchthon's opinion on organization; in 1528, public secondary education was tentatively begun by the foundation of three Latin schools on the basis of the suppressed convents, along with a school for sons of French refugees and a vulgar-tongue school for the *Burgerskinder;* yet despite this there was no over-all supervision and policy until Jean Sturm presented his plan of organization of 24 February 1538 (cf. Schmidt, *op. cit.*, pp. 23–36).

[23] Eells, *op. cit.*, pp. 46–49.

[24] Schmidt, *op. cit.*, p. 36.

pare the student for active citizenship.[25] It was at this last level that Calvin was employed as part-time lecturer during his stay from 1539 to 1541. On the basis of his exercise of both functions, he saw a difference in the pastoral and doctoral offices, for it was from Strasbourg he wrote his *Reply to Sadolet*, " In that Church [Geneva] I have held first the office of Doctor [26] and then of Pastor." [27] This self-classification, coupled with his Strasbourg background, reveals three things: that Calvin regarded the doctorate as part of the church's ministry, that he regarded it as a function distinct from the pastorate, and that he conceived of it as functioning in an academic arena. One of the first projects that came to Calvin's hands when he returned to Geneva was the submission to the magistrate of a codified polity for the Genevan Church, where for the first time he worked out a systematic scheme of a multiple ministry. However, it may be well, before we continue our research into the developments in Geneva consequent on Calvin's return, to review quickly the state of instruction in Geneva up to that point.

The Educational Situation in Geneva

When Calvin was forced out of Geneva others of his colleagues were forced out also. Among these were men who had been occupied with public instruction, most notably Antoine Saunier and Mathurin Cordier.[28]

Between 3 January 1531 and 21 May 1536 the educa-

[25] *Ibid.*, p. 90, and Charles Borgeaud, *Histoire d'Université de Genève*, Tome I, pp. 27–28.

[26] Calvin was authorized by the Genevan Council to give lectures in theology on 24 July 1536; cf. J. P. Gabarel, *op. cit.*, I:268.

[27] Cf. *Reply to Sadolet*, in J. K. S. Reid, *Calvin: Theological Treatises* (The Westminster Press, 1954), p. 222. Just when Calvin regards himself as becoming pastor is not certain; perhaps 5 September 1536; cf. *CO* XXI under that date.

[28] Gabarel, *op. cit.*, I:305–306.

tional process in Geneva was in a state of flux.[29] Classes at the *collège* were sporadic, although elementary instruction continued to be offered.[30] Sometime between 1534 and 1536 any semblance of systematic instruction broke down completely. Evangelical instruction was being offered on a gratuitous basis to the youth and citizens of the city during this period by Farel, Viret, and Fromment, but this was of a specialized nature and took the form of theological lectures on the Old and New Testaments, in private houses, which served as forums for the dissemination of their views. This was not systematic education as it had been carried on previously.

Geneva officially prohibited the Mass in August, 1535, and in September the Council ordered that the *collège* be moved to the rector's residence in the Convent de Rive.[31] The first Reformed name definitely connected with this resettled educational establishment was that of Antoine Saunier.[32]

[29] Henri Fazy, *L'Instruction primaire à Genève: notice historique* (Genève, 1896), especially pp. 8 ff., where the author notes that Council ordered the closing of the *collège* on 3 January 1531 until a new rector could be found, and that when one was secured, he, Claude Bigothier, was such an active partisan of Luther that the Council, 30 June 1532, ordered him to cease his practice of reading the Gospels. Between that date and 21 May 1536, when the city officially took its position as a Reformed community, it is difficult to know just what happened to the school.

[30] Gabarel, *op. cit.,* I:118. Cf. also evidence that the Collège de Versonnex continued to function at least until 1534, from the account of one Guillaume Messiez ("Petit Memorial," *Soc. d'hist. et d'arch. de Genève,* IX:23 [cited in J. Vuy, "Notes historiques sur le collège de Versonnex," p. 21]), who studied Virgil, Ovid, and Cicero under Master John Chrestien and others from 1532 to 1534.

[31] Vuy, *op. cit.,* pp. 21–22. Jean Martel had been named by the Council as rector in July, 1534, and did not give in his demission until April, 1536 (cf. Jules Le Coultre, *Maturin Cordier* [Neuchâtel, 1926], pp. 119–120), so was undoubtedly the individual who made the move from the old to the new location.

[32] Cf. Le Coultre, *op. cit.,* pp. 121–124, who speculates that Saunier may have been a Waldensian ("la secte des Vaudois") before joining forces with Farel in 1532.

THE REFORMED COLLÈGE DE RIVE

Saunier, on 21 May 1536, was officially named director, or regent, and carried on systematic grammar education with the help of several assistants. The curriculum was based on the medieval trivium, but the internal spirit had changed and French took its place alongside Latin, elementary Greek, and Hebrew.[33] Following Calvin's arrival in the city, a call was issued to Mathurin Cordier[34] by Farel, Calvin, and Saunier to teach in the *collège*. Thus the reform and restitution of education went on apace with the reform of the church. The initiative in the process came from the ministers, the funds for salaries came from the city authorities, and external control of the school was nonexistent, for there was no trace during this period of any oversight of curriculum, discipline, or finances.

The curriculum has been described as essentially primary.[35] Although reading and writing were taught in a number of *petit* schools scattered throughout the city, these masters were required to take their students to the *collège* once a week,[36] as has already been noted in the case of the pre-Reformation foundation.

Two questions still remain: What was the ecclesiastical status of the rector and his assistants in the *collège?* and, What, if any, was the nature of advanced instruction in connection with the secondary instruction being offered?

[33] Cf. [Antoine Saunier] *L'Ordre et Maniere denseigner in la ville de Genève au collège* . . . imprime a Genève par Jehan Gerard, MCXXXVIII (reprinted in E.-A. Bétant, *Notice sur le collège de Rive* [Genève, 1866], pp. 25–47). Charles Borgeaud, *op. cit.*, p. 16, attributes this " prospectus " to Saunier, which is controverted by Le Coultre (*op. cit.*, p. 125), who insists that the author must have been Cordier, because of the elegant style of the Latin version, " *Ordo et ratio docendi Geneauae in gymnasio.*"

[34] Le Coultre, *op. cit.*, p. 124.

[35] P. Daniel Bourchenin, *Étude sur les académies protestantes en France au XVIe et au XVIIe siècle* (Paris, 1882), p. 59.

[36] Cf. Fazy, *op. cit.*, p. 12.

Ecclesiastical Status of the Collège *Staff*

Saunier's first two assistants were dismissed by the Council on a number of grounds: chiefly that they had refused to participate in the Communion service and that they had publicly reprehended the preachers. Saunier interceded for them in vain, and himself came under attack for not doing his duty, because he was not engaged in a preaching ministry in conjunction with his educational duties. The undermasters were dismissed, but Saunier was confirmed in his salary.[37] Following this, Claude Vaultier and Jerome Vindanssy were called as assistants. However, at Christmas, 1538, after Calvin and Farel had left the city, when the Council ordered Saunier and his assistants to serve the Communion because of the lack of a sufficient number of pastors, Saunier demurred on the grounds that they had not been engaged to conduct worship, but only to teach (which they had done with regularity). The refusal of the staff of the *collège* to serve the Communion resulted in their peremptory banishment from the city on a three-day notice. Saunier appealed this hastiness of the magistrates to the Council of Two Hundred in the following terms: " The Holy Supper is an act of conscience for which one is responsible to God, neither I, nor my *bacheliers* were engaged to lead worship, but only to instruct the youth of the *collège,* and at that I am regularly busy; . . . the delay [in expulsion] of three days is very insufficient. I have numberous pensioners from the best families of Basle, Berne, and Zurich living with me, and a small daughter of 18 months, who is not able without inhumanity to go on the road in rigorous weather." [38] Vaultier,

---

[37] Cf. Le Coultre, *op. cit.,* pp. 130–131. Bétant, *op. cit.,* p. 9. Bétant (p. 10) places the call to Mathurin Cordier to be associated with Saunier in the *collège after* the discharge of the first two assistants, but Le Coultre (p. 124) places this call in the year 1536.

[38] *Registres du Conseil,* 26 and 27 December 1538, quoted in Gabarel, *op. cit.,* pp. 305–307. The banishment of the magistrates was upheld, but Saunier was given fifteen days to comply.

Vindanssy, Cordier, and Saunier had all been forced out of Geneva by February, 1539, and for the next three years the school continued under makeshift arrangements.[39] The incident, however, is interesting as a mirror of what the teaching staff considered were the limits of its ecclesiastical involvement and for the ideas of the magistracy in that regard. In the eyes of the magistrates, Saunier and his assistants, as *docteurs* of the school, were next in line to take up the slack in the absence of pastors, not as extraclerical but rather as semiclerical. In the eyes of the magistrates all the sanction they needed to administer the Sacrament was the fiat of the Council. On the other hand, it would seem that Saunier never claimed his was a function without ecclesiastical responsibilities.[40] But he specifically rejected the notion that his function was concerned with the conduct of public worship, and most specifically that by virtue of his rectorship he had any sanction to administer the Communion, not being one of *les ministres de la parole*, who were so authorized by the Articles of 1537.[41] In his defense before the Council of Two Hundred, Saunier rejected the idea that the fiat of the secular authorities was sufficient to induct him or his assistants into a pastoral function. We must not fail to mention that Saunier's rejection of magisterial fiat in this matter may have been as much controlled by the fact that they were

[39] A succession of incompetent and even brutal masters and submasters tried to continue the enterprise; cf. Bétant, *op. cit.*, pp. 11–12, and the ministers remaining in the city regularly petitioned the magistrates to take some positive action in regard to the school; cf. Gabarel, *op. cit.*, I:306, where the *Registres du Conseil* for 23 April, 25 July, 5 and 8 December 1539, and 13 January 1540 are cited.

[40] According to *L'Ordre et Manier* . . . (1538), the principal, Antoine Saunier, took time each day to instruct the whole *collège* in the Christian faith; cf. Bétant, *op. cit.*, p. 30.

[41] *CO* Xa:8; cf. also the "*3e article* . . . *de l'instruction des enfans*," which dealt only with the catechetical instruction, but in the light of daily instruction in the Christian faith at the *collège* may reasonably be regarded as a possible reference to the "ministerial" function of the teaching staff.

insisting on the use of the Bernese rite in the Communion as it was by any tender conscience over ministerial order, for Saunier had been the Evangelical preacher at Payerne in 1531; whether he administered the Communion in this capacity is not known.[42]

Ecclesiastical Status of Lecturers in Public Courses

Regarding the adjoined courses in connection with the Collège de Rive, we submit a few observations. In *L'Ordre et Maniere d'enseigner* of 1538 (attributed to Saunier), the whole system of theological lectures in Hebrew on the Old Testament (Farel) and on the New Testament (Calvin) was set forth by implication as an activity of the *collège*, although these lectures were held, not at the *collège*, but at the cathedral.[43] Evidently a third person, in addition to Farel and Calvin, was engaged as the *lecteur* in Hebrew,[44] for his duties were described as being those of a language instructor, while Farel was said to have the duties of interpreting the text in terms of life and doctrine.[45]

On the basis of these *leçons*, a system of public disputations was maintained to test the abilities of the auditors and give them experience in the arts of argument and presentation. The purpose of these public debates was that " they may prove if a person is qualified to assume the charge of instructing the people after all have diligently examined and approved of his morals and his manner of life. But if the person is to be consecrated (*ordonné*) for the government of a school, not only is he examined in the

[42] Le Coultre, *op. cit.,* p. 121.

[43] Cf. Bétant, *op. cit.,* pp. 34–35. The Old Testament lectures were given from 9–10 A.M. daily in the cathedral church of St. Peter's, whereas the New Testament was the subject of the daily instruction at 2 P.M. in the same place.

[44] Imbert Paccolet occupied this post prior to going to Lausanne (mid-September, 1538).

[45] Cf. A. L. Herminjard (ed.), *Correspondance des réformateurs dans les pays de langue française* (Paris, 1878–1897), IV:459.

faith, but also in human knowledge: To that end, he is instructed in both." [46]

Even prior to the banishment of 1538, Calvin and his colleagues in Geneva were projecting a superior course of studies and their plans had taken into account the necessity of providing the church with doctors as well as pastors. In addition, as we have seen, members of the teaching force were regarded by the secular authorities as standing next in line to the pastoral function. However much this may or may not have appealed to the masters, they did not accept the fiat of the city authorities as sufficient authorization to enlarge their functions within the church.

When Calvin finally returned to Geneva (12 September 1541) to take up where he had left off, one of his initial concerns was the re-establishment of secondary and higher education. The public lectures commenced immediately and provided no great difficulty. However, the matter of the *collège* was another thing. Calvin's first choice for rector was Cordier, but he was not in a position to leave his work at Neuchâtel. [47] Provisionally, Sebastian Castellio, whom Calvin had met at Strasbourg and whom he had secured as a regent, was made the director of the school, while negotiations were carried on looking toward Cordier's acceptance. When that appeared to be impossible, Castellio was given the appointment as *maître des écoles* in 1542 and served as a useful pedagogue until his own desires for pastoral preferment and his particular theological

[46] Bétant, *op. cit.*, pp. 35–36.
[47] Cf. Le Coultre, *op. cit.*, pp. 142–159, is of the opinion that Cordier was not really interested in returning to Geneva in view of the wretched treatment he had received in 1538–1539, and that he used his obligation to the *Quatre Ministraux* of Neuchâtel as an excuse rather than as a reason. Cf. letter of Cordier from Neuchâtel, 9 June 1541 (Arch. de Genève, *portfol. des pièces histor. No. 1263*) quoted in E.-A. Berthault, *Marthurin Cordier et l'enseignement chez le premiers calvinistes* (Paris, 1876), p. 32.

bent brought him into collision with Calvin.[48] By June, 1544, he had gone to Basel.

There is no doubt that according to the *Ordonnances* of 1541, those who instructed the youth were to be under the same discipline as the pastors,[49] but there is a real question as to which of them were entitled to the designation of doctor. Was Castellio, were his undermasters, was Enoch,[50] or were his undermasters entitled to this designation by virtue of their employment in the school (and Church) of Geneva? To these questions, we cannot at this time return a definitive answer.[51]

[48] Castellio had the additional responsibility of preaching from time to time. The magistrates wished to promote him to a pastorate, but Calvin and the other pastors did not regard him as fitted for the post, although Calvin is recorded as saying that "Castellio is a very learned man, very proper in his capacity as regent, but he has some ideas incompatible with the character of a minister" (quoted in Gabarel, *op. cit.*, II:201). It is perhaps significant that, on the basis of this rejection, Castellio resigned his position of *maître* on 17 February 1544, not to the city authorities, but to the *Compagnie de Pasteurs et Professeurs*. (*Ibid.*)

[49] *CO* Xa:22.

[50] Following Castellio's demission, Charles Damont was nominated by Calvin and approved by the magistrates, but did not prove to be satisfactory; in 1546, the Council named Érasme Cornier, then teaching at Montbéliard, who died in April, 1550. Cornier was succeeded by Louis Enoch, who became *maître* in May and carried out a thoroughgoing reorganization of the staff and discipline of the school. Cf. Bétant, *op. cit.*, pp. 16–19.

[51] A thoroughgoing study of the internal structure of the Church of Geneva during the time of Calvin would be helpful at this point; unfortunately we have failed to unearth enough detail to be helpful on the points we wish to establish. The welcome news that we may expect to have the *Registres de le compagnie de Pasteurs, 1546–1564* in printed form under the editorship of Jean-François Bergier and Robert McAfee Kingdon (Librairie Droz, Genève) comes too late to be of use to us.

Cf. also George Aiken Taylor, "John Calvin, the Teacher: The Correlation Between Instruction and Nurture Within Calvin's Concept of Communion" (unpublished Ph.D. dissertation, Duke University, 1953), p. 171, who regards Calvin's original use of *docteur* as synonymous with *Maître des ecoles*. Taylor has not adequately recognized the real distinction that existed between the *schola privata*

If unable to speak with confidence of the situation that existed in Geneva between the return of Calvin in 1541 and the formal foundation of the Geneva Academy in 1559 regarding the status of the teaching staff, we do feel confident that we are able to demonstrate by means of a parallel development in Lausanne and the Pays du Vaud what were the developing areas of relationship between the staff of the school and the evangelical ministry. The development in Lausanne is significant also in that Théodore de Bèze was intimately connected with it for a decade prior to his involvement in the school and Church of Geneva. Thus, the Lausanne episode forms a necessary introduction to the subsequent development in Geneva from 1559 onward.

THE ACADEMY AND CHURCH OF THE PAYS DU VAUD

That Calvin may have received inspiration for the Genevan Academy as much from the school at Lausanne as from his observations and activity in Strasbourg is a possibility that we cannot overlook. This is especially true in light of the influx of students and professors from Lausanne to Geneva immediately prior to the foundation of the Genevan school, an influx that contributed materially to the rapid strides Geneva made at the outset.[52]

The Academy at Lausanne had its origins in the public lectures that the first Reformed pastor, Peter Viret, had begun from his pulpit in 1537. The Synod of Lausanne (1539) passed an article on the reform of public instruction, and the Bernese regime announced in 1540 that a school was to be set up in each of the chief Vaudois cities

---

and the *schola publica*, a distinction that was articulated in the *Leges Academiae* (1559); we will deal more closely with the distinction when we come to an examination of the Genevan Academy of 1559.

[52] Cf. Borgeaud, *op. cit.*, p. 40.

and even in some of the minor towns.[53] At the same time, Berne established a foundation of twelve scholarships, the holders of which were to live in a common place, under a common master (maître des Douze), as a kind of proto-theological seminary, and as a result of this bounty were expected to serve as "ministers or as regents of a college."[54]

Less than three weeks after the victory of the Reformation in Lausanne (December, 1536) superior courses had been reorganized along Reformed lines. Two young Zurichers who had studied French at Paris were employed; Johann Fries as director of the grammar school (Ludis Litterarius) or collège, and Bernard Kienisen to instruct in Hebrew. To them were added the two pastors, Pierre Caroli and Peter Viret, to lecture on the Old and New Testament respectively. At this time a professor of Greek was being sought. By September, 1537, when one had been found,[55] the two Zurichers had been called home, Caroli had been deposed, a teacher of Hebrew had been secured but left by the end of the year to be replaced in 1538 by Imbert Paccolet, who had left a similar employment in Geneva concurrent with Calvin's demission.[56] By the time the lords of Berne got around to a really substantial reorganization of the Lausanne schools [57] the superior courses

[53] Henri Vuilleumier, Histoire de l'église réformée du Pays de Vaud, 4 tomes (Lausanne, 1927–1932), I:396–397; teachers for these schools were recruited from among the French refugees, and in some of the towns responsibility for the conduct of the school was assigned to the diacre of the parish. On the office of diacre in the Vaudois Church, cf. Vuilleumier, II:289, where the author concludes that this office was a kind of subpastor or helfer, and notes that as late as 1622 the diacres were charged with scholastic functions.

[54] Vuilleumier, I:400–402. After 1542 the maître des Douze also served as professor of liberal arts.

[55] The name of the person who taught Greek from July to September, 1537, is unknown. Conrad Gessner was secured for this work in September and served until 1540.

[56] Caroli's deposition came before he had delivered any lectures; Paccolet's predecessor is unknown.

[57] Leges schola Lausannensis, 25 August 1547; Vuilleumier, I:408, indicates that this document was never printed and that it still ex-

had been entrusted to no less than six men, one of whom was an active pastor in Lausanne (Viret), and one who had taught the school at Vevey as a deacon (J. Ribbit),[58] and three of whom cannot thus far be identified as having been pastors prior to their academic employment (Imbert Paccolet, Conrad Gessner, and Celio Secundo Curione).[59] The school laws of 1547 established an institution divided into two parts: a *schola classica sive privata,* the *collège* or grammar school of seven graded sections with a master for each;[60] and the *lectiones publicae,* for which were provided four professors in Greek, Hebrew, theology, and the arts. The term *academia* did not appear in the 1547 statutes, and reference to the school in this technical sense first appeared in a communication of the Classis of Lausanne to the pastors and professors of Berne in November, 1549. The rector of the school was to be chosen from among the pastors of the city and the professors, who in turn were nominated by the classis for appointment by the Bernese Senate. The day-by-day administration of the school was conducted by an academic council,[61] composed

ists only in MS., but it has great importance as the prototype of the School Orders of Geneva, Orthez, Orange, Sedan, Nîmes, Montauban, Saumur, and Die.

[58] The question of the relation of the *diacre* to the pastorate is not at all clear: cf. comments below, p. 73; p. 102; and Vuilleumier (I:268).

[59] Curione had been employed as *maître de Douze* in 1542 and as professor of liberal arts (rhetoric and philosophy) at a salary nearly double that of the other public professors, and had left for Basel in 1546 (Vuilleumier, I:401).

[60] Mathurin Cordier had left Neuchâtel in the early fall of 1545 and accepted the position of principal of the Lausanne school on 8 October 1545, a position that he occupied for twelve years. Although the law was drawn up by a Bernese commission, the influence of Cordier is apparent, especially in the provision for graded classes.

[61] Reminiscent of the *Conventus academia* of Strasbourg, which was the creation of Jean Sturm as a counterpart to the *Conventus ecclesiastica* only after the reticence of the magistracy had more or less effectively excluded the *docteurs* from active participation with

of the two installed pastors of the city, the professors, and principal of the *collège* (*schola privata*) presided over by the rector. Among its duties were the appointment of the regents for the seven grades of the *collège*. These regents were regularly selected from among those students who had completed their academic work and were awaiting appointments to either pastorates or professorates. Such candidates were entitled *studiosi extraordinarii* and constituted a kind of theological seminary. Their status was rather intermediate, and eventually they became known as *expectants* or *proposants;* they lived in a common under the direction of a *hospes* appointed by the pastors and professors and substituted in both school and church as replacements for the regents and as supply preachers.[62] Cordier had been the originator of the practice of employing *expectants* as undermasters, or *hypodidascali*. The fact was that the *expectants* of the Vaudois Church enjoyed a quite ambiguous status. From the very first, the Lausanne Academy had adopted the practice of ordaining certain of its graduates. However, the Academy never was the sole source of supply for the schools and congregations of the country, and so the practice grew up of the classis (after 1561, the colloquy) examining and ordaining candidates who had received their training in other centers. Between 1604 and 1621, the Academy waged a campaign to limit the right of the ecclesiastical judicatories to engage in the act of ordination, which was successful, so that from 1621 to 1839 the right of ordination was settled in the hands of the academy, investing it with a quasi-episcopal function.

Mention has been made of the organization of the Vaudois Church by classes. This ecclesiology was basically Zwinglian but had undergone some modifications both in Berne and in the Vaud, where the whole country was di-

---

the pastors and elders in the *Conventus ecclesiastica;* cf. Wendel, *L'Église de Strasbourg*, pp. 201–203.

[62] Vuilleumier, *op. cit.*, I:405, 413; II:84, 122–124.

vided into classes with definite ecclesiastical responsibilities.[63] Initially, weekly meetings were the custom, but later this was found to be inexpedient because of distances involved and each classis was subdivided into a number of colloquies, with the classis meeting as a rule only quarterly. The weekly classical meetings (Wednesday or Thursday) had been characterized by Biblical study and exegesis, examination and ordination of ministerial candidates, and discussion of administrative matters. The colloquy met as a rule once a month, except that of Lausanne, which met weekly due to its concern for the school in that city, a concern recognized even during Berne's suppression of other colloquial meetings from 1549 to 1561.[64] It is of interest to note that the composition of the classis (colloquy) was

[63] Initially (May, 1528) a *Choregericht*, or consistory, composed of two members of the Little Council, four members of the Council of Two Hundred, and two of the evangelical preachers of Berne, had been established as a disciplinary body, a practice that was emulated as the Reformation spread in Bernese territory, by the creation of other local consistories, which retained essentially a lay character. However, the clergy of Berne were under some pressure to act in concert and soon developed an Ecclesiastical Council or " Convent " of nine members (three pastors, two *diacres*, and four professors — theology, Hebrew, Greek, and liberal arts) , a development that was expanded to all German Berne in 1530. (Vuilleumier, I:255–256, 278.) Confusion arises because the Latin term *consistorium* was applied to both *Choregericht* and " convent." (*Ibid.*, n. 3, p. 256.)
The adaptation of this general organization to the Vaud was ordered by the Lords of Berne to be adopted by the Synod of Lausanne in 1537. (*Ibid.*, p. 277, where reference is made to A. Ruchat, *Histoire de la reformation de la Suisse*, IV:413 ff.) The Bernese *Choregericht* became the prototype of the Vaudois consistory, but in the Vaud this body was never popular, and although the pastor *might* be a member of it, it never developed into a truly ecclesiastical body comparable to the consistories of the Huguenot Church (Vuilleumier, *op. cit.*, I:298–300) . The classis, on the other hand, reflected the Bernese " convent " and according to Megander was to be made up of the " legitimate ministers called to the service of the church of its bounds " (quoted, *ibid.*, p. 280). In this capacity, the classis was the prototype of the Calvinistic Venerable Company of Pastors and Professors and is so denominated by Vuilleumier (*op. cit.*, II:91) .
[64] Vuilleumier, *op. cit.*, I:287.

based not only on the pastorate (pastors and *diacres*) of a given area, but also on the professors and schoolmasters.[65] In spite of the fact that the Vaudois Church never postulated the office of *docteur*, it is clear that the function was recognized by virtue of the close relationship between the pastorate and professorate at the classical (colloquial) level.[66]

From the inauguration of the *Leges Schola* in 1547 until the disruption of 1558, which was a struggle over the application of church discipline, ten men had actively engaged in conducting the "public" school courses. Peter Viret (Biblical exposition) and Zébédée (lecturer in the arts and *Maître des Douze*) were in full pastoral standing; both Jean Raymond Merlin (Hebrew) and Jean Ribbit (Greek and theology) had previously, or about that time, achieved standing as *diacres*, while François de Saint-Paul (Greek) may possibly have had standing as a pastor [67] prior to coming to Lausanne in 1547. Of the other five,[68] we can find no evidence as yet that they had previously been pastors or that they exercised pastoral functions while they were associated with the Lausanne School. Bèze later be-

[65] *Registres des Acts de la Classe d'Orbe* from the last quarter of the sixteenth century is headed by an undated document of sixty-four articles entitled *Ordonnances qui concernent le règlement de la Classe* in which the duties of "ministres, diacres, et maîtres d'Ecole" are described in relation to the classis. (Vuilleumier, II:82.)

[66] Cf. [Théodore de Bèze], *Histoire ecclésiastique des églises réformées* [1580], 3 tomes (Paris, 1883–1889), I:108–109 for evidence that the term *docteur* may have had early technical significance in Lausanne. Five scholars from Lausanne arrived in Lyons in April, 1552, carrying with them recommendations granted them at the conclusion of their study "par les Pasteurs et Docteurs de l'église de Lausanne."

[67] Eugène et Émil Haag, *La France protestante ou vies des protestants français*, 10 tomes (Paris, 1846–1859; hereafter referred to as Haag-1), IX:95–98. When the 2d edition by Henri Brodier (tomes 1–6 only, Paris, 1877–1888) is used, it is indicated as Haag-2.

[68] Imbert Paccolet, Théodore de Bèze (cf. Haag-2, II:503–540), Jean Taguat (Haag-1, IX:335–336), Eustache du Quesnoy, and Quintin Le Boiteax.

came a *docteur* and then a *pasteur* in Geneva, but of this more in its place.

We are prompted on this basis to identify the "public professors" of Lausanne (from 1537 onward, with the advent of Gessner as professor of Greek, and certainly subsequent to 1547 and the *Leges Schola*) with the *docteurs* of the Genevan *Ordonnances Ecclésiastiques* of 1541. Part of this identification is based on the involvement of both pastors and professors at a common extraparochial level, a level that is overtly ecclesiastical. One further item of evidence in support of this common extracongregational ecclesiastical involvement is contained in a list of signatures to "A Request" from the Classis of Lausanne to the Senate of Berne,[69] which included those of four professors,[70] one pastor who was a professor (Viret),[71] twenty men who can be identified as pastors, one man identified only as a *diacre* (Perrin), one identified as a *bacchelier* (regent) of the Lausanne School (J. Randon), and two who can be identified as *maîtres d'eschole* (Cordier [72] and Jacaud). This is a fact of some significance, for it indicates that at an early date even schoolmasters, along with professors,

[69] The document itself is undated, but Vuilleumier, *op. cit.*, I:757–758, who gives the whole text plus the signatures, places it in 1557. Borgeaud, *op. cit.*, p. 39, places this document in its context, which is the attempt to establish Genevan standards of ecclesiastical discipline in Pays du Vaud.

[70] Bèze, Jean-Raimond Merlin, who in addition to being professor of Hebrew in the Academy was also, at some time between 1548 and 1558, *diacré-catechèse* of the Lausanne Church (Haag-1, VII:385–387); Jean Ribbit (Ribbitus), who may have been a *diacre* when he taught at Vevey but even about this there is some question (Haag-1, VIII); and Le Gruz, whom we have not been able to further identify.

[71] The pastors at Lausanne in 1557–1558 were Viret, Valier, and Banc; cf. Vuilleumier, *op. cit.*, I:50, 51, 221, 230 f.

[72] We have been able to find no evidence that Cordier was ever regarded as a pastor of a Reformed Church, although he had been for a time one of the priests serving Notre Dame De Bonnes Nouvelle at Rouen, 1514 and after (Haag-2, IV:681–694). From 1528 onward, he engaged exclusively in teaching.

were regarded in some sense as being members of the classical organization, though they may never have been pastors or *diacres*.

THE DOCTORATE IN THE GENEVAN ACADEMY

Just five years prior to the opening of the Genevan Academy, Calvin wrote to the king of Poland that the commission of the *docteurs* was extraordinary.[73] This, coupled with the subsequent lack of clear and concise definition about the ecclesiastical nature of the office, has led Émile Doumergue [74] to conclude that this was Calvin's final word on the subject. Taken by itself, the letter to the Polish king does not really illuminate the discussion, and Doumergue admits as much when he makes reference to Calvin's concept of an extraordinary vocation of pastors and calls attention to the fact that in the reformation of the church there are a number of extraordinary ministers, quoting from *Interim adulterogermanum cui adjuta est vera Christ*.[75] The subsequent history of the office in Geneva militates against this as being the mature conclusions of either Calvin or the Genevan Church; the definitive edition of the *Institutes* (1559) made room for the doctoral office as a function allied with, but separate from, the pastorate; the *Leges Academia Genevensis* of 1559 assumed that those persons involved in the conduct of " public " courses would be a part of the *Convent Ecclésiastique* of the city; [76] and finally, the redaction of the *Ordonnances Ecclésiastiques* of 1561 preserved the text concerning the doctorate, shortened to be sure, but essentially unchanged,

---

[73] *CO* XV:335, 5 December 1554.
[74] *Jean Calvin: les hommes et les choses de son temps*, V:97–98.
[75] *Ibid.*, p. 98.
[76] It is not possible to equate exactly the *Compagnie des Pasteurs et Professeurs de Genève* with the Vaudois classes, but the similarity is too obvious to mistake. Cf. below, p. 69, for evidence that the Genevan Church used the term *classe* for the *Compagnie*.

in so far as this office was viewed as an integral part of the public ministry of the church.

The Doctoral Office in the Successive Editions of the Institutes

Earlier we have given a fairly extensive treatment of Calvin's exegetical foundations for linking the Biblical prophetic office with the doctoral ministry. In the course of that analysis, fleeting references were made to *The Institutes of the Christian Religion*. Now we wish to show that the development of the doctoral idea in the successive editions of that most influential of Calvin's writings was progressive, cumulative, and positive, and that Doumergue dropped a knotty problem too quickly when he appealed to a single letter to underwrite the proposition that Calvin was not really serious about this matter after all.

In 1541, the year of the *Ordonnances Ecclésiastiques*, Calvin published a French translation of his doctrinal classic, based on the Latin texts of 1536 and 1539.[77] In this translation, a complete ecclesiastical system was not set out; rather, the system of the medieval church was held up for examination, and on the basis of Scripture, Calvin indicated the basic directions of reform. Particularly was this true in the case of the ministry of the church. The offices of elder,[78] deacon,[79] and doctor [80] were mentioned, but in such a way as to leave the issue of the contemplated nature of the offices in doubt. Even in the case of the office of pastor, or minister *(ministre de la parole)*,[81] Calvin was more at pains to differentiate it from medieval connotations than he was to reconstruct its function in positive

---

[77] Jean Calvin, *Institution de la Religion Chrestienne*, texte établi et présenté par Jacques Pannier, 4 tomes (Paris, 1936–1939), I:xvii–xxxi (hereafter cited as: Calvin, *Institution*).
[78] Calvin, *Institution*, IV:94, 108, 179.
[79] *Ibid.*, pp.120–122.
[80] *Ibid.*, pp. 167, 183.
[81] *Ibid.*, II:142, 222; IV:151.

terms. Indeed, he used the term *ancien* in more than one place as a synonym for *pasteur*.[82]

However, he did use the term *docteur* in the 1541 translation in two places in such a way that we may be justified in thinking he had a particular office in mind. Both uses are contained in Ch. XV, *De la puissance ecclésiastique*. Initially, in speaking of the gifts, and especially the Comforter, which Christ has promised to his disciples, Calvin insisted that these promises were made not only to the corporality of the church (*à toute l'Église ensemble*) but also to each Christian. By this token, "it is necessary that those who are ordained *Docteurs de l'Église* possess the excellent gifts [of Christ's grace] along with the others they have." [83] Taken by itself, that use does not preclude the pastoral office, but some particularization was implied a few pages later when the author spoke of *Docteurs et de Pasteurs*.[84] Assuredly, there is nothing about the text of 1541 that demands that we regard the doctorate as a special ministry. But the same contention might be applied to the eldership and diaconate and even to the pastorate, for in speaking of the latter function, Calvin insisted that the whole pastoral office is "limited to ministration in the word of God, all their wisdom to the understanding of that word, and all their eloquence in the preaching of it. If they wish to decline, they are false in their sentiments, ambiguous in their language, traitors and infideles in all their office, whether they be Prophets, Bishops, Doctors, or be established in a greater dignity." [85]

Although he made a partial quote from Eph. 4:11 in

[82] *Ibid.*, IV:109. Cf. John T. McNeill, "The Doctrine of the Ministry in Reformed Theology," *Church History*, Vol. 12 (1943), p. 80, who comments on Calvin's "terminological ambiguity" in the use of *presbyteroi*.
[83] Calvin, *Institution*, IV:167.
[84] *Ibid.*, p. 173.
[85] *Ibid.*, p. 174.

1541,[86] Calvin did not follow it up as a means of distinguishing between temporary and continuing offices in the church. Such a distinction was first adopted in the edition of 1543. Here the New Testament offices of apostle, prophet, and evangelist were interpreted as being of a temporary nature, while the canonical offices of pastor and doctor were declared to be of a permanent value to the church.[87] Also, in 1543, the office of doctor was established on a Scriptural parallelism with the pastorate,[88] and Calvin contended that he " was able to distinguish between them, that doctors neither exercise discipline, nor administer the sacraments, nor engage in admonition or exhortation, but rather interpret the scripture in order that sound and sane doctrine may prevail among the faithful." [89]

Essentially, the structure and definition of the ministry as it pertained to the pastoral and doctoral offices remained unchanged in the final and definitive edition of the *Institutes* of 1559.[90] To set out that evidence independently would serve no good purpose, as in most every case it would correspond word for word with what we have already quoted from the 1543 text. We are constrained to point out that the weight and consistency of this evidence

[86] *Ibid.*, p. 168.

[87] *CO* I:562–564.

[88] *CO* I:564, sec. 39: " *Quam enim similitudinem habeant nostri doctores cum veteribus prophetes, eam habeant cum apostolis pastores.*"

[89] *Ibid.*, sec. 38: " *Sequuntur pastores ac doctores, quibus carere nunquam potest ecclesia; inter quos hoc discriminis esse puto, quod doctores, nec disciplinae, nec sacramentorum administrationi, nec monitionibus aut exhortationibus praesunt, sed scripturae tantum interpretationi, ut sincera sanaque doctrina inter fideles retineatur. . . . Pastorale autem munus haec omnia in se continet.*"

[90] Cf. *Inst.* IV:iii:2, 4, 5. Cf. especially sec. 16, where Calvin appealed to the practice of the primitive church for the use of imposition of hands in ordination and indicated his belief that pastors, doctors, and deacons had been so inducted. This section was word for word from the 1543 edition (*CO* I:571, sec. 50) ; " *Sic pastores et doctores, sic diaconas consecrabant.*"

does cast some doubt on Doumergue's use of the letter to the king of Poland as being crucial to the understanding of Calvin's own conception of the doctorate.

However, there yet remains one item with which we have not dealt. It is implicit in the *Ordonnances Ecclésiastiques* (1541). When that document is read in conjunction with the 1543 edition of the *Institutes,* the question, Where does the doctor exercise his function? ceases to be so pressing. According to the *Institutes,* qua doctor he was excluded from liturgical and disciplinary involvement. In the language of the *Ordonnances Ecclésiastiques,* the doctor was specifically to exercise his function in the academic endeavor of the church. This realization turns our attention to the founding of the Genevan Academy.

The Doctoral Office and the Genevan Academy

The early interest of Calvin in the religious instruction of the Church of Geneva had found part of its focus in the revived Collège de Rive. However, the *collège* as it stood from 1541 to 1559 did not entirely lend itself to exactly what Calvin had in mind. As early as 1542, Calvin had proposed that the Council of the city undertake the establishment of "an Academy where citizens and aliens might be able to undergo academic work both creditable and complete." [91] Although the time was not ripe, the fact that Calvin sensed the academic poverty of the *collège* was underscored. All who have investigated this institution acknowledge that in spite of the theological lectures conducted by Calvin himself, the standards of instruction were certainly no higher than secondary level.[92] But Calvin did not let the matter of advanced instruction drop, and as a result of his prodding, the Council secured in 1552 some property to be used for academic purposes. Fund-raising in

[91] Gabarel, *op. cit.,* I:498.
[92] Bétant, *op. cit.,* pp. 18–20; P.-D. Bourchenin, *op. cit.,* pp. 58–60; Gabarel, *op. cit.,* p. 500; Borgeaud, *op. cit.,* p. 36.

the sixteenth century for educational purposes was evidently no easier than it is today, for when the Council
finally got serious about the reorganization of instruction
in 1558, Calvin himself made a house-to-house canvass in
pursuit of money with which to attract the kind of faculty
that would endow the new institution with dignity from
the very start.[93] Finally, on 5 June 1559, the *Leges Academia Genevensis* [94] were proclaimed in a formal public
assembly held in the Church of St. Peter.

According to the record, these regulations had been
drafted by the ministers and were presented for ratification
to the city Council along with the designation of Bèze as
rector. Announcement was also made of the names of the
five public professors, the seven secondary instructors, and
the singing master.[95] Of some interest to us is the relation
that was conceived of existing between the two parts of the
school.

The preamble to the Latin text consistently spoke of the
schola publica and the *schola privata* within the larger context of the *Academia* and when it did so, applied the term
doctores to the instructional staff of the whole institution.
However, the French texts (1561 and 1562), under the

[93] Gabarel, *op. cit.*, p. 500; also Borgeaud, *op. cit.*, pp. 33–34,
36–38.

[94] For the text, cf. both Latin and French editions, *CO* Xa, commencing respectively in columns 66 and 65. The Latin text is also
available in a reprint (by Jules-Guillaume Fick, Genève, 1859) of
Leges Academ. Genev. issued by Oliva Rob'ti Stephani (Geneva,
1559).

[95] "*Antea vero designarant etiam iidem Antonium Cevallerium
[Chevalier] Hebraeae linguae, Franciscum Beraldum Graecae, Johan-
nem Tagautium philosophiae professores: . . . Theologiam enim
D. Johannes Calvinus multis iam ante annis profitabatur: cui nunc
D. Theodorus Beza, qui alternis hebodmadibus idem munus obeat,
collega adiunctus est.*" . . . "*Johannes Rendonium supremae classis
in privata schola doctorem: Carolum Malbueum secundae: Johannes
Barbirium tertiae, eundemque Gymnasiarchem: Gervasium Enaltum
quartae: Petrum Ducem quintae: Johannem Perrilium sextae:
Johannem Laureatum denique septimae ac postremae. Ad quos
Petrus Dacqueus cantor accessit.*" *CO* XVII:542–547.

title *L'Ordre du Collège de Genève,* exhibited a certain amount of distinction between the two parts of the school, referring in one place to " the *collège* for the young " as distinct from " the great public school " and in another referring to the total institution as " this university and *collège.*" Moreover, the French text made more of a distinction between the faculties of the two divisions by reference to the " Masters and Regents of classes " on the one hand, and the " Public Lecturers and Professors " on the other.

The text of the statutes proper demonstrated that there was a very clear division between the staff of the *collège* and that of the public courses. For one thing, the regents were responsible not only to the rector but also to the principal, who had a special oversight in regard to the inferior establishment.[96] The principal in turn was directly under the supervision of the rector, who was chosen for a two-year term, renewable, from among the members of the *Compagnie des Ministres et Professeurs.*[97] Although all members of both faculties were first nominated by the *Compagnie* and then ratified by the magistrates, it was only the public professors who were expected to attend the Friday congregation and the meeting of the ministers that followed on the heels of the congregation.[98] No provision was made for the regents, or the principal, attending these assemblies.

In connection with the festivities inaugurating the new foundation of learning, Bèze delivered a Latin address that is notable for its studious neglect of the part played in the preservation of learning by the primitive, the medieval, and the Reformed church. Indeed, he denominated Moses

[96] *CO* Xa:71: *Du Principal du College;* in the Latin text, *De Ludimagister.*
[97] *Ibid.,* col. 81.
[98] *Ibid.,* col. 85: " on Fridays that they [the three public professors of Hebrew, Greek, and the arts] attend, as much as it is possible for them, the congregation and the meeting of the ministers."

a patriarch, not because he foreshadowed Christ, but because "he had thoroughly learned all the wisdom of the Egyptians." The scholastic pedigree of the Genevan Academy was traced by Bèze from the Greeks — who had in turn received "the study of true philosophy" from the Egyptians and whose "ancient academies," it is true, were founded in accordance with God's particular design for his yet uncollected church — through the efforts of Charlemagne and other temporal rulers for the advancement of education, to the immediate concern of the city Council of Geneva for the institution about to be launched. Quite apart from the accuracy of the historical and Biblical judgments expressed by the new rector, this statement of the ideological foundations of the academic community placed its author very decidedly in the camp of those who regarded the school as being a creature of the state.

On the other hand, when Bèze had finished speaking, Calvin responded to these sentiments in a short address [99] in which he sought above all to impress upon the hearers the hand of Almighty God in the successful culmination of this endeavor to provide the society with an academy, concluding with a word of thanks to the city magistrates for the part they had played in the venture. Even in his word of thanks to the magistrates, Calvin made some allusion to the working out of the Divine Will, a thought that was carried over to a charge to the *doctores* that they be "mindful of their office."

Unfortunately, we have only the text of Bèze's remarks preserved to us or the contrast might be more profound than that which we have indicated. However, we have enough to give us some indication of the direction in which things were likely to move. A deepening interpretation and delineation of the doctoral office as a ministry of the

[99] We do not have the text of Calvin's reply, but rather a report of it, which is very evidently the work of one who heard what Calvin had to say. (*CO* XVII:546–547.)

church in an academic context would be unlikely at the hands of one who held such a high view of the civil foundations of the enterprise in which it was involved.

The Genevan Doctorate and the Ordonnances *of 1561*

In setting forth the second order of the ministry of the church in 1561, the provisions of 1541 were followed word for word, with the exception of one minor addition and a few orthographic changes. However, at the point where the 1541 provisions went into greater detail as to provisions for hiring, disciplining, and supervising the teaching staff, the statute of 1561 cut the text short with the comment that "as to the manner of procedure there [*collège pour instruyre les enfans*], it may be found in the book of *l'Ordre des Escoles.*" This was a most natural comment, in view of the following: the detailed provisions for the Academy were available in both Latin and French by this time; they had been agreed to by both church and state; and they would consume a great deal of space in an ordinance already longer than its prototype. However, the excision of the three paragraphs in question removed the statutory provision from the ordinance that subjected the teaching staff of the Academy to the same discipline as the ministers of the church. Although the *Leges Academiae* of 1559 provided standards for those selected as public professors and gave the text of the oath [100] they were required to undertake at the commencement of their labors, these standards were couched in such general terms as to be largely uninterpretable except as some appeal might be made to another document. We conclude that the *Leges Academiae*

---

[100] *CO* Xa:89: "Oath for the Professors and Regents, 'I promise and swear to acquit myself faithfully of the duty which is committed to me, to work diligently for the instruction of secondary and advanced students, to give the courses that are required of me by the statutes, our magistrates, and superiors; And to see to it, according as I am able (as I pray that God will give me grace) that the students live peacefully in all modesty and honesty, to the Glory of God and to the well-being and tranquility of the City [*Reipublicae*].' "

had in view the provisions of the *Ordonnances Ecclésiastiques* of 1541, in force at its adoption, and that the revision of 1561, intentionally or unintentionally (which we do not know), removed the very section of the document that in practical affairs tied the teaching staff of the Academy to the ministry of the church.

The Doctors of the Genevan Church

According to the *Leges Academiae,* the public professors were expected to participate in the Friday gathering of the ministers of the city. Actually, by the time of the foundation of the Academy, the Friday meetings consisted of two very distinct assemblies.[101] The morning assembly was devoted to a sermon by one of the ministers. Present at this assembly were both ministers and laymen and the technical name of "congregation" had by 1559 been applied to it in particular. Following the congregation, the ministers withdrew together to analyze the sermon and to perform other ecclesiastical duties such as the examination and setting apart of candidates for the gospel ministry, the correction of the doctrine and manners of its own members, and the general administration of ecclesiastical affairs. The seeds of this weekly meeting are to be found in the *Ordonnances Ecclésiastiques* of 1541,[102] but the first records

---

[101] Doumergue, *op. cit.,* V:108, n. 4, admits that there is a question of when a demarcation took place between the two. We are safe in assuming that it took place before 1556 as that is the pattern assumed by the *Forms of Prayers and Ministrations of the Sacraments used in the English congregation at Geneva* (see pp. 130–132) and because the distinction is evident in *Leges Academiae.*

However, one confusion we are warned against on all hands is that the Consistory of Geneva (the pastors of the city plus twelve *anciens,* chosen by the city council and the *Compagnie* together) was not the same thing as the *Compagnie* or congregation. The consistory was a civil tribunal like the consistory of the Vaudois, not an ecclesiastical judicatory of a Huguenot variety. Cf. Gabarel, *op. cit.* I:335–336.

[102] A. Bouvier, *La Compagnie de Pasteurs de Genève* (Genève, 1878), p. 4.

of its deliberations date only from Friday, 17 December 1546.[103] Thus the *Compagnie des Pasteurs et Professors* became in function what the colloquy, or classis, of the Pays du Vaud had already become.

The responsibility for instruction and the management of the Academy was vested in the *Compagnie*, where it remained until the late eighteenth century.[104] This close relationship of the academic staff with the ecclesiastical center of the Genevan Church gives us warrant, we believe, to look upon the public professors of the Academy as participating in the doctoral office that Calvin had conceived as the second ministry of the church.

Of the public professors of the first two decades of the Academy's life, there is little question that nine of them either had been pastors of Reformed congregations prior to arrival in Geneva or were concurrently serving as pastors of the Genevan Church: Calvin, Bèze,[105] Antoine-Roul Chevalier, Claude Baduel, Nicolas Colladon, Conreille Bertram, Charles Perrot, Lambert Daneau,[106] and Antoine De la Faye. With the exception of Baduel, who taught philosophy, these men made up the faculties of theology and Hebrew in the Genevan school. However, in the professorships of Greek and philosophy (*Artium*), not to men-

[103] Cf. Robert M. Kingdon, *Geneva and the Coming of the Wars of Religion in France, 1555–1563* (Genève, 1956), in his preface for a detailed account of the records.

[104] Bouvier, *op. cit.,* pp. 23–24.

[105] Bèze arrived in Geneva, 15 October 1558, was presented to the city council and accepted by them as *lecteur en grec* on 24 November, and on 15 December was given the standing of supply pastor with the understanding that he would continue *ses lectures en la Saincte Escriptue*. Then on 20 March 1559, he was named to succeed Claude Dupont in a pastoral charge. Cf. P.–F. Geisendorf, *Théodore de Bèze* (Genève, 1949), pp. 105–106.

[106] Daneau, in a work *Isagoges Christianae, Ad Christianorum theologorum locos communes* (1588), II:9:187–189, *De doctorum officio* says that some think that *simplex doctor* may administer the sacrament. He, however, does not adopt this viewpoint, but feels that they ought to be content with their vocation in the school.

tion the teaching of law, the situation was quite different. Neither François Berauld,[107] Bèze's successor in the Greek chair, nor Berauld's successor, Francesco Portus,[108] has been identified as a pastor at any time in his career. The same comment may be made about Isaac Casaubon,[109] who served in this post immediately after Portus.

The public professors of philosophy, with the exception of Baduel, were not recruited from the pastoral ranks, although at least two of them, Jacques Des Bordes [110] and Antoine De la Faye, went directly into the pastorate following their service in the *schola publica*. Of the others (Jean Tagaut,[111] Henry Scrimger, Simon Simoni, Job Veyrat,[112] Joseph-Juste Scaliger, Mattieu Beroalde,[113] and Jules Pacius [114]), we wish to single out Scrimger, Simoni, and Scaliger for further comment.

The evidence points to the probability that each of the three were members of the *Compagnie*. On the face of it and in the absence of any evidence to the contrary, this indicates the possibility that other public professors, who had not been pastors, were also included in the membership *de la Compagnie*. Such membership says little about their status in the school, but it does bear considerably on their status in the church, and indicates that their office in the school was regarded as entitling them to a place in the public ministry of the church.

[107] Borgeaud, *op. cit.*, pp. 65–66.
[108] *Ibid.*, pp. 75 ff.
[109] Haag-2, III:810.
[110] Des Bordes to the household of the Lord of Anduze at Montpellier, and De la Faye to the pastorate in Geneva. (Borgeaud, *op. cit.*, pp. 77 f.)
[111] *Ibid.*, pp. 66 ff. Tagaut was memorialized in the *Registres de la Compagnie* for August, 1560.
[112] *Ibid.*, pp. 115–116.
[113] Eugène Choisy, *L'état chrétien calviniste à Genève* (Genève, 1902), p. 129.
[114] Pacius was really a lawyer and only filled in the arts faculty. (Borgeaud, *op. cit.*, pp. 638 f.)

Henry Scrimger [115] (died 1571) was educated at St. Andrews in Scotland, 1533–1534, and studied further in Paris and Bourges. He was offered the chair of philosophy at Geneva in September, 1561, and accepted the last of December. In 1563, Scrimger became a member of the Council of Two Hundred and, although in the same year he took over the courses being taught by his colleague in philosophy, Jacques Des Bordes (when the latter was ordained to the pastorate and sent as a chaplain to a noble house in Montpellier), he seems to have found it difficult to serve both state and church well, for we find the *Compagnie* expressing dissatisfaction with his divided loyalty two years later. He turned over the philosophy courses to Simoni in 1565 and turned to lecturing in law as a direct result of the dissatisfaction, but his involvement in legal and diplomatic business did not cease and in October, 1568, he was advised by the Council to request a dismission from his academic duties before he got " sacked." Later in the month, he made his request, not to the Council, but to the *Compagnie,* who granted it provided the magistrates would agree. [116] The evidence does not prove conclusively that Scrimger was a member of the *Compagnie,* but it is suggestive. The force of the *Compagnie's* complaint of 1565, and the Council's suggestion of 1568 would seem to be that both bodies recognized the claim the *Compagnie* had on this man, a claim that extends beyond mere employment in the Academy. Weight is added to this point of view when we deal with Scrimger's successor in the chair of philosophy.

Simon Simoni [117] (? — after 1582) was from Lucca and an elder-catechist of the Italian refugee congregation. He

[115] Cf. Borgeaud, *op. cit.,* pp. 73–78, 92–94; quoting *Reg. Comp.* for 1 March 1563, 8 October 1565, 1 October 1568, and 1 November 1568.

[116] Bèze reported to the Council that Scrimger had approached the *Compagnie* for his dismission.

[117] Cf. Borgeaud, *op. cit.,* pp. 94–100.

had been giving public lectures for about a year when the question was raised as to the propriety of this activity in the early part of 1565.[118] Initially, the idea seemed to have been that Simoni would be given a blessing and told to go ahead with his teaching, but dissatisfaction with Scrimger changed the picture and Simoni was given a position as a titled professor and admitted to the *Compagnie*.[119] Of this there seems to be no doubt; neither does there seem to be any doubt about Simoni's capacity to foment trouble and difficulty and the *Registres du Conseil* for 1566 are replete with his protestations of poverty and pleas for assistance in averting impending financial doom. Finally, in 1567, Simoni thought up a scheme to augment his wages, and offered to give medical lectures if the Council would give him half again as much as he was getting, which was finally agreed upon after Simoni had demonstrated his capacity as a teacher of medicine before an audience that consisted of " pastors, professors, physicians and surgeons, and some of the Magistrates."

Everything seemed to be settled and going well when, in the summer of 1567, Simoni got into a brawl with the pastor of the Italian congregation, Balbani, and was brought before the Consistory. This outrage finished his usefulness in the eyes of the *Compagnie,* and it recommended his dismissal from his professorship and his ouster from *la classe des ministres*.[120]

Joseph-Juste Scaliger [121] (1540–1609) had been won completely to the Reform while a student in Paris and had fought in the ranks of the Reformed forces during the Third War of Religion. Following the war, he had gone to

[118] *Ibid., Reg. Comp.* for 26 January 1565.
[119] *Ibid., Reg. Comp.* for 20 June 1567, where it was specifically minuted that Simoni had been a member for two years of the *collège des ministres et professeurs.*
[120] *Ibid.,* p. 97, quoting *Livre du Conseil des affaires criminalz et consistoriaux,* 19 June 1567.
[121] Cf. Borgeaud, *op. cit.,* pp. 132 f.

study law at Valencia and had escaped out of France to Geneva after the Massacre of St. Bartholomew. His arrival coincided with the necessity of finding a successor to Job Veyrat, professor of philosophy, who had just died. By 31 October, the Compagnie [122] had elected him to the post and four days later the Council confirmed his appointment.[123] Scaliger did not get along with Bertram, who had that same year taken on some of the responsibilities in the theology lectures as well as continuing to read Hebrew. At a later date, after Scaliger had left the city, he wrote to Bèze, protesting some attacks on himself by Bertram in which he spoke of de paroles outrageantes l'un de nostre Compagnie et ministre.[124] It is significant that he should use nostre, indicating his own involvement, rather than vôtre, which would have been entirely natural if he had never been included in the Compagnie. Two decades later, when he was under attack from another source, the Compagnie came to his defense on the basis of prior association.[125]

Again, as in the case of Scrimger, our demonstration is not absolute. However, arguing on the basis of the overt testimony we can present in the case of Simoni, we believe that the threads of evidence showing in the cases of Scrimger and Scaliger lead to the conclusion that the chair of philosophy at the Academy of Geneva was regarded at this time as being a fit occupation for a doctor of the church, and furthermore, that the occupant of the chair was picked with an eye to his acceptability in the public ministry of the church, and even more to the point, that by induction into this office he became a doctor and thereby took his place along with the pastors and other doctors of the

[122] Ibid., p. 132, quoting Reg. Comp. for 31 October 1572.
[123] Ibid., quoting Reg. Con. for 3 November 1572.
[124] Seitz, Joseph-Juste Scaliger et Genève (Genève, 1895), pp. 21–22, quoting Reg. Comp. for 8 June 1576.
[125] Seitz, op. cit., p. 31, where the Reg. Comp. for 3 January 1597 is quoted.

church in the *Compagnie* or *classe des ministres* as it exercised episcopal functions and responsibilities in the Reformed Church of Geneva.

This, then, was not a temporary or extraordinary office of the Church: [126] neither in Calvin's Geneva, nor, as we shall demonstrate, in the Reformed churches of France, Netherlands, the Rhine Valley, Scotland, nor even in the Puritan settlement of New England and the halls of the Westminster Assembly. However, by the banks of the Charles and the Thames, some of Calvin's heritors forgot that the church on the banks of Lac Loman employed its doctors in the Academy.

[126] Bouvier, *op. cit.*, p. 12, gives evidence that *La Compagnie* in the Church of Geneva maintained "lay" professors and individuals certified as competent to be pastors on its roll until 1834, pastors emeritus until 1847, and professors of theology by virtue of their office until 1874. Unfortunately, however, M. Bouvier did not cite a great deal of evidence from the early period.

IV

The Huguenot Church and the Doctoral Office

NEITHER THE GALLICAN CONFESSION OF FAITH of 1559 nor the first Discipline[1] of the French Reformed Church made reference to an ecclesiastical office of doctor. Yet the corporate nature of the ministry was quite evident in both documents,[2] and doubtless this allowed an early introduction of the doctoral office with no apparent sense of strain. In addition to this, there was an evident lack of complete uniformity in the French Reformed churches as to the exact composition of the public ministry.[3]

[1] Cf. Jacques Pannier, Les origines de la Confession de Foi et la Discipline des églises réformées de France (Paris, 1936), pp. 164–167.

[2] Philip Schaff, The Creeds of Christendom (New York, 1919), III:376, Art. XXIX: " C'est qu'il y ait des pasteurs, des surveillants et des diacres." Pannier, Les Origines de la Confession de Foi, Art. 3, " Que les Ministres amèneront avec eux au Synode chacun un Ancien, ou Diacre de leur Église, ou plusieurs." Also, Arts. 5, 6, and 20, " Les Anciens et Diacres sont le Sénat de l'Église, auquel doyvent présider les Ministres de la parole."

[3] Cf. [Théodore de Bèze], Histoire ecclésiastique des églises réformées au royaume de France, 3 tomes, edition nouvelle (Paris, 1883–1889); I:119–120, noted that by 1555, congregations at Paris, Poitier, and Meaux were governed by consistories of Anciens et Diacres; however, in 1561, at Montauban, Cestat was ordained diacre catechiste (p. 927) and on 3 August, de Biron was ordained diacre & catechiste eleven days prior to Carvin, who had preached previously at Villeneuve in 1541, and was similarly listed (p. 929). Also, at Orleans and Gyen in 1562, the consistory was said to consist of Diacres et Anciens, transposing the usual way of listing the offices. (Bèze, II:196, 548.)

THE HUGUENOT CHURCH AND THE DOCTORAL OFFICE   73

However, the influence of the Genevan Church Order was strong, for at the second National Synod (1560) [4] both matters came under consideration. First, the Lausanne practice of denominating vicars or associate pastors as *diacre* was rejected in favor of the Genevan conception of that office. Second, the church felt called upon to add to its discipline a new article, specifically denying the authority of a *docteur* to administer either sacrament, unless he was at the same time a pastor (*ministre*).[5]

What is interesting here was not so much the prohibition, which had for authority the writings of Calvin (cf. *Inst.* IV.iii.4), but rather that the church recognized the existence of a group of men so closely related to its liturgical life that their office was in danger of being confused with the pastoral office. Even more interesting was the recognition of their existence and (by implication) their status without the trouble being taken to formalize the office and fit it into the already established structure of *pasteur, anciens,* and *diacres.*

The Role of the Doctor Reflected in Synodical Records

For our purposes, the Acts of the French Reformed National Synods may be divided into three major periods: (1) 1560–1581; (2) 1594–1617; and (3) 1620–1645. During the first period, the references generally indicated increased concern for a more exact delineation of the office in terms of its ecclesiastical nature and relationship. During the second stage, the doctorate was subjected to further

[4] Text in Aymon, *Tous les synodes nationaux des églises réformées,* 2 vols. (La Haye, 1710), pp. 13–22; hereafter referred to as Aymon. For English translation of these records dependent on different MSS., see John Quick, *Synodicon in Gallia Reformata* (London, 1692); hereafter noted as Quick, cited only when there is a divergence from the Aymon text.

[5] Aymon, *op. cit.,* I:16.

delineation, and certain limitations to its prerogatives began to appear. In the third period (post-Dort), a real aura of suspicion became apparent as the church sought to bring the doctorate under a more rigid control in the name of " orthodoxy " and pure religion. During the initial phase especially, some quite important actions were initiated. In 1563, it was decided that professors of divinity might be admitted to consistories and serve as deputies to synods (national as well as provincial, presumably).[6] Thus, professors (of theology) were not automatically included in the pastoral office. If such had been the case, there would have been no point to this action. The only logical explanation is that there did exist a group of public office-bearers who may never have been pastors,[7] but who, because of their function as instructors in a particular discipline, were recognized as being the doctors of whom the Genevan Church had spoken in its *Ordonnances Ecclésiastiques* of 1541 and 1561.

The synodical actions of 1571 and 1572 reinforce our point that the doctorate and pastorate were regarded in the French Reformed Church not only as separate in function but as separate in status, i.e., a distinct " order " of the public ministry of the church. The National Synod at La Rochelle (April, 1571), with Théodore de Bèze as moderator, decided that when matters of doctrine were up for consideration in the colloquies the elders and professors of

---

[6] Aymon, I:33: Organization of the provincial synods into classes or colloquies did not become uniform until 1572; cf. G. V. Lechler, *Geschichte der Presbyterial- und Synodalverfassung* (Leiden, 1854), p. 83, although both terms were used in 1563. *Colloque* was synonymous with the *Ministres du voisinage* and the *Ministres de la Classe de Nîmes* were delegated to be board of censors for books. (Aymon, I:34, 36, arts. xv, xi.)

[7] " *Ceux qui sont esleus une fois au ministère de la parole* [pastorate], *doivent entendre qu'ils sont esleus pour estre ministres toute leur vie.*" Art. 12, Discipline, 1559 (Pannier, *Les Origines de la Confession de Foi*, p. 165). The principle of status for the pastor, apart from office, was clearly indicated from the beginning.

divinity might be present to give their voice in judgment, but only the ministers and professors of divinity were to have determining vote. The assumption here was twofold: the doctor's office was similar to but not identical with that of elder; by the same token, it was similar to but not identical with that of the pastor.

Finally, in 1572 the National Synod made some definition of the doctorate in the following words: " The Article [8] concerning professors of divinity shall be thus enlarged, [Doctors] and Professors of Divinity shall be chosen by a synod, or colloquy [9] after good proof, and sufficient trial of their life and doctrine. And they shall be acquainted, that they be wholly dedicated for their lives under the service of God and His Church, and to be employed according to the appointment of the classes or synods, to whose authority they shall yield obedience. Moreover they shall subscribe our Confession of Faith, and Church Discipline. And whenever any difficulty in doctrinal points does occur they shall be called forth, if they be upon the place, to assist in the decision. The Regents also shall make the same subscription." [10]

By this enactment, professors of *théologie* (" divinity " is perhaps a good translation, as it is a broader term consistent with the actual practice of the church) were given a kind of status, similar to the pastors, in that their office was *pendant toute leur vie.* The synod or colloquy was charged

[8] What article? The only ones of which we have record are: that of 1560 prohibiting serving of the sacraments; the one of 1563, allowing the professor of theology to sit on consistories and in synods; and the one of the previous year, legislating both voice and vote for the professors in the colloquies. From the records of the National Synod of 1571 (Aymon, I:98:111; Quick, I:91–101), it is apparent that some copies of the Discipline had been divided into at least ten " headings " or *titre,* these in turn subdivided into articles. We possess no absolute evidence of the text of the Discipline before that of 1590. (Pannier, *Les Origines de la Confession de Foi,* p. 105.)

[9] Quick (I:106) used " classis " in the text and supplied " colloquy " in the margin.

[10] Aymon, I:115. Word in brackets does not appear in Aymon.

with their trial, induction, and employment, and they were charged with the specific responsibility (echo of the previous year) of participating in the settlement of controversy, but only when they were immediately available.

Two other pieces of evidence from the same Synod will perhaps give us a clue to the general tenor of the church's mind. First, the question was raised whether or not doctors and professors of divinity were obliged to put away (de repudier) wives who had been guilty of adultery, as was incumbent on pastors, or be deprived otherwise of their "positions as professors in our schools and our churches." The answer was interesting: No, because the canon in question dealt only with pastors and not professors, the parity (parité) is not equal; professors are not involved in the administration of pastoral discipline as the ministers are, and it is possible for them to cover up the unfaithfulness of their wives as they continue to teach.[11]

Second, the question was raised, specifically in regard to the University of Orange, but as a general query also, as to the legitimacy of docteurs en droit participating along with a minister of the Word of God in the creation and admission into their dignity and office of the docteurs en théologie. The answer of the Synod was: that such a procedure is allowable for lawyers and medical men in the induction of their candidates but that for theologians it is not, because " our Church has expressly provided against such an abuse as this."[12]

Thus, by the close of the National Synod of 1572, we may say that the French Reformed Church regarded the professor of divinity (doctor) as an officer of the church with specific responsibilities for instruction in the schools; that in some minds this office was identical with that of the pastor, but that in important respects (exemplary moral

[11] Aymon, I:119.
[12] Aymon, I:121. Quick (I:110) has "our Discipline" for nôtre Église in Aymon.

demands of the family life, administration of discipline and of the sacraments) the whole church judged this not to be true. The evidence leads us to believe that the professor of divinity was regarded as taking his place in the institutional organization of the church at the consistorial, classical, and synodical levels, not by virtue of being a pastor, elder, or deacon, but by virtue of his doctoral status. What is more, by 1572 the church may have delivered itself of a pronouncement regarding the mode of inducting a doctor into his office that, while based on an academic pattern, was not completely academic in its intention.

The first period closed with the Second Synod of La Rochelle in 1581. Only one item occurred there that was of importance, but it is interesting, for it gave evidence of two developments. " To the Heading of Professors shall be added Regents and Schoolmasters "; [13] thus in some copies of the discipline the provisions for the doctoral office had been grouped under a single heading, giving it status (by implication) distinct from pastors or elders. At the same time, all instructors of the French Reformed secondary schools were recognized as exercising a quasi-ecclesiastical function. The Synod of 1572 had established the church's duty of subjecting the teachers of the secondary schools to ecclesiastical control in the form of subscription to the doctrinal and disciplinary formulas of the church; now, in 1581, they were included, by implication, in the doctoral office of the church.[14]

The second period opened with a notation that Jean Baptiste Rotan, " pastor and doctor of the Church at la

[13] Aymon, I:149.

[14] The best study of the universities and secondary schools of the French Reformed Church, P.-D. Bourchenin, *Étude sur les académies protestantes en France au XVIe et au XVIIe siècle* (Paris, 1882) does not discuss the doctoral office at all, and in outlining the relation of the school to the church assemblies (pp. 297–301) does not take up the question of the relation of the individual faculty members to the organs of church government.

Rochelle," was seated as a deputy of a provincial synod.[15] This was the first instance of the term being used as the description of the status of a deputy to the National Synod. The exact meaning of the usage escapes us. Rotan is known to have taken his doctoral degree at Heidelberg in 1583, to have taught at the Genevan Academy before coming to France in 1589, and to have taught theology at La Rochelle while serving as pastor.[16] However, La Rochelle was never the seat of a French Reformed university or theological academy, although a *collège* was supported by the Reformed church of that place.

However, it was in the seventeenth Synod at Gap (1603) that we find the most illuminating legislation on the office of the French Reformed doctorate. " Article 3 of Chapter 2 shall be couched in these words. Provincial synods, in which are our universities (*Academies*), shall choose their own Doctors, [Pastors], and Professors of Divinity whose ability shall be proved by public lectures (*Leçons*) on some special text out of the original Hebrew and Greek Bible, given to them for that purpose, and by disputations in one or two days following, as may be most advisable. And if they are found to be capable, and in case they were never in the ministry (*& qu'ils ne soient point Pasteurs*), the right hand of fellowship shall be given them (*la Main d'association leur sera donée*) after they have first promised to discharge their office with faithfulness and diligence, and to handle the sacred scriptures with all sincerity (*pureté*) according to the analogy of faith and the confession of our Churches which shall be subscribed by them." [17] Doctors were assumed to be a class separate from pastors; the wording of the French text is significant here,

[15] The thirteenth Synod held at Montauban, 15–28 June 1594. (Aymon, I:173.)
[16] Haag-1, IX:8.
[17] Aymon, I:260; Quick, I:229. Aymon's text did not include mention of pastors; cf. brackets. Parentheses indicate Aymon's text.

for we have already seen with what ease the terms "minister" and "pastor" were used interchangeably. Specific provision for a formal admission of the new doctor by the Synod into ecclesiastical association (*la main d'association*) was not based on prior service as a pastor. A man who had previously been a pastor would already have had imposition of hands *and* the hand of association; repetition would be superfluous. The provision for academic and exegetical trials of the candidate indicated that the procedure was viewed as being analogous to the trials of a pastor, and the choice by the provincial synod, although it may have been merely prudential, was closely patterned on the election of a pastor by the consistory of the congregation.

The church was divided on the question of the necessity of laying on of hands in pastoral ordination. Initially, this, together with prayer, had been deemed necessary to confirm pastoral election.[18] However, this position was alternately challenged and defended in 1565, in 1567, and 1571, at which time the Synod declared that laying on of hands "would not be necessary . . . although it would be holy and a good [thing]" and then proceeded to formulate a liturgical order that presupposed just such an act of induction. The Synod of 1594, refusing to ratify the text of prayers to be used in the service of ordination, nevertheless called for strict observance of the controverted ritual.[19] As to the act designated as *la main d'association*, the Synod of 1609 approved a text relating to pastoral ordination that gave this symbolism a parallelism with the laying on of hands by way of signifying the acceptance of the newly ordained pastor in the wider community of the Synod. The *main d'association* (or "right hand of fellowship") can be traced as a symbol of ministerial reception as early as

[18] Pannier, *Les Origines de la Confession de Foi*, p. 165; Aymon, I:2.

[19] Aymon, I:64–65, 73, 101, 179.

1576 in the reformation of the Church of the Channel Isles.[20]

The intimate relationship existing between school and local church at this period was contained in the provision that made it lawful for professors, pastors, and consistory together to name a temporary substitute to conduct the lectures of an academic professorate that had become vacant, until such time as the provincial synod could name a permanent successor. The concern of the church for proper regulation and standardization of the academic institutions found voice at the same session in the establishment of a commission to draw up a body of regulations for the academies and colleges to be presented at the next National Assembly.[21]

The National Synod of 1598 recorded the first distribution of the king's bounty toward "the relief of our churches." [22] The use to which this money was put was indicative of the educational concern of the French Reformed body. The first provision was directed at two universities (Saumur and Montauban) and two theological academies (Montpellier and Nîmes) and only after this had been allocated was the dole divided among provincial synods on the basis of the number of parishes in each. From this time on, no National Synod was held at which the matter of this monetary division was not an issue. From the way this money was used, and the instructions accompanying its di-

---

20 Peter Heylyn, *A Full Relation of Two Journeys* (London, 1656), pp. 343, 368; and Baron Ferdinand de Schickler, *Les églises du refuge en angleterre*, 3 tomes (Paris, 1892), III:315.

21 Aymon, I:274; Sonis, Béraud, Giraud, Ferrier and Chamier were the commission.

22 Aymon, I:225. Quick (I:xcvi) explains that this money represented a cash payment from the public purse in exchange for the surrendering of the tithes to the Crown (or to former ecclesiastical holders) of those parishes which had become Reformed (arts. 3, 4, 5, of the Edict of Nantes, April, 1589; English text in Quick, I:lxiii-lxiv), and was necessitated by the fact that the Reformed were prohibited from levying imposts on their own people by synodical action, even at the parish level (art. 77 of the Edict, Quick, I:lxxx).

vision over the years, we are able to gain insight into the place and importance of schools of higher education to the French Reformed churches, and we are given evidence of a particular kind on the doctoral office. Three years following the initial division of the crown money, the National Synod pressed its provincial synods to utilize a part of their bounty to extend and undergird schools within their boundaries. Quercy was charged to see to it that the University of Montauban was provided with *de bons Professeurs,* and the other colloquies *sont pareillment chargës de tenir la main à tout ce qui concerne l'utilité de leurs Universités.*[23]

The very act of assuming part of the financial burden of the schools gave the National Synod an instrument with which to attempt a greater conformity.[24] The directive to report on the performance of the professors and regents, and a limitation imposed on students as to what Reformed schools they might attend,[25] was illustrative of a widening breach between the pulpit and the podium, and the failure to take seriously the prophetic demands of the doctoral office.

[23] Aymon, I:251, the allocation to the University of Sedan (although not a part of the French Church) may have been a nudge in this direction, for it was declared to be *"fort commode aux Provinces voisines."*

[24] *"Les Academies de Montauban, Nîmes, Montpellier, & Sedan très censurable, pour avoir manqué d'aporter à ce Synode les Comptes des Deniers qu'elles ont reçû pour l'entretien des Professeurs & Regens,"* and the provision that *"les Synodes Provinciaux sont chargés de rendre en conscience temoignage aux Synodes Nationaux du devoir que sont les Professeurs & Regens des Academies qui sont dans leurs Provinces,"* were the entering wedges. (Aymon, I:309, Synod XVIII, 1607.)

[25] *"Les Ecoliers en Theologie, & specialement ceux qui seront entretenus aux dépens des Provinces, & des Eglises particulieres, seront le cours de leurs Etudes dans les Academies dressées en ce Roiaume, entre lesquelles sont comprises celles du Bearn, de Sedan & de Genève; & il ne leur sera pas permis d'aller aux Academies étrangeres sans permission des Synodes Provinciaux."* (Aymon, I:312.)

From time to time evidence comes to light that in the mind of the church a clear-cut distinction between the pastoral and doctoral office was the exception rather than the rule, and that the action of 1603 was perhaps as much hypothetical as real. Thus, the pastors of congregations in the vicinity of schools (*Academies*) were urged to prepare themselves by means of occasional lectures in case the need for their full-time employment in the schools should arise. The presumption behind this enactment was that recruitment into the doctoral function was to be made from the ranks of incumbent pastors.[26]

However, the National Synod did recognize some need for a certain amount of autonomy in the school to carry on its functions unmolested. It instructed the pastors living in Montauban but serving outlying charges not to meddle in the affairs of the church and university of that place unless the *Consistoire ou Conseil Academique*[27] were to request their aid and assistance. Nor was this the only unpleasantness at Montauban.

Béraud, the younger, and William Duncan, regent of the first class in the *collège*, were both competitors for the vacant professorship in Greek. The details of the matter were not recorded, but because the Colloquy of Lower Quercy had instructed Duncan to take the matter into civil court, both Duncan *and* the colloquy were put under the shadow of ecclesiastical censure. Moreover, the Synod decided that neither Béraud nor Duncan was to get the post. It was to be given to a third person.

Due to these evidences of dissension, and also to a desire to strengthen the school at Saumur, a move to reduce the number of Reformed universities was made in the

---

26 Aymon, I:311 (1607).
27 Aymon, I:325. We are not certain of the composition of the academic council of Montauban; in 1609 the National Synod ordered that the " *Conseil Academique sera composé seulement des Pasteurs & Anciens nommés par le Synode Provincial* " (Aymon, I:378).

closing days of this Synod.[28] This was but the first of a
number of such moves,[29] and had coupled with it a demand that those provincial synods which had the means of
self-support for their educational endeavors should so declare themselves, that funds available from the public
purse might be spent where needs were greatest.[30]

Two actions relative to the doctoral office were taken in
1609. One concerned the competency of professors of theology participating in certain kinds of assemblies; the other
was a limitation on how the crown bounty might be used
to support the teaching staff of a university. The first was
somewhat ambiguous; on the one hand it exempted professors of theology from being included by the provincial
synods in deputations to political assemblies and to court,
and then left it up to the discretion of the synods as to the
wisdom of sending professors in theology as commissioners
to the National Synod.[31] Probably this enactment was
merely prudential, in that the professor ought not to spare
time away from the classroom. The events of the next three
years would indicate as much,[32] but there can be no doubt
that the second half of the enactment seriously compromised the doctoral office's involvement by right and status
in the ongoing work of the church at the synodical level.

The question as to which professors were to be paid out
of the royal bounty gives us evidence of what academic
functions were regarded as being part of the doctoral min-

----

[28] Quick, I:297, Art. 6; Aymon does not record this text.
[29] 1609, Aymon, I:378; 1614, II:26; 1617, p. 122; 1623, p. 286.
[30] Aymon, I:315.
[31] Aymon, I:374.
[32] Synod XX, 1612, ordered that a professor of theology accepting
deputation to a political assembly should be suspended for 6 months
from his charge (Aymon, I:405, art. viii), and specifically censured
" Monsieur Jeremie Ferrier, Pasteur de l'Eglise de Nîmes . . . pour
avoir beaucoup negligé sa Charge de Professeur en Theologie,
n'aniant pû l'exercer tandis qu'il a fair divers Voiages en Cour &
aux Assemblées Politiques, contre l'Ordonnance du Synode National
de St. Maixent " (Aymon, I:413–414).

istry of the church. For example, the professor of law at the
University of Sedan might not be paid out of monies provided by the Synod,[33] and this in spite of the fact that as of
1609 this was the only place where law was taught in any
of the Reformed academies of the kingdom. More specifically, the following professorships only were to be sub-
sidized in each school out of the crown funds: divinity,
Greek, Hebrew, and philosophy (two only). The wages
of the *Regens Classiques* were not to be drawn from this
fund.[34]

When it came to detailed salaries for individual schools,
the National Synod regarded itself as competent to stipu-
late them. For the University of Montauban, it provided
that " at Montauban, two Professors in Theology, of whom
one being Pastor, will have only 350 *Livres,* and the other
700 *Livres.* One Professor in Hebrew, who being Pastor,
will keep only 200 *Livres* for half Wages of the Professor
in Hebrew. One Professor in Greek receiving 400 *Livres.*
Two Professors in Philosophy who will have 100 [400]
Livres each." [35] In addition, the Synod took action in regard to the university at Sedan, stipulating that it would
support a single professor each of divinity, of Hebrew, and
of Greek in that school.[36]

Admittedly, the whole matter of the financial concern
of the National Assembly in the affairs of the academies
does not prove a great deal. But it does demonstrate the

[33] Aymon, I:378.
[34] Aymon, I:377. Only the Academy of Nîmes, for a brief period,
followed the Strasbourg pattern of a *Collège des Arts,* (superior to
the elementary institution) capped by a faculty of public professors
or an *academie.* All the other schools followed the pattern of Geneva
and had only the two divisions: *collège* and *academie.* The instructors in the *collège classique* were the personnel referred to here.
(Bourchenin, *op. cit.,* pp. 155–159.)
[35] Aymon, I:378. Quick's text I:330 has the larger figure for the
philosophers. Aymon's summary of the *Academie* accounts (p. 392
[par. 6]) supports Quick's figures.
[36] Aymon, I:379.

proximity of status of those involved in the teaching of Greek, Hebrew, and superior courses in philosophy to professors of theology, in contrast to the outright exclusion of the professor of civil law and the regents of the secondary schools from this association. It also demonstrates the responsibility the *whole* church felt for the proper exercise and efficient conduct of these offices as a doctoral function of the *whole* church.

As the period closed, we are able to demonstrate that all of the threads we have tried to lay bare up to this time were not completely unrelated; that the *docteur* of the French Reformed Church existed not only in the deliverances of the General Synod, but was an operative status in the life of the church, and further was not relegated solely to those entitled *professeur en théologie.* John Cameron,[37] a Scotch *émigré*, had been nominated for the post of professor of theology at the University of Saumur, being at the time copastor in the Church of Bordeaux. When the post at Saumur became vacant, he and Josué LaCosta [38] were in competition for the position. The examination was conducted by the Synod of Anjou.[39] Twelve pastors and four professors [40] were in attendance at the examination. Of the twelve pastors, Bouchereau, the vice-moderator, was professor of theology, and Louis Cappel du Tilloy [41] was pro-

[37] Cf. Haag-2, III:658 and *Fasti* VII:393.
[38] Cf. art. "LaCosta" in Haag-1, VI. LaCosta had been temporary supply in the post for a year.
[39] The record for 8 August 1618, at Mans is quoted in article "Cameron, Jean," Haag-2, III:658. The procedure recorded is precisely that set down by the seventeenth National Synod at Gap in 1603 (cf. pp. 78–79 above).
[40] [Marc] Duncan, M. D., professor of math and principal of the *collège;* [Jean] Benoist, professor of Greek; Guillaume Geddé and [?] Franco, professors of philosophy.
[41] Haag-2, III:720; following two years at Oxford, had been called to the chair of Hebrew at Saumur in 1613, and in 1616 had been named as a pastor of the Saumur church with reservations regarding his pastoral duties. He was not named professor of theology until 1633. On being named rector of the Academy in 1617, had

fessor of Hebrew at Saumur. However, Marc Duncan,[42] Jean Benoist,[43] and the two professors of philosophy, Guillaume Geddé and Franco,[44] have not been identified as ever holding pastoral office in the French Reformed Church, and so far we have not been able to identify Duncan in the Scotch Church prior to his coming to France. The presence of Duncan, Benoist, Geddé, and Franco, as professors in this synodical assembly, accorded perfectly with the enactments of the National Synods regarding the nature of the doctoral office in its exercise of juridical authority.

During the final quarter century of our study, four trends were observable that had a bearing on the Huguenot doctorate. First, and not unexpectedly, was the emphasis on doctrinal orthodoxy following on the heels of the Synod of Dort (1618–1619), with concomitant limitations placed on the free exercise of the doctoral office, especially that involved in the teaching of philosophy. Second was the emergence of a sort of anti-intellectual piety that found it difficult to accept the use of "pagan" Greek authors as texts in the training up of the church's ministry. Third, we note during this period an attempt to define certain of the traditional doctoral offices (theology and Hebrew) in

---

ceased to function as a pastor, but continued to be listed as such until 1626, similar to the record with which we are dealing here. These circumstances lead us to believe that the rectoral office was not regarded as having ecclesiastical status; certain professorships were.

[42] Cf. Haag-2, V:834; Scots medical man, called to Saumur in 1606 to teach Greek, metaphysics, and philosophy; made principal of the *collège* in 1616 with duty of lecturing twice each week in philosophy, twice in history and eloquence, and also in Euclidian geometry.

[43] Cf. Haag-2, II:279; a *medicine;* professor of Greek at Saumur in 1611. Had appeared in the National Synod in 1617 with a petition from the University of Saumur requesting that academies have authority to call pastors as professors of theology under certain conditions. (Aymon, II:125.)

[44] Bourchenin, *op. cit.,* pp. 463–464.

terms of the pastorate. And lastly, not unrelated to the third factor, we shall see how the church began to limit doctoral involvement in the life of the church.

Post-Dort orthodoxy. John Cameron's admission as professor of theology at Saumur, which has already supplied us with such excellent evidence in this study, was not received with complete approval in the neighboring synods.[45] Although Cameron was accused of being too liberal in his views of salvation, his appointment was ratified in the National Synod of 1620, but the Synod took the occasion to demand, that " it [oath of allegiance to Dort Canons] be fully publicized to them [the provincial synods], the National Assembly has ordered that it will be printed and joined to the Canons of the said Synod of Dort, to be read and published in all Provincial Synods, and in all the Academies, and that it will be approved, sworn to, and subscribed by the Pastors and the Elders, and by the Doctors and Professors and the Regents, and by all who wish to be admitted into the holy Ministry, or into the Professor's Chair in any of our Academies." [46] Further, any who were to reject the doctrines of Dort would be ejected from their office or employment, whether in congregation or school.

Simultaneously with the Canons of Dort being made a standard for the Huguenot Church, the National Synod gave warning to the professors of philosophy that " they were to take care in dealing with Physical or with Metaphysical questions, which have some Relation with Theology, to do it in such a way that they do not do any Violence to the Principles of True Religion, and never implant Scruples in the Spirits of the Youth which are contrary to Piety." [47] As would be expected, this was easier

---

[45] Aymon, II:173. The Synod of Poitier was the plaintiff.
[46] Aymon, II:183–184.
[47] Aymon, II:203.

to legislate on than it was to accomplish. The philosopher was severely limited in the way he might handle his material, especially trying in view of new knowledge and new thought patterns becoming current. So, once more, in 1631, it was necessary to remind the professors of philosophy that, although they were to teach metaphysics, they were to stay out of the domain of the professor of theology.[48] In 1637, all pastors and professors were forbidden to treat " curious questions " in their sermons, lectures, or writings. These questions were identified as those subjects which " may be the occasion for the fall or stumbling of students in divinity or private Christians." [49]

The church's concern for orthodoxy and piety was re-emphasized, and its working definition of the doctoral office further restricted, when on query from the Provincial Synod of Dauphiny, " if a pastor (Ministre) be able to exercise the charge of Professor in Philosophy with the Pastorate (Ministere) [?] " it gave answer that " the two Employments are not mutually compatible." [50] This was but further evidence that the French Church was gradually divorcing itself from a comprehensive doctorate as a necessary ministry of the church, and was relegating the teaching of so-called " secular " subjects to a profession, as such, apart from a public ministry. If pastors ought not to teach philosophy, then it would not be long until a definition of the doctorate could be drawn in such a manner as to exclude professors of philosophy,[51] and this, in spite of what

[48] Aymon, II:510; both metaphysics and logic were regarded as essentially useful for their polemical value, vis-à-vis the Church of Rome.

[49] Aymon, II:566. Censure and deposition " du Ministere, aux Pasteurs des Eglises, & aux Professeurs de nos Universités," was promised.

[50] Aymon, II:180 (1620).

[51] The reasoning here is based on the first part of Calvin's contention that all pastors " ought to be doctors," and the subsequent efforts on the part of the French Reformed to classify theologians and teachers of Hebrew as pastors.

the National Synod had implied by providing for the payment of professors of philosophy out of the funds for the public ministry, along with pastors and the others of the doctorate — theologians and teachers of the sacred tongues. Neither would the example of such as Geddé, Franco, Duncan, or Benoist carry much weight in the face of such an attitude, and the teaching of philosophy would become but another area of " secular " employment removed from the church's active concern.

Piety and the Greek language. What Calvin, Bèze, and other Reformers would have thought of the pious efforts to protect the minds of theological candidates from the corrupting influences of "pagan" Greek literature by proscription of the whole language is not difficult to imagine in view of their classical training. The initial move in this direction came in 1620 when the National Synod gave as its opinion that " it is not seemly that he [*un Ministre*] exercise the charge of Professor in the Greek language, if he be not discharged from the Holy Ministry [*Saint Ministere*], because it only uses for the most part the Exposition of Pagan and Prophane Authors: but the Professors in Theology and in the Hebraic Language, who are *Ministres*, . . ." [52] Evidently this prohibition could be removed if the man in question demitted the pastoral office. *Saint ministere* probably referred to active functioning as a pastor of a particular congregation, but we must not forget that in the French Reformed Church, pastoral status was interpreted as " for life " from the very beginning. Obviously, *saint ministere* was not broad enough to include doctors of the church who taught Greek, for Jean Benoist was still incumbent in that chair in Saumur. It would seem, then, that this usage bears witness to an increasing penchant in Reformed circles to confuse the term *ministre* with that of *pasteur,* and thus refer to the pastorate as *the*

[52] Aymon, II:204.

ministry, to the exclusion of the other ministries. The action was but a prelude to that taken in 1623 when the teaching of Greek was prohibited on the grounds of poverty and that teaching Greek did not produce enough profit.[53] This kind of anti-intellectualism did not go unchallenged, and although it resulted in the termination of the employment of at least one man — Jean Benoist as professor of Greek at Saumur — who has been identified as a doctor of the French Church, it did not remain on the record in this fashion. Subsequently, the Synod of 1626 permitted instruction in Greek, but provided that only the writings of the fathers of the church were to be used as texts.[54] The Synod of 1631 recognized that a knowledge of the Greek language was necessary for the proper instruction of candidates for the ministry and made provision that in those cases where a school was too poor to have the instruction carried on by a separate professor, regents of the *collège* would be given the duty of preparing ministerial candidates.[55]

Coalescence of the doctoral into the pastoral office. We have already touched lightly on this matter when we noted that subsequent to becoming professor of Hebrew in 1613, Louis Cappel du Tilloy was inducted as a pastor of the church at Saumur, with special reservations as to pastoral duties. The Synod provided that " Professors in Theology & in the Hebraic Language, who are *Ministres,* nevertheless will be considered as Pastors of the Place where they are located in order to preach the Word of God, with the Consent of the Church which will have assigned them certain days for that, without obligating them for other routine Functions of the *Ministere,* from which they ought to be relieved, such as that which concerns Ecclesiastical Dis-

53 Aymon, II:286.
54 Aymon, II:402.
55 Aymon, II:511.

cipline under the Articles of Pastoral Duties; and as to those other *Ministres* who exercise currently the said Charges of Professors, without having any Flock which be assigned to them in particular, they ought never to be placed in the rank of the Pastors in the Place of their Residence; that is why it will pertain to the next National Synod by the Testimonies of those who know them, to the end that they be given some Church, however, they will be tolerated where they presently are: it being well understood that the above concerns those who do not have any fixed position in the Academies and who are only occasionally & voluntary Professors & Preachers." [56] Two groups of men were being considered in this action: those actually serving in academic posts of theology and Hebrew, and another class of free-lance operators, evidently graduates in theology who had been certified by their colloquies, synods, or schools,[57] who taught and preached occasionally without ever having been assigned a pastoral charge. On the one hand, theologians and Hebraists were to be given status by simulation into the pastorate; on the other, men not yet called and ordained as pastors were to be forced to take up pastoral employment, yet were accounted as *ministres*.[58] The total impression received from such an account is of a rather fuzzy and unclear concept of the nature of the public ministry of the church, which was only able

[56] Aymon, II:204.

[57] The National Synod (1620) warned against an insufficiently serious view of ordination and blamed the entry of some unworthy men into the ministry because " *les susdits Inconveniens proviennent fort souvent des Temoignages avantageux qui sont donnés aux Ecoliers par les Docteurs & Professeurs des Academies*," who were warned to be more exact in the future (Aymon, II:178).

[58] In actuality these individuals were *proposans*, who occupied a rather indeterminate status; cf. the practice in the Vaudois Church and also the regulation of the French National Synod of 1644 that " *Conformement à la Coutûme reçûë depuis plusieurs Années dans l'Eglise de Saumur, . . . ordonna que nos Proposans aprocheroient de la Table du Seigneur immediatement après les Professeurs, & qu'ils precederoient tous les Regens des classes* " (Aymon, II:697).

to recognize ministerial status on the basis of the pastorate. Evidently the language employed in 1620 was not clear to some of the French churches. In the next National Synod (1623), the Synod of Anjou requested an explanation of what had been said and was especially concerned about the function of those professors who had been denominated pastors of churches where universities were established. The explanation was forthcoming that "the Churches shall not be obliged to give them Wages, nor employ them in such frequent Service as their ordinary Pastors, but leaves to the Prudence of Consistories to agree with the said Professors about their work and maintenance as they shall judge most consonant to reason and equity." [59] Quite plainly, the National Synod did not force the local congregations to accept professors of theology and Hebrew as *their* pastors, nor even expect that they would function as such. But it was indicative of the fact that need was felt to more exactly define the status of these men than had been done. That their status as pastors might be largely honorary was not discussed. Based on the church's own earlier practice, obviously their main function was doctoral; but it was equally obvious that the concept of the doctoral office by this time had grown so thin as to make it hard for the French Church to utilize the office in its full Calvinian connotation. Evidently the only course considered by the Huguenot Church was that these men were to be classed as pastors regardless of whether they were exercising a pastoral function or not.

Concurrent with the church's concern over the status of men teaching in its academies, it was also concerned with recruiting men for the doctoral office. The matter had been raised in 1607, and the provincial synods had been directed to discuss the matter of the supply of professors of divinity to the universities. In the Synod of 1620 the matter was raised once again, and it was ordered that selection

[59] Aymon, II:249.

be made of competent pastors who were both available and mature.[60] This indicated on another front that the church was coming to an equation between the doctoral and the pastoral office. Especially in the teaching of theology, the church was of the opinion that a man ought to have been a pastor before taking on the instruction of future pastors. The prudential factor was unmistakable. But in view of the drive toward orthodoxy, the church felt that it could expect greater loyalty to its doctrinal standard from men who had served a pastorate than it could from those who had spent their whole life in a professorate.

In 1637 the Synod referred once again to the action of 1620, preferring pastors as professors of divinity,[61] and in 1644–1645 it reinforced this sentiment by instructing pastors of churches in cities in which universities were located to take part in the public exercises or disputations of the theological students.[62] They were to do this together with the professors of theology, as colleagues of the professors. Here we may recognize the practice of Calvin's dictum that although all doctors were not pastors, all pastors ought to be doctors.

Thus we may say that the high-water mark of the doctoral office in the French Reformed Church came immediately prior to 1620, and that following that date there was a gradual coalescence of the pastoral and the doctoral functions, especially in the office of professor of theology. Furthermore, after 1620 the fact that a man was professor of Hebrew, Greek, or philosophy did not automatically class him in the public ministry of the French Reformed Church.

Limitations on doctoral involvement in ecclesiastical affairs. The Synod of 1609 had legislated on doctoral par-

---

[60] Aymon, II:152.
[61] Aymon, II:577.
[62] Aymon, II:696.

ticipation in the proceedings of the National Assembly, but had left the matter up to the wisdom of the particular synod. But the 1620 Assembly took a much more stringent position, denying to professors of theology, even though they might be pastors of congregations, right of free access to church judicatories, except under strict limitations.[63] This action seriously compromised the function of professors as office-bearers of the church, and practically eliminated the possibility that nonpastors would regard themselves as office-bearers in their doctoral capacity, or that the church itself would remember for long that doctors, apart from pastoral status, were to be reckoned among its public ministry.

At the same time it limited the ecclesiastical involvement of its doctors, the French Church promulgated *Statuts Generaux, . . . pour les Academies des Églises Reformées de France,*[64] which bore witness in some of its provisions that the doctorate had not been completely misplaced. These General Laws are quite interesting, for they show that the church was beginning to understand the school as a separate and distinct institution with specific needs.

Each academy was to be under the control of two councils. One was known as the Ordinary Academic Council and was composed of the local pastors, the public professors of theology, Hebrew, Greek, philosophy, rhetoric, and mathematics in the academy, and the first regent, or principal, of the *collège* attached to the academy. The rector of the academy was moderator of the council. This council met once each week and had for its specific duty the supervision of all of the public professors, the regents, and the scholars in the school. The Extraordinary Council was chosen generally by the consistories of the locality, along with the pastors, and the professors of the school. It was to

[63] Aymon, II:203.
[64] Aymon, II:209-212.

choose its own moderator in accordance with the local custom and was to be called to meet only on important occasions, and when the Ordinary Council asked that it be convened. It had the duty of nominating professors and naming regents of the various classes, deposing them or discharging them if they were negligent, dealing with those of the teaching staff who would not obey the Ordinary Council, and administering the funds that were due to the academy.

" Doctors and professors in theology " who were nominated by the Extraordinary Academic Council were to be notified to the provincial synod for examination and reception. The provisions of 1603, providing a form of inducting doctors and professors into office, did not receive recognition in the Academic Law of 1620. But in 1631 this matter came up for specific elucidation and it was provided, " Les Docteurs & Professeurs en Théologie having first been picked by the Extraordinary Council of the University, the said Selection will be notified to the Provincial Synod for its judgment; & in Case that it approves, the Order for the Examination and Reception of the Professors-elect will be given, according to the 3rd Canon of the 2nd Chapter of our Discipline " [Synod of Gap, 1603].[65]

In the establishment of academic councils in the universities of the church, analogous to congregational consistories, the National Synod had removed academic problems from the regular processes of ecclesiastical consideration. For the academies this was without doubt the only sensible action. Yet one result of this action must have been that those engaged in instruction within these institutions would no longer regard themselves, or be regarded by the churches, as possessing status in the church qua church but rather in the school qua school. Their loyalty would tend to center on the academic council and they would cease to consider the exercise of their doctoral office as an exercise

[65] Aymon, II:510.

of a public ministry in quite the same way as they would if their first court of appeal were to the local consistory or to the colloquy of which their church and university were a part. Only for the " doctors and professors in theology " was provision made for examination and reception in the Synod itself. Academically the professor of Hebrew, Greek, or philosophy, might rank with the professor in theology, but ecclesiastically they were not of the same stature — this in spite of the fact that a few short years before, Marc Duncan, Jean Benoist, Guillaume Geddé, and one Franco, the professor of philosophy, had sat in judgment, with the Synod of Anjou, on Pastor John Cameron to determine his fitness for the doctoral office of professor of theology in the University of Saumur.

Doctors of the Huguenot Church

Enough has been said so far about the permissibility of pastors assuming a doctoral office to indicate that this involved the individual in no radical change of status; his place in the ministry of the church was assured on the basis of his pastoral status. However, this was only partly the case for men involved in the doctorate who had not been pastors. If our interpretation of the history of this office in the French Church is correct, doctoral status per se had become pretty much of a dead issue by 1644, though there had been some slight effort in 1631 to preserve it.

However, prior to this date when doctoral status was still a theoretical possibility, the French Reformed Church included within the ranks of its public ministry not only pastors, elders, and deacons but also working doctors, who assumed their place within the life of the church on the basis of their academic involvement in preparing the youth of the church, not only for employment in the pastoral ministry but also for service in and to the larger community. On the basis of the clear and the implied statements in the documentary remains, and because of the synodical involvement of such men as Benoist, Duncan, Geddé, and Franco, it is possible to identify a number of others as doctors of the French Church who exercised a public professorship in theology, Hebrew, Greek, or philosophy (including eloquence, rhetoric, and mathematics) prior to assuming a pastorate or who, at this point, we are unable to classify as ever being pastors.

A detailed inventory and description of approximately forty individuals would serve no purpose beyond extending the text. Therefore, we will be content to call to mind a roll of those who exercised their ministry as *docteurs*. Those who cannot be identified with a pastorate include: Adam Abernathy, Charles d'Aubus, Samuel and Jean Benoist, Toussaint Berchet, Gilbert Burnat, Alexander Colville, William Craig, Crozier, François de Bons, David Derodan, Marc and William Duncan, Isaac Escoffier, Franco, Guillaume Geddé, Didier Hérault, Claude de la Grange, Jean-Rodolphe Le Fèvre, Alexander Morus (*sr.*), Claude Pethoys, Jean-Antoine Rudavel, Anne Rulmann, and David-Theophile Terrisse. In addition we are aware of the names of sixteen individuals who were elevated eventually to the pastoral office. In some cases, as with Bèze in Geneva, the interval was short, but in a number of cases, as in that of Louis Cappel du Tilloy, the pastoral charge (title) was something of an honorific addendum to their prior and primary doctoral responsibility: Alizier de Langlade, Robert Boyd of Tochrig, Jacques Brissac, John Cameron, Louis Cappel du Tilloy, Claude Baduel, Isaac Casaubon, Robert Constantin, Jehan Dragon (Sr. de Choméane), Pierre du Molin, Jules Feuot, Josué de La Place, Bernard Majandie, Archibald Newton, Alexander Morus (*fils*), and Jean de Serres.[66]

[66] For detailed evidence and description, cf. my "Doctoral Ministry in the Reformed Tradition" (Harvard University, Ph.D. dissertation, 1959), pp. 121–128.

The overwhelming majority of these men taught as professors of philosophy. However, at least two who never became pastors taught theology, six instructed in Greek, three taught Hebrew, and several worked in a combination of the disciplines either simultaneously or in succession. It also needs to be emphasized that this inventory is not exhaustive; rather, it is demonstrative of French Reformed practice and indicative of those who occupied a teaching office within this communion.

V

Prophesying, Prophets, Doctors, and the Dutch

S TRANGE AS IT MAY BE, the immediate forerunners of the
Dutch Church Orders of the sixteenth century were
formulated, not on the Continent, but in England among
the refugee congregations of weavers and other artisans
from the Lower Rhine and the Low Countries (both Flem-
ings and Walloons) . Products of the work of John à Lasco [1]
and Valerand Poullain [2] during the Edwardian regime,
these two orders were not completely independent; neither
were they absolutely dependent documents. Both were intended as pragmatic ecclesiastical disciplines for refugee
congregations served by these leaders.

[1] *Forma ac ratio tota ecclesiastici Ministerii in perigrinorum,
potissimum vero Germanorum Ecclesia instituta Londini in Anglia,
per Pietissimum Principem Angliae, Regem Eduardum ejus nominis
sextum.* Aucotre Jo. à Lasco, Poloniae Barone. London, 1550. Francf.
ad. M. 1555. The Latin text of 1555 may be found in A. Kuyper,
Joannis à Lasco Opera tam edita quam inedita, 2 vols. (Leiden,
1866) , II:52–285, and the German text, edited by Martin Micronius
(1565) in A. L. Richter, *Die evangelischen Kirchenordnungen des
sechszehnten Jahrhunderts,* 2 Bde in 1 (Weiner, 1846) , II:99–115.

[2] *Liturgia sacra, seu ritus ministerii in ecclesia peregrinorum
Francofordiae ad Moenum cet.* Francofordiae, 1554. Text found in
Richter, *op. cit.,* II:149–160. Cf. also Baron Ferdinand de Schickler,
op. cit., I:59 and 62, who identifies this work as a translation of the
liturgy of the French congregation at Strasbourg made prior to 19
February 1551, or before Poullain became the superintendent of
the Glastonbury congregation, and also cites a more extensive trans-
lation, to which Poullain added some of his own ideas and some
ideas drawn from à Lasco, known only to Schickler in a single copy,
*La Forme de Ordre des Prières et Ministère ecclésiastique avec
Forme de Pènitence publique et certaines Prières de l'Église de
Londres et la Confession de Foy en l'Église de Glastonbury en
Sonerset, à Londres 1552.*

99

À Lasco and Poullain

The offices of the ministry displayed in both documents conformed to the essential structure of the Reformed ministry as it had been worked out in Strasbourg and Geneva and was taking shape in the Huguenot Church. Both orders included the offices of pastor, elder, and deacon.[3] À Lasco included, in addition, the office of superintendent,[4] which was conceived as much on prudential lines as on theological. Poullain also used the term " superintendent," but it is obvious that in the Glastonbury congregation the superintendency was simply another name for the pastorate.[5] In theory, à Lasco established two levels for the ordering of the ministry, that of elder and that of deacon. He interpreted the order of elders to include bishops, pastors, and doctors. Although in matters of ecclesiastical discipline these two levels remained constant, when it came to the practice of worship there were three levels to à Lasco's ministry, the pastor being different in function from the other elders. As a teaching office, the doctorate in à Lasco's discipline was indistinguishable from the pastor or the superintendent. Pastors and doctors were spoken of indiscriminately as elders of the church; the doctor had the same functions as to worship, the sacraments, and discipline as the pastor had, meaning that in practice there was no recognizable distinction.

However, there was another activity of the Refugee congregations in London with a distinct bearing on the office of instruction per se. These were the weekly sessions for prophesying which were held on Tuesday and Thurs-

---

[3] *Forma ac Ratio,* cap. I, Richter, *op. cit.,* II:99 a–b. Also, " De ordine ministrorum et eorum institutione ac disciplina ecclesiastica . . . De electione ministris . . . De electione seniorum . . . De electione diaconorum." *Liturgia sacra,* Richter, *op. cit.,* II:159 a–b.

[4] Cf. Louis Herminjard, *Jean de Lasco et son ecclésiologie* (Lausanne, 1901), p. 90.

[5] Schickler, *op. cit.,* I:61.

day in both the Flemish and the French congregations.[6]
À Lasco followed the general interpretation of the other
Reformed fathers that prophesying, or the activity known
as the prophetic, was an activity of instruction rather than
irresponsible speaking in tongues or prediction of future
events.[7] The organization of the prophesying sessions in
both congregations was similar.[8] However, the procedure
in the two groups differed slightly. In the Flemish congregation, the practice was for the assembly to discuss theological and doctrinal questions, raise matters of moral im-
port for discussion, criticize the sermon of the previous
Sunday, and in a general session of give-and-take, instruct
itself in the more deeply involved questions of doctrine
and the Christian life. On the other hand, in the French
congregation a more systematic system was followed, and
the meeting was generally devoted to a formal exposition
of some specifically selected Biblical book.

In both congregations, the congregation at large formed
the auditory for these sessions. In the French congregations
the pastors, elders, and deacons were specifically mentioned as being among the leaders involved in this type of
educational activity. However, there were others designated as " specially selected of the faithful " who were to
take part in this activity with the aforenamed officers.[9] In
the Flemish congregation, the session of prophesying was
to be conducted by " good men, grave, modest, and versed
in scripture." There is no reason to make more of this than
the text will bear. But it is evident that there were in both
Flemish and French congregations men not called or appointed to any of the enumerated offices who nevertheless
were considered to be of such a stature, to be so well versed
and learned in the Scriptures that they were to be given

[6] *Forma ac Ratio,* A. Kuyper, *op. cit.,* II:100–105.
[7] Cf. Louis Herminjard, *Jean de Lasco,* p. 57.
[8] Following Schickler, *op. cit.,* pp. 47–48.
[9] A. Kuyper, *op. cit.,* II:101; Richter, *op. cit.,* II:106.

the responsibility of participating in these prophesying sessions. It is too much to say that we have here a doctoral office. However, it is equally evident that we are faced with a regular teaching situation and with a class of people who were recognized for and by their learning as occupying a specific position within the general Christian community.

In Poullain's Glastonbury congregation, the offices of pastor-superintendent, elder, and deacon were also present in their normal Reformed connotations. In addition, the discipline of this group mentioned a special office of deacon,[10] not elected as the others were by the congregation, but appointed by the pastor. This deacon was to conduct the catechetical session at noon on Sunday, and also was given the prerogative of conducting the worship of the congregation and administering the sacraments in the absence of the pastor. This fourth office probably reflected the usage of the Church of Strasbourg, where the term " deacon " was used to denote men serving as assistants to the senior pastors of large parishes.

In addition to the prophetic meeting as an integral activity of congregational life, à Lasco also called for weekly, monthly, and quarterly meetings of the ministry of the congregations as integral to the existence of the church.[11] Each week the congregational council or consistory of both the French and the Fleming congregations would meet. This council consisted of the pastor and the elders together, and one was not competent to meet without the other, except in the case there was no pastor installed. Each month, the pastors and elders of both congregations were to meet together in a formally assembled coetus. Once each quarter, just prior to the celebration of the Holy Communion, all the officers together with the superintendent

[10] Cf. Schickler, *op. cit.*, I:65.
[11] Schickler, *op. cit.*, I:50–51. Also Louis Herminjard, *Jean de Lasco*, pp. 86–89, and Gaston Bonet-Maury, " John à Lasco and the Reformation in Poland 1499–1560," *American Journal of Theology,* 4 (1900), pp. 314–327.

of the Refugee churches in London would meet in a session known as the *censure*. At the weekly meetings of the consistory the deacons of the congregation might be called upon to meet with the pastor and elders in arriving at decisions. At the monthly meetings of the coetus the deacons of both congregations might be called upon to render account of their stewardship of the funds for the poor. At the quarterly *censure*, the deacons, along with pastors, elders, and superintendents, were equally liable to have their conduct and their doctrine called into question. The pattern of a collegiate responsibility of elders and pastors had already been established formally in the Strasbourg Synod of 1532–1533, but the whole body of the Strasbourg eldership had not been involved. At Geneva, the consistory was made up of elders as representatives of the city council, and representatives of the pastors from the Venerable Company, and its responsibility consisted largely in the enforcement of moral and cultural standards in the community. In the French Reformed Church, the primitive text of the discipline included a congregational consistory as a component part of the church's judicial function, and the consistory included both pastors and elders, and on occasion, deacons. But note: the discipline of the French Church reflected a state in the development of Reformed Church polity at least nine years after à Lasco had instituted the same type of arrangement in the French and Flemish congregations of London, which shows à Lasco's priority in the development of the congregational consistory in Huguenot and Dutch Reformed practice.

This extended introduction to the Dutch Church Orders, and the structure of the ministry which they mirror, by way of the Refugee congregations of Edwardian England, is justified on several grounds. First, the Refugee congregations, their congregational life, and attendant Church Orders returned to England following the death of Mary Tudor, to provide a ready channel for Calvinian and Reformed ideas to circulate from the Rhineland into the body of English Puritanism. As such, their descendants will be met again when we deal with the debates of the Westminster Assembly nine decades later. But most of all, they are important to us here, as we seek to understand the nature of the initial documents of the Reformed churches of the Low Countries and the Rhine Valley. It has been noted that of the three principal groups identified at the Synod of Wesel in 1568 one of the most prominent were members, pastors, and elders of the Flemish congregations resident in England.[12] Wesel was the first of a series of synods held by the Reformed churches of the Netherlands and from it can be traced a series of documents we will now study. That the Wesel document owed much to the French Reformed discipline of nine years previous has also been noted,[13] for another of the major groups identified as taking part in this Synod represented the French-speaking Walloon Church located in the Low Countries.

THE CHURCH ORDERS

The meeting held at Wesel in 1568 has been described as more of a conference than a formal synod of the Dutch Church.[14] Be that as it may, the meeting did produce a document that became the prototype ecclesiastical discipline for the Netherlands. In this document five offices were described as " public ministries " of the Reformed Church: (1) minister or pastor; (2) doctor; (3) elder; (4) schoolmaster, and (5) deacon.[15]

The office of doctor was specifically separated from that of pastor and was partly assimilated to the office of

[12] Jan De Jong, *Historische Studiën over het Convent te Wezel (1568) en de Synode te Emden (1571)*, (Groningen, 1911), pp. 198–199.

[13] *Ibid.*, p. 24, and G. V. Lechler, *op. cit.*, pp. 116–118.

[14] Jong, *op. cit.*, p. 26.

[15] F. L. Rutgers, *Acta van der Nederlandsche Synoden der zestiende eeuw* (Utrecht, 1889), pp. 1–36.

prophet,[16] although it was stated that doctors and prophets were added to the office of minister or pastor, but that they had a specific teaching office (docendi munus). The writers of the Articles of 1568 evidently envisaged a difference between the doctor and the prophet for they stated that "of the doctors, we are unable to say anything at this time," by implication leaving a definition to the future. But they spoke of the prophets as " those, who in the meeting of the Church propose and explain the ordinary places of scripture, and this ability of explaining scripture is a teaching office." [17]

The activity of prophesying was also recognized here as a specific and distinct exercise of the gospel teaching function, and it was stated definitely that in the meetings for prophecy " not only the pastor but also the doctors, the elders, and the deacons, and also those from the people are to be heard." [18] The prophets and doctors were also to have their place in the consistory or Senate [19] of the church, and it was considered to be part of a prophet's office to conduct the catechizing of the congregation.[20] The correlation of this material with the previous work of à Lasco in London is too close to be mere coincidence, especially in view of the fact that this kind of clear-cut delineation of the doctoral office had not yet found its way into the French Reformed discipline. As far as the Articles of Wesel were concerned, the doctoral office was a separate and distinct position in the church co-ordinate with the status of minister or pastor, and superior in function to the status of deacon or elder. The function was equated with the pro-

[16] Rutgers, op. cit., p. 15, par. [18] "Prophetae seu Doctores."
[17] Ibid., p. 16, "Ministris adjuncti sunt Doctores ac Prophetae, quorum unum quidem est docendi munus, sed diversa functionis ratio." The teaching office was thus seen as shared by pastors and doctors, while the diversity of function was recognized in a typically Calvinistic manner.
[18] Ibid., p. 17, par. [19].
[19] Ibid., par. [20].
[20] Ibid., p. 20.

phetic office as this had been formulated in general Reformed terms. Although it may not be conclusively argued that an academic arena as such was contemplated, there is some evidence that the framers had a school in mind.[21] A distinction between the pastorate and the doctorate was evident, and we are justified in saying that the writers of the Wesel Articles had in view a separate and distinct office of the church.[22]

In the Wesel Articles we have merging at least two separate streams of influence. On the one hand, there was positive reflection of the previous work of à Lasco and Poullain in the Refugee congregations of England. This influence was most evident regarding the gatherings for prophecy for the instruction of the whole congregation. All the early Reformers had exercised a type of prophetic-doctoral ministry in the manner in which it was organized in this document. But none of the disciplines prior to this time (with the exception of à Lasco's) had placed the gathering for instruction within the context of organized congregational life so clearly as was done at Wesel. The gatherings for prophecy in the Wesel Articles were not synonymous with the act of catechizing, nor with formal schooling.

Wesel's recognition of the doctorate as an order of the church's ministry was a witness to the situation as it cur-

---

[21] *Ibid.*, p. 10, par. [4], which spoke hopefully of the "foundation of schools" and the "teaching of theology" as among the benefits to be derived from the implementation of a church order.

[22] The terminology of the Articles was not clear-cut. However, the usage of "minister," as synonymous with "pastor," in contradistinction to "doctor" or "prophet" was common enough to allow us to conclude that two orders, not one, were in the minds of the framers. Although "ministers" are to be inducted by imposition of hands (Rutgers, *op. cit.*, p. 15, par. [11], as well as "elders," *ibid.*, p. 23, par. [7]), no mention was made of the mode of induction into their office of either "doctors" or "prophets." Are we to assume then that they too received laying on of hands? It is impossible to say, and in the light of Huguenot practice (cf. pp. 79 f.) and subsequent strictures in the Dutch Church (cf. p. 108 n. 27), we are inclined to think not.

rently existed in the French Church. In 1563, the French
Church had legislated on the admissibility of professors
of divinity into the various courts of the church. According to Wesel, the prophets and doctors were to have a place
in the councils of the church whenever matters of doctrine
or ceremony became matters of controversy.[23] Thus, in
1568, the Dutch conception of the doctoral office drew
both on the tradition of à Lasco and on the tradition of
the Huguenot Church (as an interpreter of Geneva) and
conceived of the doctorate not only in the sphere of education, but also as a ministry of the church, taking its place
alongside the pastorate and the seniorate in the business of
doing the work of Christ, in discipline [24] and the temporal-
ities as well as in word and sacrament.

Emden (1571) to s'Gravenhage. The prophetic ministry
and the doctoral office received no further confirmation
during the next ten years in the Dutch churches. The
Acts [25] of the Emden Synod of 1571 made no reference
whatsoever to the activity we have denominated the " gathering for prophesying " written so large in the Wesel Articles. The only reference to the doctoral office was a rather
backhanded remark that the professors of theology, together with the ministers of the classis, were to be the
agents of censorship for those who wished to publish or
print any books dealing with religious or philosophical
questions.

The Provincial Synod of Dort (1574) [26] entertained an
overture from the Classis of Walcheren in which the classis
requested the synod to take action to stimulate the magistracy in the reformation of the schools so that adequate instruction in theology, law, medicine, and " professors in
the three languages " might be established in an existing
school to the end that a more adequate ministry might be

[23] Rutgers, *op. cit.*, p. 17, par. [20].
[24] *Ibid.*, p. 31, par. [4].
[25] Text in *ibid.*, pp. 42–119.
[26] Text in *ibid.*, pp. 120–220.

trained.[27] Reference to professors of language was important because of the position taken at Wesel that it was the
duty of the church to work for the establishment of schools
and theological colleges where these languages would be
taught.

Although the Church Order of 1578 [28] made no mention
of the doctoral office as a constituent ministry of the
church, " it specifically stipulated that: No professor of
theology may preach nor administer the sacraments except
he be called as a minister of the Word (*dienst des
woordts*)." [29] Under these terms, we must recognize the
doctoral office, limited though it was to the professorship of
theology, and we must also recognize the same forces at
work circumscribing the nature of the office that we have
seen previously at work in the Genevan and French
Churches. However, it was a new stipulation that the professor of theology, or doctor, might not *preach* unless he be
called to a specific pastoral charge.

Under the same heading, the Church Order of 1578
maintained the place of the professors of theology in the
judicatories of the church. No provision was made for their
sitting on the local consistory, but it was specifically legislated that they should have representation, through one of
their number, at such time as the classis or synod would
meet in the place where their university happened to be
located.[30] This perhaps reflected some of the concern expressed previously that the schools of the church would

----

[27] *Ibid.,* p. 213. The Classis of Walcheren, along with the Classes
of Voorne, Putten, and Overflakke were also concerned with the
matter of induction of ministers (*dienaren*) into their charges,
specifically with the practice (or lack of it) of the imposition of
hands.

[28] Text in Rutgers, *op. cit.,* pp. 211–338.

[29] *Ibid.,* pp. 246–247 [cap. III], "Van de Scholen" pars. 1–6,
specifically, art. 51 [par. 5].

[30] Rutgers, *op. cit.,* 247. The representative professor was specifically allowed the vote (" *een wt den name der anderer stemme
hebben sal* ").

have representation in the synodical or classical meetings of the body. It may also be reflective of a prudential concern (already noted within the French Church) tending to limit time given by the doctorate to activities of the courts of the church.

The National Synod of Middelburg (1581) [31] amended the Church Order to return to the classical fourfold Calvinist definition of the public ministry. Under the heading " Of the Ministry " the ministers were declared to be four: " the Ministers of the Word, the Doctors, the Elders, and the Deacons." [32] The stipulation against preaching or sacramental administration was extended from the professor of theology specifically by name to the doctor, and also to the elder and the deacon. Such a stipulation obviously established the term *Dienaren des Woordts* as synonymous with " pastors." This action definitely tied the concept of the doctor of 1581 (by virtue of the prohibition against preaching and sacramental administration in the church) to that of the professor of theology of 1578. We are also given some reason for projecting the office beyond simply the professorate of theology, for in speaking of the care that the communion should exercise over professors and schoolmasters, Middelburg specifically mentioned that professors of liberal arts and learned speech (literally, *vrije consten ende spraecken leeren; humanas disciplinas et politiores literas*) and those who teach the catechism were to be considered in the same category as professors of theology.[33]

The Synod of Middelburg dealt with specific questions propounded by provincial synods and their classes. One of these raised the question of the ability of the professor of theology to act in the classical assembly; whether or not the professors of theology were permitted, as the resident pastors of a place, to appear in the classical assemblies when

[31] Text in *ibid.*, pp. 339–480.
[32] *Ibid.*, p. 376: " *De Diensten zijn vierderleij; Der Dienaren des Woordts, der Doctoren, Ouderlinghen ende Diaconen.*"
[33] *Ibid.*, p. 381.

matters of doctrine were under discussion, and whether it was proper for them to vote on these matters. The answer given by the synod was a short and affirmative yes.[34] This is the first positive proof of doctoral involvement at the classical (presbyterial) level.

The mind of the Dutch Church on the office of doctor at the end of the sixteenth century was contained in the Acts of the National Synod of s'Gravenhage (1586).[35] Once again the ministry appeared in its fourfold Calvinistic pattern: the ministers of the word, the doctors, the elders, and deacons. The Church Order indicated, by implication, that the office of doctor was that of professor in theology and stated that the office was " to explicate the Holy Scripture and to stand for doctrine against heretics and wrongdoers." [36] In this document, as in that of Middelburg, the correlation between all the professorial offices was made to appear quite close, for the " other professors " were indicated as being in stature vis-à-vis the church in the same relationship as professors in theology regarding the necessity of taking the oath to the Confession of Faith of the Netherlands Church. Similarly, they were to be ousted from their posts by their consistory or their classis if they refused to take the oath.[37]

Acts of the Synod of Dort (1618–1619). The Synod of

[34] *Ibid.*, p. 454.
[35] Text in Rutgers, *op. cit.*, pp. 481–643.
[36] *Ibid.*, p. 491: "*Het Ampt Doctoren ofte Professoren in der Theologie is, de heylighe Schriftuere uyt te legghen, ende de suyvere Leere Teghen de Ketterijen ende Doolinghen voor te staen.*" Note addition of "*ofte Professoren*" as a correlative description.
[37] *Ibid.*, p. 498, par. 47: "*De Dienaers des Woorts, item die Professoren in de Theologie (twelck oock den anderen Professoren wel beg betaemt) sullen de Belijdenisse des Gheloofs der Nederlandtscher Kercken onderteeckenen.*" Identical wording in the *Kerkenordening* of the Provincial Synod of Zeeland (1591). Cf. Joh. Reitsma en S. D. van Veen (eds.), *Acta der Provinciale en Particuliere Synoden, gehouden in de Noordelijke Nederlanden gedurende de jaren 1572–1620*, 8 dln. (Groningen, 1892–1899), V:19, par. 18 (referred to hereafter as Reitsma en van Veen).

Dort must be divided, for our purposes, into two distinct parts. The first, or International Session, held from November, 1618, to 9 May 1619,[38] does not immediately interest us here. Although called by the authority of the States General of the United Provinces,[39] it was in effect an international doctrinal council of the Reformed churches.[40] However, following the one hundred fifty-fourth session on 9 May 1619, the foreign theologians were dismissed, and on Monday, the thirteenth of May, at the one hundred fifty-fifth session, the Dutch delegates proceeded to consider the revision of the existing Church Order. Kuyper reminds us that the Church Order re-edited at Dort was what had been adopted at Emden in 1571, and it was received at Dort as it had been re-edited in the Synods of 1578, 1581, and 1586.[41] Thus the Church Order to be remodeled in 1619 had, as a prior assumption, a fourfold ministry. And because the church in 1619 made no alteration in this pattern, we must conclude that the doctrine of a fourfold ministry was received without too much question.

What the Dutch churches did do between 13 and 29 May was to define more closely the relation of the church to the schools and, at the same time, define the relation of the professors to the church.

[38] Text of the first 154 sessions in Richard Jean de Nerec, *Actes du Synode National, tenu a Dortrecht, l'An MDCXIIX & XIX. Ensemble les jugemens tant des Theologiens Estrangers que de ceux des Provinces Unies des Pais Bas, sur les points de doctrine y debattus & controverse*, 2 tomes (Leyden, MDCXXIV).

[39] H. Kaajan, *De Groote Synode van Dordrecht in 1618–1619* (Amsterdam, n.d.), pp. 11–13.

[40] De Nerec, *op. cit.*, I:16–17, lists delegates from Great Britain, Palatinate, Hesse, Geneva, Zurich, Berne, Basel, Schaffhausen, Bremen, and Emden. Delegates from Nassau were late arriving; those from the Huguenot Church and Brandenburg never did appear. (Kaajen, *op. cit.*, pp. 25–27, 49, 50.)

[41] H. H. Kuyper, *De Post-Acta of Nahandelingen van de Nationale Synode van Dordrecht in 1618–1619 gehouden* (Amsterdam, 1899), p. 95 (referred to hereafter as *Post-Acta*).

The church was not ready to relinquish its position of authority and control over the professorial or doctoral offices in the university. In so far as the Estates of each province were the objects of the church's appeal for university reform, the articles displayed a reluctant recognition by the church that the political authority was involved in the academic enterprise, and also was the agency by which reform would ultimately be achieved. However, the church had a point of view as to the manner in which the professors in the academies were to be chosen, as to their responsibilities toward the church in their method of instruction, and of the church's responsibility toward what was to be taught in the classroom. It is too much to say that we have here an explicit concept of the doctoral office. However, it is evident that the church's concern for the professorate of the schools and colleges was based upon a definite consciousness that the doctoral office in the school has some relationship to the work of the church, and the recognition by the church that this office came under the jurisdiction of the whole church represented in national and provincial synods. Once again we have evidence of the church's special concern for the instructors in theology, in Hebrew, in Greek, and in philosophy, a concern already demonstrated in the life and action of the French Church. A close relationship was recognized, as in previous Netherland Church Orders, between professors of " sacred subjects " and the professors in the faculties of the arts, law, and medicine. These men were all required to subscribe to the Confession and Catechism of the church.[42]

The evidence cited to this point indicates that the Netherlands *kerkenordening* (1568–1619) endowed the office of doctor with a distinct place in the life of the church. Equally apparent was the fact that this church never spelled out the status or nature of this office. Aside from his role in the classroom, did the doctor, by virtue of his

[42] *Post-Acta*, pp. 167–170, especially Arts. IV, V, VII, VIII, IX.

office, have a part to play in the ongoing life of the church similar to that of the pastor (*diener des woordts*) or the ruling elder (*ouderling*) ? It was of the essence of the pastoral office that its incumbent not only interpreted the Word and administered the sacraments, but also joined with his church council of elders and deacons in administering the total life of the congregation, and on other occasions joined with other pastors and elders from neighboring congregations in administering the life of an even larger portion of the church (in classes and synods). It was the essence of the eldership that it shared the pastoral oversight of the congregation with the pastors, administered the affairs of the local congregation, and from time to time individual members from its ranks took their place, by virtue of their office, within the superior judicatories of the church.

Because the Church Order was silent on this aspect of the doctorate, hinting only occasionally at involvement beyond the academic precincts, we will now show that doctors of the Netherlands Church were, in fact, over a considerable period of time regarded *in practice* as possessing the right of participation in the judicatorial life of the church, by virtue of their doctorate. That we possess the well-printed records of the provincial synods of the Netherlands churches from 1572 to 1620 (and in the case of the Synod of South Holland, continuing to 1656) is fortunate.[43] On the basis of these documents, together with the catalogues of professors of the five oldest Dutch universities (Leiden, Franeker, Harderwijk, Groningen, and Amsterdam),[44] we believe that it is possible to show something of

[43] W. P. D. Knuttel (ed.) *Acta der Particuliere Synoden van Zuid-Holland 1620–1700* (s'Gravenhage, 1908–1916), 1st dl, 1621–1633; 2d dl. 1634–1645; 3d dl. 1646–1656 (referred to hereafter as *Acta Syn. S. Holl.*).

[44] Univ. van Leiden, *Album studiosorum academiae Lug-duno-Batavae, MDLXXV–MDCCCLXXV* (Hagae Comitum, MDCCCLXXV); W. B. S. Boeles, *Frieslands Hoogeschool en het Rijks Athenaeum te Franeker*, 2 dln. (Leeuwarden, 1878–1889);

the nature of the doctoral office in the church apart from
its purely academic involvement, and more, to demonstrate the way its purely academic activity was regarded *by*
the church as qualifying it to be considered in the church
as an integral ministry *of* the church.

The synodical records allow us to witness some activities
of those Dutch professors for whom we have as yet found
no evidence of pastoral status.[45] This group of seventeen
church officers is made up of Hendirck Alting, Petrus Bertius, Henricus Bredius, Johannes Coccejus, Willem Coddaeus, Petrus Cunaeus, Joannes Drusius, Ubbo Emmius,
Constantijn l'Empereur, Bernadus Fullenius, Jacob Go-
lius, Johannes Maccovius, Paulus Merula, Hermann Ravensperger, Claude de Salmasius, Daniël Sinapius, and Johannis Gerardus Vossius.

Of these, six received little more than a passing reference, either by attention called to some aspect of their work
or by mention of them in connection with some contemporary situation, and need detain us no further. However, a
number were actually given duties to perform as a result
of synodical determination. Paulus Merula, the Leiden historian, was made the agent for collecting histories and historical materials of the several churches during the latter
years of his life,[46] while William Coddaeus was placed on

D. G. van Epen, *Album studiosorum academiae gelro-zutphanicae
MDCXLVIII–MDCCCXVIII* (Hagae Comitis, MCMIV); Hist.
Genootschap te Groningen (ed.), *Album studiosorum academiae
Groninganae* (Groningen, 1915); Univ. van Amsterdam, *Album
academicum van het Athenaeum Illustre en van de Universiteit van
Amsterdam* (Amsterdam, 1913).

[45] The distinction is crucial for this period. Exercise of and induction into a pastorate were regarded as that which conferred upon
an individual the status of a pastor; cf. distinction accorded status of
Caspar Barlaeus vs. Petrus Bertius and G. J. Vossius (below, pp.
116–119).

[46] Reitsma en van Veen, III:228, 245; in 1605 and 1606 the classes
were directed to send historical material to Merula that he might
have better sources for the history he was writing for the Estates-
General.

a commission from the Synod of South Holland (1606) to secure the signatures of the professors of the university to the Confession and Catechism of the church.[47] Just prior to the National Synod of Dort, both Johannes Maccovius and Hermann Ravensperger were given specific commissions by their respective synods.[48] In the middle of the seventeenth century, two professors of the University of Leiden were directed to perform synodical duties in connection with church groups outside the synod, Salmasius[49] being a part of a commission of the Synod of South Holland to that of North Holland, l'Empereur being named an agent for the transmission of benevolent moneys destined to relieve the situation at the *Illustre Schola tot Herborn.*[50]

Nine of these professors attended synodical sessions. Three of these served as classical commissioners from a specific classis to the synod of which the classis was a part. Both Paulus Merula and Willem Coddaeus served in the office of elder-commissioner from the Classis of Leiden to the Synod of South Holland.[51] Merula's service extended over six separate sessions from 1594 to 1606,[52] while Coddaeus served in the Synods of 1603, 1606, and 1608.[53] In

[47] *Ibid.,* p. 255.

[48] *Ibid.,* VI:245–246; VII:335, 367.

[49] *Acta Syn. S. Holl.,* III:28 (1646).

[50] *Ibid.,* I:41. There is no indication that either Salmasius or l'Empereur carried out these synodal commissions other than by virtue of their status as professors in the universities.

[51] The provincial synods of the Dutch churches were not consistent in the ratio of pastors to elders deputized from each classis to its respective synod; in North Holland (1588) it was two *dienaer* and two *ouderlinghen* from each classis (Reitsma en van Veen, I:144); South Holland (1589) deputized two or three *Predicanten* and one *ouderling* (*ibid.,* II:330–331); Drente, on the other hand, as late as 1615, was a synod of the whole, with each pastor expected to be present, and with no *ouderlingen* in attendance (*ibid.,* VIII:190–191).

[52] *Ibid.,* III:17, 39, 78.

[53] *Ibid.,* pp. 197, 240, 276. In 1608, Coddaeus was the only elder-commissioner designated by initial "D." On basis of previous usage in the Synod it is impossible to know whether this stood for honorific

both cases, the records were at pains to identify the men
involved not only as elders but also as professors of the university. Bernardus Fullenius, in the middle of the seventeenth century, is known to have served the Synod of Groningen as an elder-commissioner from the classis where the
university was located.[54] Sixteen years prior to the founding
of the university at Groningen, a fourth, Ubbo Emmius,
served in the synodical assembly as " an elder " represent-
ing in this case, not a classis, but the magistracy of the
province.[55]

Two who participated, however unwillingly, in the deliberations of the Synod supply by the circumstances of
their participation some crucial evidence of how the church
regarded the doctoral office vis-à-vis the university.

Both Petrus Bertius and Johannis Gerardus Vossius were
cited by the Synod of South Holland in 1619 [56] to defend
themselves before the Synod on charges growing out of
their refusal to support the Canons of the National Synod
of Dort. Both were suspected of sympathy with the views

dominus (reverend) or title of academic degree; cf. below, p. 122,
n. 71.
   [54] Boeles, op. cit., II:137.
   [55] Reitsma en van Veen, VII:21.
   [56] Synod held at Leiden, July 23 to Aug. 17, 1619, Art. 71. " Alsoo
D. Petrus Bertius ende D. Gerrardus Vossius, gewesene regenten des
collegii theologici, ende Casparus Barleus, onlanckx subregent des-
selvigen colegii . . . is goetgevonden de voornoemde persoonen voor
dese vergarderinge te ontbieden om met haer te spreecken, off sij
gesint souden sign de kercke van dese dingen satisfactie te doen ende
wederomme met deselvige te versoenen." (Reitsma en van Veen,
III:375–376.) The same Synod (Art. 75, ibid., p. 385) directed that
" Petrus Cuneus, professor juris ende politices " be called to account
by the commissioners of the Synod for the embarrassment he had
caused the church by certain passages in his Satyra Menippea (1612
— on educational reform) and his De republica Hebraeorum (1617).
Cunaeus never appeared in the Synod, but was dealt with by the
Commission of the Synod, either to his face or by letter. He finally
" satisfied " the Synod by promising to put out a book that would
modify his previous work, and his excuse was that he had done the
objectionable writing when he was young (26) " ende geen professie
der religie en dede " (Acta Syn. S. Holl., I:9 [1621]).

of Jacob Arminius, and both men initially denied that the Synod had any hold on them,[57] although the Synod from the first maintained that it cited them as " being regents of the Theological College."

The immediate answer of both men was that the Synod did not have control over them and that they were not responsible to the Synod. Vossius put the matter very succinctly in stating that " he was not a pastor." [58] The committeemen from the Synod who had approached the two regents in this matter (and also Casper Barlaeus, subregent of the theological college) [59] reported that Bertius had flatly refused to make his appearance, stating to them that he was responsible only to the trustees of the university. Though Vossius had made the statement quoted above, nevertheless the committeemen stated they had urged all those men to make their appearance and Barlaeus had promised he would.

Following the midday recess, the moderator of the Synod informed the assembly that the burgomasters and trustees of the city and University of Leiden had addressed him, and that their excellencies had informed him that neither Bertius nor Vossius were *Kerchendienaren*.[60] The political authorities of the city and university granted that the Synod had authority over Barlaeus, but they insisted that the authority and discretion of the Synod extended only so far as Barlaeus was a minister of the church, and that anything that the Synod did would leave his professorship (as subregent of the theological college) unaffected. What was more, their excellencies informed the moderator of the

[57] Reitsma en van Veen, III:376.

[58] *Ibid.: D. Petrus Bertius seydem dat hij eerst met de heeren curatoren soude speecken ende soo sij tegen sijn comparitie wiet en hadden . . . D. Vossius seyde verwondert te sijn, dat, daer hij geen predicant en was ende oock van sijn regentschap verlaten."*

[59] Barlaeus *" geantwoort hadde, dat hij geen kerchendienaet was "* (Reitsma en van Veen, III:377).

[60] *Ibid.*, p. 376.

Synod, and through him the Synod, that *they* would under-take the work of reforming the university.

In this incident, we have a clear-cut case of secular au-thority attempting to define the nature of the church's ministry. For the burgomasters of the city or the trustees of the university, either singly or together, to say that any individual was *not* a minister of the church in the face of the current Church Order indicated the extent to which the church's own concept of the doctorate was misunder-stood outside its boundaries; it was also evidence of the essentially ambiguous nature of the doctoral office in the mind of the church itself.

However, what was not ambiguous was the attempt by the church to discipline the regents of the theological col-lege of the University of Leiden, not on the basis that they were pastors, but because, in fact, they were " students of Christian truth." [61] All three did appear on the floor of the Synod, answering to the citations of the Synod for their ap-pearance and made answer to the Synod. Bertius contended to the end that he was *suppoost* (usher) of the university and as such was under the jurisdiction of the curators and burgomasters.[62] Vossius, on the other hand, argued his case before the Synod. Even if he was not exonerated com-pletely, the charges against him did not bring about his dismissal. The next year (1620) the Synod recorded that his action in defending himself before the Synod had not been received with great acclaim by the trustees of the uni-versity, who protested that he had no business to be in con-ference with the Synod, as he was " yet a member and usher

[61] *Ibid.*, p. 379, Art. 73.

[62] *Ibid.*, p. 379. Bertius would not acknowledge the authority of the Synod, steadfastly refused to subscribe to the Dort Canons, and was ejected from the Synod (p. 382). Excommunicated by the Leiden Church, he went to Paris, was refused Holy Communion by the Reformed Church there (cf. *ibid.*, p. 420 [1620]), and abjured the Reformed to get a post as professor of eloquence in the College of Concourt.

of the University, being under a yearly wage." [63]

In practice, the secular authorities were telling the church of what its ministry did and did not consist. That the Synod resisted this kind of treatment may be cited as further evidence that, as of the National Synod of Dort, the Reformed Church of the Netherlands had a consciousness of the nature of the doctoral office,[64] even if a clear-cut definition of its status was lacking and even if, in the course of events, the office was to fall into disuse.

Having touched on the doctoral office in its relationship to the secular authorities, it will now be of interest to review two situations in which the doctoral office is viewed *within* the context of the Reformed Church. Hermann Ravensperger, of Groningen, and Johannes Maccovius, of Franeker, both came to the chair of theology in their respective schools about the same time. Neither man had ever held a pastorate in a church of the Reformed persuasion in the Netherlands. Ravensperger had served for a few years (1612–1614) as inspector of the Church of Steinfort in Germany.

The question of Maccovius' participation in the ministry of the church was raised at the Synod of Frisia in 1616. Maccovius brought the issue to the fore himself by complaining to the Synod " that he as yet had not been separated to examine theological candidates who present themselves for the ministry of the Church, and makes representation whether or not his promotion to the Doctorate

[63] *Ibid.,* p. 456. By 1621, Vossius had made his peace with the Leiden Church, promising not to teach against the Dort Canons. (*Acta Syn. S. Holl.,* I:10.)

[64] Interestingly enough, there is some evidence that at least one of these men had some kind of formal induction into his office; formal, that is, in the eyes of the church. The commissioners of the Synod of North Holland reported at Hoorn, in November, 1608: " 2. Dat. D. Petrus Bertius wierde geexamineert, also hy nu simpelycken is aengenomen tot een regentem des theologischen colegii tot Leyden," which action is reported by the Synod of South Holland for the approval of North Holland, which was granted. (Reitsma en van Veen, I:437, Art. 35.)

is not sufficient, or whether the Synod or the commissioners of the Synod require more from him, in order to properly function in this capacity." [65] Such a request for status spread upon the records of the Synod indicated clearly that there was some question, both to the church and to the professor, of his standing relative to the examination of candidates for the church's ministry. It also demonstrated that mere promotion to the doctoral grade was not viewed by the church as being the same thing as ability to function within the ecclesiastical life of the church community, that there were other considerations necessary before this individual, academically qualified and holding the position of professor of theology in the university, was able to function fully in the ordination of candidates for the ministry.[66]

As is so often the case with representative assemblies, the synodal directive of 1616 produced no action. The following year the matter came up for discussion again and was handled in a more peremptory fashion. On the basis of a review of the record of the previous year, the Synod determined that " on the question of whether D. Maccovius, not being a pastor, may participate in the examination of new pastors who are to be ordained to the pastoral office, it is decreed that inasmuch as the resolution of a

[65] *Ibid.*, VI:238. The reaction of the Synod was to require each classis at its next meeting to discuss the matter and return opinions to commissioners of Synod, who in turn were to consult the magistrates and " *heeren Scholarchen.*"

[66] A. Kuyper, Jr., *Johannes Maccovius* (Kampen, 1899), pp. 70–71, recounts the whole incident without reflecting on its relation to the Reformed doctorate, or even to the ministry. He does, however, comment on the fact that Maccovius' colleague, Sibrandus Lubbertus, accused him before the Classis of Franeker of being less than loyal to Holy Scripture by distinguishing between historical fact (*historische kennis*) and theological knowledge (*Theologische wetenschap*) in *God's Woord,* and that the classis cleared him from the charge of heterodoxy (pp. 65–69). The possibility that he had been excluded from the function of examining candidates by his colleague because of their differences must not be overlooked. However, there is no evidence to support it.

previous Synod has not been complied with, it shall be debated, and that the opinions of the classes through the synodical commissioners shall be forwarded as was intended, which shall be determined by majority vote, to make representation to the excellent Lord Commissioners of the Estates and the Excellent Lord Scholars as therein shall occur." [67]

The matter was resolved at Dokkum (June 2–9, 1618) in favor of Maccovius and his legitimate place in the examination of candidates for the office of pastor in the Reformed Church: " On the question whether or not dr. Maccovius, doctor of theology, but not a pastor, may examine and ordain candidates for the Church's service, it is by the majority vote of the classes found acceptable that he lawfully function in such a manner along with the other professors of theology." [68] The only conclusion we may legitimately draw from the record was that the Synod of Frisia recognized the existence in fact of the doctoral office as an integral part of the public ministry in that church.

Although the situation with regard to Hermann Ravensperger was not nearly so clear-cut, yet his status was ambiguous enough for it to raise questions in the Synod of Groningen. It was apparent Ravensperger had functioned in the act of examining candidates for the gospel ministry.[69] However, in the Groningen Synod of 1617 the matter was brought up for discussion on the basis of the fact

[67] Reitsma en van Veen, VI:241.
[68] Ibid., p. 254.
[69] Ibid., VII:293. That the theological faculty of the university might function in place of the classis in the examination of candidates for the pastorate was specifically recognized by action taken, at behest of Synod, by the " E. E. Heeren Gedeputeerden der stadt Gronningen ende Ommelanden," which decreed that " geene persoonen van den collatoren totten dienst des predichampts gepromoveert, die niet van den professoribus academiae offte classibus eerst behoorlick sull wesen geexamineert, ende van heur bequaemheyt tot alsulcken hoegen ampt goede blycke conden verthoenen." This practice was neither original with, nor confined to, the Dutch Church; cf. H. Vuilleumier, op. cit., II:84.

that Ravensperger had conducted the examination of two candidates, one from the Classis of Dammonen and one from the Classis of South Horn. The fact that he had conducted the examinations raised questions as to their validity, and the testimonials he had provided the candidates were subjected to reexamination by the commissioners of the Synod. The Synod declared in a series of acts: (1) that the examination certificate should include not only the testimony of the professor of theology conducting the examination but also the testimony of the synodical commissioners who were present at the examination itself,[70] (2) that those commissioners who were present at the examination were at liberty to act independently of Ravensperger, and (3) that the certificate recognizing the completion of the examination would not be valid without the signatures of those synodical commissioners who were present at the examination itself. In a further action (1618) the Synod legislated that " whenever any theological student must be examined in the University of Groningen by the Professors of Theology, the same shall be made known to the reverend synodical commissioners, that they may have *dominum doctorem Ravenspergerum* keep them [the credentials], that they [the commissioners] might have a copy and that . . . [he] . . . has promised to place the same in the hands of the synodical commissioners." [71]

70 Reitsma en van Veen, *op. cit.,* pp. 302-303.
71 *Ibid.,* p. 326. This passage provides one of the clearest demonstrations to be found in the synodical records of the precise meaning of the " D. D." found so frequently appended to the name of these seventeen representative professors. Pastors were regularly and consistently denominated " D." for *dominus;* a suitable translation might be " reverend." Used alone in the case of the professors, it could conceivably stand for either *dominus* or *doctor.* However, based on the examples of Emmius, Merula, Coddaeus, Bertius, Vossius, and Maccovius (cited above), we are of the opinion that instead of standing for *doctor* in the sense of academic status, it was used to call attention to the ecclesiastical status of these individuals as doctors of the church, and stands for the honorific *dominus.* It was never used as a title with the names of elders, regardless of their position or status

The exchange was brief, but it was indicative of some question in the mind of the Synod as to the relationship of a professor of theology in the university with the process of calling and ordaining men to the ministry of the Reformed Church in the Synod of Groningen.[72] The Synod was concerned to identify the professor of theology with the ongoing work of the public ministry of the church. The procedure called in question here was evidently one of common occurrence and is more evidence that the professor of theology of the university was regarded as occupying a public ministry within the church, quite apart from any status he may or may not have had as a pastor of the church. By virtue of his professorate in theology, he was assumed to partake of the public ministry of the Reformed Church, and as such was deemed competent to examine students who were preparing for the public ministry. When we call to mind the high place that examination played in the creation of the public ministry of the Reformed Church, we are aware that this was not a peripheral consideration.

In addition to those members of the teaching faculties who have been mentioned so far, we ought to list others who were engaged in teaching theology, Hebrew, and Greek, yet have not so far been identified as pastors. Hubertius Sturmius at Leiden, Johannis Antoinius Cluto at Franeker, and Matthias Pasor at Groningen are to be added to the theologians. Thomas Erpinus, Franciscus Raphelinghien, and Hermanus Rennecherus at Leiden, with Sixtinus Anama and Johanne Hachting at Franeker,

---

in the community or the state, except when the individual was also a professor in the university.

[72] There still remains the question of Ravensperger's inspectorship of the church at Steinfort during the period when he was professor of theology (1612–1614) in that school as successor to Conrad Vorstius, *Allgemeine deutsche Biographie* XXVII:470. It is impossible to tell just what the ecclesiastical status of this office was and whether the Dutch churches regarded it as equal to a pastorate.

bring the total of nonpastoral professors of Hebrew to thirteen. In Greek instruction, the following were active, although they had never been pastors: at Leiden, Daniel
Heinsius, Jeremius Hoelzlinus, Johannis Meursius, Petrus
Tiara, and Bonaventure Vulcanius; at Franeker, Sixtinus
Arcerius, Petrus Moll and Tiara; at Harderwijk, Christo-
pher Mathaeus and Janus Erasmius; and at Groningen, Jan
Gebhard and Tobias Andreae. It does not seem to be
worth-while to list the names of professors of the arts faculties for a number of reasons: first, there are over fifty
such names prior to 1650; second, there is little evidence of
participation by this group in synodical affairs (those participating have been mentioned) ; and third, there is no
evidence from the latter part of this period that the church
solicited their participation in its councils.

In connection with this last point, the Synod of Groning-
en (1618) [73] and the Synod of South Holland [74] (the latter
also in 1629 [75] and again in 1639 [76]) raised the whole issue
of synodical participation by professors of theology. In each
case, it is of interest that the Synod chose to quote as authority Article 52 of the Church Order of 1578.[77] According to Groningen, that article had decreed that whenever

[73] " Dat soo classes oft synodi quamen tho vergaderen in plaetsen,
daer professores theologiae syn, deselve sullen begroetet werden
sulcken classicalen of synodalen vergaderyngen by tho wonen und
met haren raedt und instemmingen tho assisteren, of deswegen D. D.
Gomarus, synde van den theologis alleen tegenwoordig in Groning-
en, niet solde begroetet worden. Res. Welckes, dewijle synodus sich
heeft laten gefallen, syn D. prases und D. assessor belastiget sulckes
nomine synodi aen D. D. Gomarus te versoecken." (Reitsma en van
Veen, VII:339, Art. 5.)
[74] Cf. Post-Acta, p. 485.
[75] Acta Syn. S. Holl. I:293, Art. II.
[76] Ibid., II:185, 229.
[77] Compare both the Dutch and French texts of the 52d article
of the "K.-O." of 1578; Rutgers, op. cit., p. 247; Commission de
l'histoire des églises wallonnes, Livre synodal contenant les articles
résolus dans les synodes des églises wallonnes des Pays-Bas, Tome
I (1563–1685), p. 50.

a classis or a synod should meet in the place where the professors of theology were located, they should be invited to appear in the classical assemblies and provincial synods, to take part in its proceedings by their voice and also by their vote. Specifically, Professor Gomarus was to be informed of this fact in order that he should make his presence felt in the Synod. Apparently, both Groningen and South Holland interpreted Article 52 with some freedom, for the provision of one professor speaking or voting for his colleagues was not mentioned. Actually, this omission is one more pragmatic demonstration of common doctoral status, inasmuch qua doctor, the professor of theology was on an equal footing in the Synod with every other member of it.

The fact that this admonition was repeated is evidence that professors of theology as a class and, under this circumstance, professors of Hebrew and Greek or of philosophy, probably had ambiguous notions relative to the ecclesiastical status entailed in their academic office. Yet, the very presence of this reminder by the synodical body indicated that the church, through its assemblies, did accord the professor of theology a legitimate place in classis and synod by virtue of the academic office exercised and that this office in some sense bore a status entitling its holder to sit, deliberate, and vote in the assemblies of the church side by side with those whose status was that of pastor or ruling elder.

SUMMARY

In concluding this survey of the Dutch Reformed communion in the middle years of the seventeenth century, we are able to make several statements regarding the doctoral office in those churches. First, the Church of the Netherlands definitely embodied the doctoral office in its Church Order. This evidence is not completely consistent, but it is certain that from 1578 onward, the professor of theology had a distinct place in the judicatories of the Reformed churches, and from 1581 onward, the Dutch churches held to the traditional Calvinian fourfold public ministry of the church.

Secondly, the Dutch Church delivered its mind on the place of the doctoral office within the framework of the church, when at Dort it recognized the close alliance existing between professors of theology and the teachers of philosophy, Greek, and Hebrew.

Most important of all, however, we have shown how the Reformed Church in the Netherlands actually accorded status to the doctors of the church, qua doctor, not as a suborder of the pastorate, by its treatment in particular instances of individuals who had never been accorded the status of pastor. To be sure, all the ramifications and implications of doctoral status were never defined by a general deliverance of the church, no mode of induction into the office was made a matter of synodical enactment, nor were the ecclesiastical rights and responsibilities of its holders defined beyond specific legislation in regard to specific cases.

Rather, the office was allowed to remain ambiguous, so ambiguous indeed that in 1618 and 1619 the burgomasters of the city and the trustees of the University of Leiden were able to challenge the church's definition of its own ministry, implicitly contending that the public ministry of the church was limited to the office of pastor, elder, and deacon, and explicitly that the doctor qua doctor was no minister of the church but, rather, an employee, a member of the secular and university order. Except for professors of theology, this would seem to be the point of view prevailing in later emendations of these Church Orders. In this case, the development we have noted in the Lower Rhineland in the seventeenth century seems to preview the situation as it was to develop in the American churches of a Continental background.

VI

The Doctor in the Church of Scotland

IN PASSING FROM THE CONTINENT to the British Isles, it
may seem strange to make landfall north of the Tweed.
However, there is justification for this procedure. The Reformed Church in Scotland arrived at a formulation of the
doctoral office prior to any comparable situation in the
English Church. Influenced as it was by the practice of
the Genevan, Vaudois, and Huguenot Church Orders, the
kirk presented a fair example of Continental Reformed
thought and practice regarding the doctrine of the church
and ministry transplanted to the British scene. Furthermore, many English Puritans made frequent reference to
the practice of the kirk as they sought a further reformation of the English Church.[1] Not without cause, the practice of the kirk concerns us before we turn to England.

There are three basic documents to be dealt with in discussing the ministry in the Church of Scotland: (1) *Forms
of Prayers and Ministration of the Sacraments, used in the
English Congregation at Geneva* — 1556; [2] (2) *The First
Book of Discipline,* or the *Policies and Discipline of the*

[1] Scotland was an example for the " Puritan " faction in the
Church of England, and at the deprivation of the nonconsenting
clergy, 26 March 1566, a number of the deprived went north and
took charges in the kirk; cf. John Brown, *The English Puritans*
(Cambridge, 1912) , p. 45.

[2] Original February, 1556; text found in David Laing (ed.), *The
Works of John Knox,* 6 vols. (Edinburgh, 1846–1864) , IV:157–214;
hereafter cited as Genevan Order.

Church — 1560; [3] and (3) *The Second Book of Discipline,* or *Heidis and Conclusions of the Policie of the Kirk* — 1578, 1581, 1592.[4] The *Form of Prayers and Ministration of the Sacraments* was a church order, dating from the Marian exile in Geneva, that a number of Scottish Reformers shared with their English brethren on the Continent. This document is basic for an understanding of the Presbyterian Church Orders throughout the British Isles, and is also important because of its witness to the exiles' understanding of the nature of the public ministry of the church as it was practiced in the home of John Calvin.

Following a Preface and a Confession of Faith, the exiled congregation in Geneva set down a section entitled "Of Ministers and Their Election." [5] Here we find the typical Calvinistic offices of pastors, elders, and deacons, the manner of their election, the term of their service, and the nature of their duties. Following these three offices came a long section indicative of the understanding of these refugees on the doctoral office.

" We are not ignorant that the Scripture make mention of a fourth kind of ministers left to the Church of Christ, which also are very profitable, where time and place doth permit. [But for lack of opportunity, in this our dispersion and exile, we cannot well have use thereof; and would to God it were not neglected where better occasion serveth.] [6]

" These ministers are called Teachers, or Doctors, whose office is to instruct and teach the faithful in sound doctrine, providing with all diligence that the purity of the

[3] Text found in Walter Steuart of Pardovan, *Collections and Observations Concerning the Worship, Discipline, and Government of the Church of Scotland,* 4 books in 2 vols. (Aberdeen, 1830), I:29–94; hereafter cited as Pardovan.

[4] Text found in Pardovan, I:107–137.

[5] Genevan Order, p. 174: " What things are chiefly required in the Pastours and Ministers " was the subtitle of the section, but the 1561 and 1562 editions printed in Edinburgh omitted the words " Pastours and."

[6] This sentence omitted in Edinburgh editions of 1561 and 1562.

Gospel be not corrupt, either through ignorance, or evil opinions. Notwithstanding, considering the present state of things, we comprehend under this title such means as God hath in His Church, that it should not be left desolate, nor yet His doctrine decay for default of ministers there of.

" Therefore to term it by a word more usual in these days, we may call it the ' Order of Schools,' wherein the highest degree and most and next to the ministry of the Church, is the exposition of God's Word, which is contained in the Old and New Testaments.

" But because men cannot so well profit in that knowledge except they be first instructed in the tongues and humane sciences, (for now God worketh not commonly by miracles) it is necessary that seed be sewn for the time to come, to the intent that the Church be not left barren and waste to our posterity; and that schools also be erected and colleges maintained with just and sufficient stipends wherein youth may be trained in the knowledge and fear of God that in their ripe age they may prove worthy members of Our Lord Jesus Christ, whether it be to rule in civil policies, or to serve in spiritual ministry, or else to live in Godly reverence and subjection." [7]

There can be no doubt whatsoever of the close dependence of this document on the *Ordonnances Ecclésiastiques* of Geneva of 1541. The third paragraph dealing with the " Order of Schools," the second paragraph outlining the duties of the doctoral office, and the reference to instruction in the Old and New Testaments being the office nearest the ministry (pastorate) are all close paraphrases of the language of the Genevan document.

One or two things may be mentioned, not only as an exposition of what was to become the rule in Scotland, but also as a way of interpreting the situation in Geneva during the Marian exile. First, we note that the doctorate was

[7] Genevan Order, p. 177.

described as " a fourth kind of minister," thus heightening our impression that the Genevan Church regarded the four *offices* as all participating in the total public ministry of the church. Also to be noted was the expansion on the " Order of Schools." This expansion specifically included, within the orbit of the doctoral ministry, instruction in " tongues and the human sciences," tending to show that the actual scope of the doctorate of the Genevan Church was broader than a narrow limitation to professors of theology, and also pointing the way to the inclusive educational system outlined in the *First Book of Discipline*. Thus, even in exile the Reformed communities from the British Isles recognized the responsibility of the church in the institutional education of its people.

Interestingly enough, the English congregation felt under a certain kind of restraint in not being able to support the whole ministry of the church. Few in number, in alien surroundings, and with the expectation of returning once again to the homeland, the exiles did not feel that they were in a position to establish among themselves a doctorate separate from the doctoral office as it was then exercised in the Church of Geneva. Subsequent editions issued in Scotland from 1562 onward significantly omitted the apologetic sentence. No longer operating under exile conditions and with the *First Book of Discipline* before them as an active product of their own life, it was not deemed necessary to apologize that in an exiled condition the precursors of the kirk had not been able to do something they regarded as necessary.

Immediately following the section on the doctoral office, the English-Genevan Church Order included two sections, the contents of which are now familiar to us. The first of these was entitled " The Weekly Assembly of the Ministers," [8] which was a meeting of the pastors to be held

8 Genevan Order, pp. 177–178.

on Thursday of every week. The choice of this particular
day, of course, reflected the day on which the "colloquy of
the ministers" of the Church of Geneva was held, indicating that the ministers of the English congregation copied the formal assembly of the ministers of the Genevan
Church, yet remained free to join the Genevans on Friday. The nature of this assembly was described as being
disciplinary as well as instructive. It is perhaps significant
that the Edinburgh editions of 1561 and 1562 included in
the title for this section the words "elders, and Deacons."
This indicated the transference of this type of meeting
from Geneva to Scotland, which resulted in the formation
of a body within the congregation known later as the
"Kirk session." [9]

In addition to the weekly meeting of the ministers, the
congregation was to be assembled once a week, in addition
to Sunday worship, to "hear some place of the Scriptures
orderly expounded." Congregational participation in this

[9] Janet MacGregor, *Scottish Presbyterian Polity* (Edinburgh,
1926), pp. 50–53, by neglecting *The Form of Prayers* (Geneva, 1556)
failed to recognize this source for Scottish practice, and has concen-
trated on the Lascian model and the practice of the Huguenot
Church. A Lasco was influential, but it was by way of influence on
Poullain and the Frankfort congregation that this example was
manifested; cf. W. D. Maxwell, *The Liturgical Portions of the
Genevan Service Book* (Edinburgh, 1931), p. 5, rather than directly.
Miss MacGregor presents no evidence that the French Reformed
Discipline of 1559 was known in Scotland when Winram, Spottis-
wood, Willock, Douglasse, Row, and Knox edited the *First Book* in
1560; although it did not call the kirk session, or consistory, by name,
it did provide that perpetrators of "publick, . . . heynous" crimes
were to be called "in the presence of the minister, elders and deacons," and "if the offender called before the *ministerie* be found
stubborn . . . then must he be demitted . . . to consider the dangerous estate in which he stands; . . . if he within a certain space
shew his repentance to the *ministerie, they* may present him to the
kirk" (Pardovan, I:68-69, chap. ix, secs. 4 and 5 [italics mine]). On
the other hand, the *First Book* (1560) specifically acknowledged and
presupposed the use of the English Genevan Order. (Chap. ii, sec.
2, Pardovan, I:33.)

meeting was not only contemplated but expected. But the proceedings were to be carried on in a spirit of mutual edification "rather than [any] seeking to profit or to contend." In the cases of disagreement, the decision of the matter was left up to the " moderators " and if that did not satisfy the contending party, they were exhorted to keep silent so that final judgment might be rendered by the ministers and elders in the weekly assembly just mentioned.[10]

The English-Genevan Church Order served the emerging Reformed Scottish Kirk from 1557 until 1560 as its basis of organization and discipline. However, the Genevan document, drawn up on the basis of a single city, was not adequate for a growing church of large territorial extent. Therefore, in 1560, Knox and five others of the General Assembly were commissioned by the Assembly and the Privy Council to draw up what has become known as the *First Book of Discipline*. Never formally ratified by the Privy Council (although subscribed by a number of its members), this book served as the basis of the organization of the church until the adoption of the *Second Book*. The style of the work was rather diffuse, and there was no single place where a consistent structure of the ministry was formulated. However, by usage and implication the offices in the church were fivefold: the ministers, the readers, the superintendents,[11] the elders, and the deacons.

Although the *First Book* made no mention of the doc-

[10] Genevan Order, pp. 178–179. No sharp distinction was drawn in the English text between the meeting for prophecy and the stated worship of the congregation beyond a change in type size. However, the Latin edition of the work, in the *actual* arrangement of its contents, did draw a sharp distinction, and Maxwell regards the meeting for the "Interpretation of the Scriptures" as distinct from the Sunday public worship of the congregation. A parallel between à Lasco and the English congregation at Geneva is too close to have been mere coincidence. (Maxwell, *op. cit.,* pp. 84, 104.)

[11] MacGregor, *op. cit.,* pp. 42–47, suggests that the chief function envisaged by the framers of the *First Book* for the superintendent was that of itinerant preacher, and that administrative and disciplinary duties were decidedly auxiliary.

torate as such, it did provide a thorough and detailed system for the public education of the Scottish nation.[12] The rationale of the educational system was proclaimed to be the cessation of miraculous illumination " suddenly changing [men] as he did the apostles and others in the primitive Kirk," and the desirability of the " continuance of His [Christ's] benefits to the generation following." To this end, the Scottish Church made representation to the magistrate that " we ought to be careful that they [the youth] have knowledge and erudition to profit and comfort that which ought to be most dear to us, to wit, the Kirk and spouse of Our Lord Jesus." [13]

However, the kirk did not leave the matter of education exclusively up to the magistrate, but declared that each congregation ought to support a schoolmaster. In the country parishes where distances were great and the people would meet for worship and doctrinal instruction " but once in the week," the office of schoolmaster would fall on either the reader or the parish pastor. However, in the larger towns there were to be instituted schoolmasters " such a one at least as is able to teach grammar and the Latin tongue, if the town be of any reputation." And in the larger towns, especially those places that were large enough to support a superintendent, it was contemplated that a college " in which the Arts, at least logic and rhetoric, together with the tongues, be read by sufficient masters." This was an ambitious program and system for the newborn Reformed Church of Scotland to seek to establish in the land. Its framers were so naïve as to think that two years was sufficient for elementary work (the Catechism and the first rudiments of grammar) , and that three or four years would be all that would be required to prepare the student in the arts " *to wit,* to logic, to rhetoric, and to the Greek tongue." Beyond that period of from five

[12] Chap. vii, "Of Schooles." (Pardovan, I:52–62.)
[13] *Ibid.,* pp. 52–53.

to six years, the years from the age of 13 to 24, were " to be spent in the study, wherein the learner would profit the Church or commonwealth, be it in the laws, physics, or divinity." The remainder of Ch. VII, " Of the Schools," was given over to detailed legislation on the nature of instruction in the three universities of St. Andrews, Glasgow, and Aberdeen.

Following the English-Genevan Order, the kirk in the *First Book* included a section on " For Prophesying, or Interpreting, of the Scriptures." This meeting for Scriptural edification was regarded as being " most expedient . . . in every town, where schooles and repaire of learned men are." [14] Scheduled to be held once a week, it was contemplated that the Scriptures would be read, that first one would give his judgment for the instruction and consolation of the hearers, and that following the initial explanation, one or perhaps two others would be called upon to " add . . . or . . . gently correct or explain more properly " the portion of Scripture that had been read and initially expounded upon.

Because of the possibility that such an exercise of mutual edification might lead to altercation and unseemly dispute, it was specifically stated that the interpretation might not digress from the " principles of our faith," be out of line with " charity, or stand in plain contradiction with any other manifest place of Scripture." Furthermore, " the interpreter in this exercise may not take to himself the liberty of a public preacher, (yea, although he be a minister appointed) but he must bind himself to his text." Here it

---

[14] *Ibid.,* p. 81. The location of the Exercise in the places where the universities and "Colledges" were located is interesting evidence of two developments: (1) that the academic atmosphere was regarded as normal for this kind of meeting, and (2) that the role of the congregation in it had become secondary. This is in direct contrast to Miss MacGregor's affirmation that the Scottish practice was modeled largely on Lascian congregational prophesying (*op. cit.,* pp. 53–54) , she having neglected to mention the academic context.

would seem we have echoes of two previously noted Reformed traditions in regard to the meeting for prophesying. In connection with audience participation, we must look to à Lasco's Discipline of 1550; to the matter of the interpreter of Scripture not being properly qualified or commissioned to perform the office of a public preacher, we must turn specifically to Calvin's definition that the doctor may interpret Scripture but not apply it.

Prophesying was further hedged around with the stipulation that persons who were noted for their " curiosity or bringing in of strange doctrines " were to be dealt with by the " moderator, ministers, and elders immediately after the interpretation is ended." Furthermore, the sessions for prophesying were organized on a territorial basis rather than a congregational, by the provision that the ministers and the readers in the country towns surrounding each chief place were to appear and assist at these meetings in order that they themselves might be taught or, out of their own illumination, teach others. In addition to pastors and readers of parishes, " men in whom is supposed to be any gifts which might edify the Church if they were well employed must be charged by the ministers and elders to join themselves with the session and company of the interpreters," [15] in order that they might be also a means of distributing God's grace and knowledge through their gift of interpretation. The actual day to be used for the exercise of interpretation was left to the wisdom of the ministers and the elders in each particular place. Originally designed as it was to serve a particular peculiar function of instructing the newly reformed Kirk of Scotland in the contents of Scripture, the " Exercise," organized on a territorial basis, was the forerunner of the organization of the Church of Scotland into territorial presbyteries.[16]

[15] Pardovan, I:83.
[16] Cf. G. D. Henderson, *The Burning Bush* (Edinburgh, 1957), p. 53.

Although the *First Book of Discipline* made no provision for the doctorate, there is no doubt that in the " Exercise " there was an incipient doctorate of the Genevan pattern. For the " Exercise " was most strongly contemplated in the towns where the projected educational institutions of the church were to be located.

Because the *First Book* was never formally approved by the magistrate,[17] a second attempt was begun eighteen years later, which issued in the production of the *Second Book of Discipline*. This document, a much more tightly knit work, included in its second chapter the statement that there were " four ordinary functions or offices in the kirk of God; the office of the pastor, minister or bishop, the doctor, the presbyter or elder, and the deacon." [18]

The office of the doctor was described to be that of opening " up the mind of the spirit of God in the Scriptures, simply without such applications as the ministers [pastors] uses, to the end that the faithful may be instructed and sound doctrine taught and that the purity of the Gospel may be not corrupted through ignorance or evil opinions." [19] The doctor was declared to be different from the pastor " not only in name but in diversity of gifts." And in addition to his Scriptural role as prophet, bishop, and elder, he was also described as a catechizer " that is, teacher of the Catechism, and rudiments of religion." For the first time in any of the Reformed Church Orders the doctor was

[17] Pardovan, I:96–106, "*Ane schort Somme of the Buik of Discipline for the Instruction of Ministers and Readaris in thair Office.*" The *First Book* was never formally ratified by the Privy Council, although a number of its members subscribed the January following its presentation. As a result of this subscription, a " short sum " of it was circulated for the use of the church. This brought into juxtaposition the sections on " The Exercise," " Schulis," and " Universities," indicating the relationship existing in the minds of the framers even more clearly than the *First Book* itself had done.

[18] Pardovan, I:113.

[19] *Ibid.*, p. 117.

specifically given the designation " elder " and was also charged to assist the pastor in the government of the church and to " concur with the elders, his brethren, in all assemblies." [20] However, he was specifically forbidden to preach to the people, to administer the sacraments, or to perform marriages, as these were regarded as functions not specifically related to his teaching office and not to be indulged in unless he was " otherwise called ordinarily " thereto.

Unlike the *First Book*, the *Second Book* subsumed the whole detailed arrangement of schools, colleges, and universities into a single paragraph included under the chapter on doctors. " Under the name and office of a doctor, we comprehend also the order in schools, colleges, and universities, which has been from time to time carefully maintained as well among the Jews and Christians as among the profane nations." [21]

In common with the Church Orders of the Continental Reformed communions, the *Second Book* of the Scottish Church established a series of church judicatories on a territorial basis.[22] There was some vagueness in the use of the term " eldership," but it is obvious from subsequent enactments that two sorts were envisaged, one of a congregational nature (the consistory or kirk session), and one based on a broader territorial organization for which the

[20] " The Doctor being an elder, as said is, should assist the pastor in the government of the kirk, and concurre with the elders his brethren in all assemblies, by reason the interpretation of the word, which is the only judge in ecclesiastical matters, is committed to his charge." (*Ibid.*, pp. 117–118.) John Cunningham, *The Church History of Scotland*, 2 vols. (Edinburgh, 1882), I:356, interpreted this passage to mean that in case the doctor was *also* an elder, he was to join with the courts of the church. This is a possible interpretation, but we believe, on the basis of evidence we will subsequently present, that this was not so in the beginning, and that the doctor qua doctor participated in ecclesiastical assemblies.

[21] Pardovan, I:117.

[22] *Ibid.*, p. 119.

existing " Exercise " formed the basis.[23] Above the Exercise was the provincial synod and the General Assembly, or the Synod of the whole church. Membership in each case of these judicatories was limited to " pastors, doctors, and such as we commonly call elders." [24]

Thus by the *Second Book of Discipline,* first introduced in 1578 and finally ratified in 1592, the office of the doctor was given a specific status in the Scottish Church, both as to function (which was regarded as academic) and ecclesiastical involvement in the government and work of the whole church.

It remains then to show the way the office was exercised in the life of the kirk, and to identify the men who participated in the office. One difficulty we face may be found in the concluding section of the chapter on the doctorate of the *Second Book,* which specifically allowed that " the pastor may teach in the schools, as he who has the gift of

[23] " Assemblies are of four sortis. For aither are they of particular kirks and congregations one or more, or if of a province, or of an whole nation, or of all and divers nations professing one Jesus Christ." (*Ibid.,* Art. 2.) The ecumenical assembly of the last phrase was to be convoked " at command of godlie emperours . . . for the avoiding of schismes within the universal kirk of God," but the Scottish Kirk did not press the issue farther " because they apperteine not to the particular estate of one realm " (*ibid.,* p. 123) .

However, there can be no doubt of the vagueness of language used regarding the " eldership " (G. D. Henderson, *op. cit.,* p. 51) , but this problem was solved by reference to the Acts of the October General Assembly of 1578, which legislated that the " tulchan " bishops must not overlord " above particular Elderschips, but be subject to them," and in a separate item, " that they usurp not the power of the Presbyteries " (Church of Scotland, *Acts and Proceedings of the General Assemblies,* 3 parts, plus Appendix [Edinburgh, 1839–1844], II:419) .

In answer to a question raised by the Synod of Lothian about the advisability of " a general Order to be taken for erecting of Presbyteries in places where publick Exercise is used, unto the time the Policie of the Kirk [2d Book] be established by law," the General Assembly of July, 1579, answered, " The exercise may be judged a Presbytery " (*B.U.K.,* II:439) .

[24] Deacons were specifically excluded from both of the lower courts. (Pardovan, I:124.)

knowledge oft times meet therefore, as the examples of Polycarpus and others testify." [25] Thus even in the Scottish Church with its rather complete definition of the doctoral office we find that the offices of pastor and of doctor were not clearly distinguished. According to the *Second Book*, the pastor, as pastor, might teach in the school; but the doctor, as doctor, had no business in the pulpit. This provided the basis for a measure of distinction in the status of individuals involved in each office.

THE PRACTICE OF THE DOCTORAL OFFICE IN THE KIRK, 1560–1578

Although there was no mention of the doctorate in the Scottish Church Order until the *Second Book* of 1578, it is demonstrable that in fact the Scottish Church recognized the doctorate prior to that date. Evidence for this may be cited both out of the records of the General Assembly for that period and by a scrutiny of the status of men involved in teaching at the university level. Based on the detailed scheme for education of the *First Book of Discipline*, the General Assembly repeatedly petitioned the civil authorities to undertake only the employment of teachers who were of the Reformed faith, decreeing the same practice for its parishes.[26] This applied not only to teachers of the elementary and the secondary schools, but was specifically in each case extended to university teachers. This particular kind of activity came to a head when, in 1568, the General Assembly petitioned the civil magistracy to appoint a joint commission for the reform of the University of Aberdeen.[27] The result of this commission was a report rendered the following year [28] specifically naming Alexander Anderson,

25 *Ibid.*, p. 118.
26 *B.U.K.*, I:33–34 [1563]; pp. 59 f. [1565]; pp. 109–110 [1567].
27 *Ibid.*, pp. 127, 129.
28 *Ibid.*, pp. 141–144 [5 July 1569].

principal; Andrew Galloway, subprincipal; Andrew Anderson, Thomas Owsten, and Duncan Norris, regents, as being incapable of further service to the church and to the school because of their refusal to subscribe to the Articles of Reformed Religion before the " Lord Regent and Privy Council."

The same year in which a reform at Aberdeen was called for, the General Assembly specifically noted that commissioners from the universities were to be sent to the General Assembly,[29] pausing to discuss the doctor of theology degree and how it was to be given.[30] Evidently the Assembly took seriously its desire that the universities be represented in the General Assembly by their commissioners, for in 1575 it was a matter of note that the University of St. Andrews was not represented.[31]

But most important of all was the item contained in a petition by the General Assembly addressed to the Lord Regent in August, 1574. Among the articles enumerated was this one: " Item, in respect that in the ecclesiastical functions there is two only distinct offices of teaching, the doctour, that interprets the Scriptures, and the Minister to preach and apply the same: That his Grace will take order, that Doctours may be placed in Universities, and stipends granted unto them; whereby not only they who are presently placed, may have occasion to be diligent in their cure, but also other learned men may have occasion to seek places in Colleges within this realm." [32] There is no doubt that the use of the technical term here was significant. More significant, was the specific relationship drawn between the doctoral office and the university. Equally important was the distinction drawn between " Doctors " and " Ministers," highlighting the fact that there existed in the

[29] *Ibid.*, p. 124.
[30] *Ibid.*, p. 140 [March, 1568].
[31] *Ibid.*, p. 334 [August].
[32] *Ibid.*, p. 305.

kirk a distinction between the status of the academic and
the parochial office, permitting us to equate " minister "
with the Continental terms " *pasteur*," " *predikant*," or
" *diener*."

However, we are not entirely dependent upon the records of the General Assembly for our demonstration of the
doctoral office in the Scottish Church prior to 1578. We are
able to distinguish prior to the actual establishment of the
doctoral office within the Scotch Church Order twelve or
thirteen individuals who exercised it and were not pastors.
Some of these men had held academic or pastoral livings
in the pre-Reformed Church, others had been engaged in
academic endeavor on the Continent in churches and
schools with a Reformed outlook. Most of them were active
in the affairs of the General Assembly prior to 1578. The
list includes John Rutherford, James Martin, John Dun-
canson, Robert Hamilton, William Ramsay, George Buchanan, James Melville, and Patrick Melville, of St. Andrews; Walter Steward, of Aberdeen; Andrew Melville, of
Glasgow and St. Andrews; Patrick Sharp, of Glasgow; and
Robert Rollock, of St. Andrews and Edinburgh.[33] The
most interesting, and in some ways the most important sto-
ries are those of George Buchanan, Andrew Melville, and
his nephew, James.

George Buchanan (1506–1582),[34] had studied in Paris
and St. Andrews; 1529–1534, taught grammar at the Collège St. Barbe in Paris; 1536–1538, tutored James V's natural son; 1539 taught at Bordeaux in the Collège du
Guienne; 1544–1547, was in Paris teaching at the Collège
de Cardinal la Moine; 1547–1552, taught in the newly established University of Coimbra (Portugal) ; between 1552
and 1562 was in England and France with five years as a
tutor in the family of Maréchal du Brisson. Buchanan was

[33] Cf. R. W. Henderson, *op. cit.*, pp. 209–217, for detailed analysis of careers.

[34] Cf. P. Hume Brown, *George Buchanan, Humanist and Reformer* (1890) .

active in the affairs and meetings of the General Assembly from December, 1563 to 1567, when he served as the moderator.[35] In 1566 Buchanan was appointed as principal of St. Leonard's College, St. Andrews, which included the function of preaching in the parish church attached to the college. As such, there would be no doubt of his right to sit as a commissioner of the General Assembly, even though there is some doubt as to whether the charge of the church associated with the college can be denominated a pastorate.[36] However, there is no escaping the fact that George Buchanan served as a member of the General Assemblies of 1563, 1564, 1565, and 1566, without holding any pastoral charge in the Scottish Church, and without ever having held, as far as we know, any kind of a pastoral charge in any Reformed Church.[37] We think that George Buchanan served the kirk in General Assemblies from 1563 to 1566 in his capacity as a doctor, an office that his whole previous employment fitted him to occupy.

Andrew Melville (1545–1622) was educated in the grammar school at Montrose, the University of St. Andrews, and at the University of Poitiers. He became in 1566 a regent in the Collège du Marceon, a position he held for three years. In 1569–1574 he was regent of the second class of the collège at Geneva, and on returning to Scotland, was appointed principal of the University of Glasgow. On re-

[35] *B.U.K.*, I:41, 49, 50, 58, 60, 77, 93, 113.

[36] P. H. Brown, *op. cit.*, p. 242, calls it a " tradition " that he undertook a preaching ministry, and attributes this tradition to the possibility that as principal he was obligated to deliver divinity lectures on Wednesdays and Fridays.

[37] *Fasti*, VII:437, injects a long explanation on his moderatorship of the General Assembly of June, 1567, that he served " [not as a lay man, as commonly represented, but in virtue of his office as Principal of St. Leonard's college, St. Andrews (to which he was appointed in 1566), min. of the parish and Professor of Divinity]." Interestingly enough, when dealing with the parish involved (*Fasti*, V:229–245), no mention is made of Buchanan's incumbency, although his successor in the principalship, James Wilkie, is listed as the first Reformed pastor of that charge.

turn to Scotland, he was immediately active in the affairs
of the General Assembly, being ordered by it in August,
1574 to be, with George Buchanan, a censor for Patrick
Adamson's work on The Book of Job and in March of
1575 the General Assembly ordered Andrew Melville,
" Principal of the Pedagogie of Glasgow," to be the con-
venor of the commission that was to determine whether
the Bishop of Murray was to be tried. In the General Assembly of August, 1575, he was ordered to be part of a
commission along with Alexander Arbuthnet, principal of
Aberdeen, and four others, to answer bills and complaints
presented to the General Assembly. The General Assembly
of April, 1576, made him a member of its committee to
write an answer to the Lord Regent and also made him
part of a commission for reading and answering bills and
reviewing the reports of the visitors of the church. He
continued to be active in the affairs of the General Assembly even after his translation to St. Andrews in 1580, but
for our purpose this activity must be listed as that of a pastor, for he was admitted minister of the Parish of Govan
on 13 July 1577,[38] removing him from the roll of those university professors who were not pastors.[39]

[38] The relationship of the parish of Govan to the University of
Glasgow was such that the income of the parish was assigned to the
school with the provision that the principal of the college exercise
ex officio the preaching and ministerial office. The terms of this were
modified in December, 1621, so that rents of the parish were still
applied to the school, but the principal was relieved of the ministerial duties and the school retained the patronage of the parish.
(Fasti, III:409–410.)

[39] Fasti, VII:417, and B.U.K., I:310, 315, 317, 321, 337, 352.
Thomas McCrie in his Life of Andrew Melville (Edinburgh, 1824),
II:10, makes the gratuitous assertion that Melville "acted for a
number of years as a ruling elder in the congregation of St. Andrews." Unfortunately, he does not document this except by way of
citing other professors, both at St. Andrews (St. Andrews Kirk-Session Records, 1559–1600, Scottish Society Publication, vols. 4 and 7)
and at Glasgow who so served, and by referring to James Melville's
"Diary" (in manuscript). Evidence from the "Diary" (R. Pitcairn,
ed., Autobiography and Diary of Mr. James Melville, pp. 124–125)

James Melville (1556–1614) had been between 1572 and 1574 regent in St. Andrews and in 1575 regent at Glasgow, teaching Greek, logic, and mathematics. In 1580 he went with his uncle to New College (St. Mary's) at St. Andrews to be professor of Hebrew and Oriental Languages until 1586, when in November of that year he was ordained to the parish of Anstruther Wester. Prior to ordination, he was a member of a committee of the General Assembly (1583) to draw up articles and questions regarding the ordination of one John Graham,[40] and in April, 1586, just six months prior to his assuming the pastorate at Anstruther Wester, he had attacked Archbishop Patrick Adamson on the floor of the Synod of Fife with the result that the Synod excommunicated Adamson.[41]

The " Second Book of Discipline " and the Doctoral Office, 1578–1592

Although the *Second Book of Discipline* was agreed to by the General Assembly of 1578, and was again inserted in the register of the Assembly in 1581, not until 1592 was it approved by the civil authority and made the standing law of the church. Although the church found it difficult

---

may be cited which tends in just the opposite direction, that after coming to St. Andrews " the Session of the Kirk haid a custome to send twa of thair eldars everie ouk to desyre Mr. Andro and me to helpe them on the Sabbathe," when they were without regular pastoral leadership. However, McCrie rightly assessed the place of the doctoral office in the total life of the kirk (McCrie, *op. cit.*, I:141–143), except that he did not elucidate its full importance, nor its Continental background.

[40] *B.U.K.*, II:637.

[41] *Fasti*, VII:212; *Dictionary of National Biography*, XXXVII:241. In connection with the action against Adamson, cf. *The Autobiography of Mr. James Melville*, 2 vols., ed. by Robert Pitcairn (Edinburgh, 1842), I:245, where, in describing the circumstances of this action, Melville comments that the Provincial Synod of Fife had not been held for two years, and that he had been moderator of the last session (1583), a further proof of doctoral participation and involvement in the organs of church government.

to conduct its affairs the way it felt was necessary for lack of a clearly defined " policy of the kirk," nevertheless, it did appeal to and use, if we may trust the evidence of its records, the *Second Book* from 1578 onward.[42] Repeated deliverances of the General Assembly reflected the usage of the *Second Book*, and occasionally the language was such as to indicate that the *First Book* had been supplanted in the mind of the church by the *Second Discipline*. Cognizance was taken of the nature of the ministry; the office of bishop, of reader, and exhorter, were declared to be no offices of the Scottish Kirk, and the Assembly delivered itself of certain formulas regarding the offices of elder and deacon.[43]

The October Assembly, 1580, held at Edinburgh, raised the question of the doctoral office. Andrew Melville had been ordered by the king to become a member of the University of St. Andrews, having been the principal of the College at Glasgow. The church, however, did not feel that such unilateral action on the king's part might pass without some comment: " In the meantime, the question being moved, If the Kirk might concurr with the King's Magesty in transporting of Doctors from one University to another for weighty and necessary causes; the Kirk and Assembly present, for the most part, voted to the affirmative of the said question." [44] This was based exactly on the language of the *Second Book of Discipline* in regard to the doctoral office. No account was taken that Melville was acting as the minister, or pastor, of the parish of Govan. What concerned the Assembly was that his office as a doctor of the church had been the subject of royal attention.

Melville's translation from Glasgow to St. Andrews

[42] Cf. the " answer to certain doubts proponed concerning the Presbyteries " (*B.U.K.*, II:567–568, 1582) which demonstrated that the frame of reference was the *Second* rather than the *First Book of Discipline*.

[43] *B.U.K.*, II:453, 455 [July, 1580, at Dundee]; p. 464 [Oct., 1580, at Edinburgh]; p. 472 [1580]; p. 601, sess. 16, item 2 [1582].

[44] *Ibid.*, p. 466.

raised a number of questions in the mind of the Assembly. Subsequently, the question was put, " If in respect of the present necessity, that there is no Doctours within this realm, a minister may supercede the office of Pastorship for a time, and use the office of a Doctour [?] It was answered by the kirk, That it may, by the command of the General Kirk, and upon good consideration." [45] Thus Melville's translation to St. Andrews produced in the minds of some a concern that the church did not have within its ministry sufficient men of doctoral status to man the universities, and the question was raised whether a pastor might perform this function.[46]

Alexander Arbuthnet was ordered to demit the principalship in the College of Aberdeen in favor of Nicolas Dalgleisch because he had taken on a pastorate in the city of Aberdeen.[47] The king did not take kindly to this direction of the General Assembly and ordered Arbuthnet to disregard the " acts of the Kirk " and to remain in his post in the college under pain of royal displeasure.[48] The Assembly protested this interference by the king in the church's business along with a number of acts in a document drawn up in 1583. Showing that he had again changed his mind, the king indicated that he considered that the matter of placing ministers in the kingdom was his prerogative quite

[45] *Ibid.,* p. 469 [1580].

[46] An echo of this came two years later when some "doubts and difficulties proposed by Mr. Thomas Buchanan, as weale concerning his acts in the law, as if a Minister for a season leave the Ministrie and execute the office of the Doctor, being discussed as follows, to wit, that the brethren above mentioned [Andrew Hay and John Duncanson] should be direct to the Lords, to seek performance of their promises made for expedition of the said Mr. Thomas his cause, and that it is leisum for a Minister for a season to superseid the Ministrie, and use the office of a doctour; therefor the Assembly has concluded & ordained Mr. Thomas Buchanan to enter in the New Colledge, and use and exercise the office of a Doctour there for the support of the same " (*Ibid.,* p. 597 [1582]) .

[47] *Ibid.,* p. 475.

[48] *Ibid.,* p. 634.

apart from what the General Assembly might think. He gave answer to the Assembly: " The removing of the principal of the College of Aberdeen to be minister of St. Andrews, His Majesty trusts will not think that matter, (the substance is well considered) either so proper to the Kirk, or so improper to the civil estate, but that His Highness and the Council had good ground and reason to direct his letters as he did upon the generals of the North Country." [49]

The creation and stabilization of presbyteries became of prime importance to the kirk, as it sought to preserve its freedom.[50] The *Second Book* had not been specific on either the nature or composition of such bodies. However, the General Assembly, in the period under discussion, gradually interpreted the presbytery to be that which had been denominated the " Exercise " in the *First Book*. Basic authority in the church, however, was to be exercised through the General Assembly, and toward this end, because of the lack of statutory Church Order, the General Assembly in 1586, in conference with the king's commissioners, decreed: " [1] It is found that all such as the Scripture appoints Governors of the Kirk of God as namely, Pastours, Doctours, and Elders, may convene to General Assemblies and vote in Ecclesiastical matters; and all others that have any suit or other things to propose to the Assembly may be there present and give in their suits and propose things profitable to the Kirk and hear reasoning, but shall not vote. [2] There are four offices ordinary set down to us by the Scripture, to wit, Pastours, Doctours, Elders, Deacons. The name of a Bishop ought not to be taken as it has been in Papistrie; but it is common to all Pastours and Ministers." [51] Previous to this, the General Assembly had defined the presbyteries as " consisting of

[49] *Ibid.*, p. 644.
[50] *Ibid.*, p. 568.
[51] *Ibid.*, p. 658.

Doctours, Pastours, and such as are commonly called Elders." [52]

The Scotch Parliament specifically annulled the Discipline of the Church in 1584,[53] and James got his way with the " tulchan " bishops in 1586,[54] but in 1592 the tide had turned and the church, through its Assembly, was once again able to bring forth its discipline and get it adopted by the Parliament. Thus arriving at another watershed in the history of the kirk, we pause to identify those men who were occupying doctoral status in the church.

Andrew Melville, Walter Stewart, Robert Rollock, Patrick Sharp, and James Martin, although still engaged in academic work, had all become involved in pastoral status at some point prior to this date. Robert Wilkie, principal of St. Leonard's College, cannot be counted because of his participation in the ministry of St. Leonard's Church. This leaves but five men to be mentioned: David Rait; Henry Charteris; Patrick Sands; John Robertson; and John Caldcleuch, who can be shown to have participated in the activity of the General Assembly prior to the time when he was inducted into a pastorate.[55]

---

[52] In 1582, *ibid.*, p. 601.

[53] No record of General Assemblies for the years 1584 and 1585 are extant today; cf. *B.U.K.*, II:644–645, although absence of records is not conclusive proof that no meetings were held, for the present work known as *The Buik of the Universal Kirk* is a " retrieving, from such secondary sources as yet exist, the broken and disjointed fragments of the original Registers " (*B.U.K.*, III: Appendix, pp. ix–x) .

[54] Under the pressure of the King in Council, clergymen were nominated to assume the title of bishop and sit in bishops' places in Parliament, with the understanding that they would remain subject to the discipline of the kirk and its judicatories (*B.U.K.*, II:652–653) . The term " tulchan " was derisive and derived from the practice of herdsmen using the skin from a dead calf to entice the mother to give milk.

[55] Third master of St. Mary's College, 1583–1593, and as such sat on a commission of the General Assembly of 1586 along with seven others to try the Bishop of St. Andrews. Charge of the parish of Abdie (Presbytery of Cupar) 1594–1612. *Fasti*, V:123; *B.U.K.*, II:667.

THE SCOTTISH DOCTORATE, WANING PRESBYTERY,
AND JACOBEAN EPISCOPACY, 1592–1606

In spite of the fact that the kirk had gotten the *Second Book of Discipline* enacted into law in 1592, its troubles were not over. The struggle by the king for ascendancy and domination in the church continued unabated throughout the succeeding fourteen years, until in 1606 [56] the General Assembly through its commission became little more than a rubber stamp for royal demands. Initially, the kirk seemed to make some headway in bringing its ministry into what it considered a more vital relationship with the demands of the gospel.[57] But soon the king returned to his previous practice of convening the General Assembly at his command. He presented a series of questions to the General Assembly to be debated at its next meeting, prescribed by him as February, 1597, in Perth.[58] A number of these questions bore directly on the Reformed doctrine of the ministry, and as such they are worth quoting here:

" Q.   6. Is he a lawful Pastour who wants *impositionem manuum?* "

. . .

" Q. 15. Why should not Elders and Deacons of any particular Session be elected *ad vitam?* "

. . .

[56] Cf. *B.U.K.*, II:iv, Appendix.

[57] A report of the Commission for listing the " corruptions and enormities in the Ministrie," presented at the General Assembly of March 24, 1596, in Edinburgh (*B.U.K.*, III:864–865).

[58] The questions raised by the king were ordered to be discussed at a General Assembly that he ordered to be convened in February, 1597, at Perth. However, the actual meeting did not take place until March (*ibid.*, p. 889) and even then was attended by many commissioners with instructions from their judicatories to regard it as a convention of individuals with the king, rather than a legitimate General Assembly, the meeting of which had been ordered at the last adjournment to be for April, 1597.

" Q. 17. Should not the Elders and Deacons of any particular Session have vote in the Presbyteries or the
Pastours only? "

. . .

" Q. 22. Should any University or College, or any Master
or Regent within any College have vote in the
Presbyteries or Synodals in the towns or countries where they are: and so like, what form vote
should they have in General Assemblies? " [59]

The crux of the matter was " Question 6," where the issue of imposition of hands in ordination was raised by the
king.

The king's intrusion of his political authority into the
church was resisted by many, and the provincial Synod of
Fife directed its commissioners to regard the projected assembly at Perth in March as no lawful General Assembly
by virtue of the fact that it had been ordered by the king
and was therefore not a free convocation of the church, but
only a convention between certain members and the king
himself. The Synod of Fife reasoned that the discussion of
the Discipline of the Church was a matter that had been
settled by the church in the *Second Book* and that it was
not the king's business or prerogative, especially inasmuch
as the General Assembly had decreed its meeting would be
for 26 April at St. Andrews and not for February in Perth.
The commissioners from Fife were charged that if the fore-
going protest did not work, they were to confine their discussions with the king to the specific questions that he had
raised for debate,[60] and in case of debate or private discussion, they were to hold fast to the following points:
" 1. That the whole external government must be taken

[59] *Ibid.*, pp. 903–907.
[60] The suspicion was abroad that the special meeting in Perth in
February had ulterior motives such as removal, under royal pressure,
of the excommunication under which the Earl of Huntly lived.
(*Ibid.*, p. 908, art. 4.)

out of the Word of God. 2. That the ordinary Pastors and
Doctors of the Kirk must show the Will of God out of his
Word; and that only to be followed. 3. That the Pastors
and Doctors of the Kirk of Scotland have, with long and
grave deliberation, set down and constituted the whole external discipline and government of the Kirk; according to
the which it has been for many years so happily governed
and ruled, that no heresy, schism, or dissention has had
place therein unto this hour; and that there is none bear-
ing-office in the Kirk, who calls the same in doubt." [61] Instructions given to the commissioners from the Presbytery
of Edinburgh were of a like nature.[62]

The April Assembly of 1597 was postponed until May at
Dundee because of lack of attendance at the April meeting. At the May meeting, the Assembly made answer to a
portion of the king's question that had been set before the
convocation at Perth in March. The only question of those
directly concerning us to which we have a specific answer
was the sixth, and at Dundee the Assembly " ordains that
there be an uniformity in the ordination of the Ministry
throughout the whole country, imposition of hands." [63]
The Assembly's answer reiterated the basic positions of Reformed polity regarding the responsibility of pastors,
sessions, presbyteries, and provincial and National Assemblies. The king pled that it was necessary for the well-
being of the church that " ane General Commission
should be granted to certain of the most wise and discreet
of the brethren to convene with his majesty." What the
king had been unable to do through the attempted imposition of bishops on the church he sought to attempt by the
device of a Commission of the General Assembly.[64]

No sooner had the General Assembly adjourned than the

[61] *Ibid.*, pp. 908–909.
[62] *Ibid.*, pp. 909–911.
[63] *Ibid.*, p. 925.
[64] Fourteen men were appointed to serve; " any seven of them "
could act for the whole. (*Ibid.*, pp. 927 f.)

king called its Commission into session, ostensibly to settle the matter of the complaint of one John Rutherford
against the Presbytery of St. Andrews.[65] One action led to
another, and within two months the Commission was sitting in judgment on the university. As a result of the king
working through the Commission of the General Assembly, Andrew Melville was deposed from his place as rector
in the university, the course of studies in the New College
was rearranged to suit the fancy and expediency of the
king, and furthermore, " Lest they should be distracted by
any other employment, it was concluded, That all the Doctors, Professors; and Regents, not being Pastors in the
Church should be exempt from keeping of Sessions, Presbyteries, Synodical or General Assemblies, and from all
teaching in Churches and congregations, Exercises ex-
cepted: with a discharge to all and every one of them, to
accept any commission prejudicial to the said exemption,
under the pain of deprivation and rebellion, at the con-
servator's instance, the one exception not prejudging the
other. Yet that they should not be thought excluded from
the General Assembly, it was appointed, That the Masters
and Regents of the University should meet when any such
occasion did offer, and condescend upon three persons of
whom one should be elected by the aforesaid Council, to
be present at the General Assembly for that year; which
persons so chosen should not for the space of three years
thereafter be employed in that Commission." [66] The whole
weight of this action was so obviously aimed at Andrew
Melville that we are not surprised when, in the Synod of
Fife meeting in St. Andrews in February of 1598, Thomas
Buchanan challenged Melville, " that he should not have
place in the Assembly (meaning by reason of the Act which
the King and Commissioners of the General Assembly had

[65] Rutherford had been deposed from the ministry by the Presbytery of St. Andrews, but the commission reduced the sentence in
June, 1597. (B.U.K., App.: 931.)
[66] Ibid., pp. 934–935.

made at the last visitation of the Universities, debarring
the Masters thereof, namely of theology, from the Assemblies) he answered, my profession was to resolve questions
in the Kirk of God out of His Word and to reason, vote,
and moderate in Assemblies when your's was to teach the
Grammar rule." [67]

When the General Assembly convened in March of 1598
at Dundee, the king challenged Melville on the basis of
the fact that he was prohibited from attendance on such a
meeting. Melville answered that " he had a calling from
the Kirk; the King's discharge being civil, touched the constitution and rents of the College, but not his doctoral
charge, which was ecclesiastical, he would not betray the
Kirk for his part." [68] In this exchange, John Davidson answered the king with the famous reply of a free church to
an overbearing civil magistrate: " Sir, ye are to remember;
that you sit not here as Imperator, but as a Christian." Melville and John Johnston were ordered to leave Dundee two
days later under pain of prosecution. [69]

When Melville had been unseated as the rector of St.
Andrews (1597), the move was made to elect him dean of
the Faculty of Theology in order that his fame and erudition might be used as a drawing card for foreign students.
His tenacity in keeping the General Assembly of 1598 was
rewarded a year later by the king's visitation to the university and his promulgation of the statute curtailing the
rights, privileges, and tenure of all the deanships. [70]

Melville was not easily silenced, and in 1602 when he
was " making the exercise upon Eph. 5:11 . . . touched
the present corruptions of the Kirk; and namely of the

[67] The question of ministers voting in Parliament had been
brought to the floor of the Synod, and it was when Andrew Melville
rose to speak against this motion that Buchanan challenged him.
(Ibid., App.: 942–943.)

[68] Ibid., App.: 944–945.

[69] Ibid., p. 946. John Johnston was at this time second master in
St. Mary's College. (Fasti, VII:428.)

[70] Ibid., p. 984.

ministry of St. Andrews." The offended ministers made complaint to the king, and Melville was ordered to keep within the bounds of his college,[71] but the kirk had not been beaten into complete submission quite yet, and before the November General Assembly, one Synod cited as an item conducive to the low spiritual and moral level in the church, " that the Doctours bearing ordinary calling in the Kirk, by the discipline and custom thereof, are debarred from the Assemblies." [72] The Assembly in answering this petition of particulars from the Synod of Fife, " finds that Doctours have had, and may have, vote in the General Assembly, they having a lawful commission for that affect, according as it has been found by the General Assembly held in Edinburgh May 10 [1586] and at [Glasgow] 1581, where it is found and declared by the act of the General Assembly that Doctours should concur with the Elders as brethren in all Assemblies." [73]

This was the last mention of the doctoral office by the General Assembly prior to 1638. Four years later, presbyterian polity was overthrown in the Scottish Kirk and the rule of the king became supreme in the church as well as state. No longer was James troubled by the unco-operative doctor from the University of St. Andrews who spent the last eleven years of his life as professor of Biblical Theology at the University of Sedan. The stage was set for the subsequent common endeavor that brought commissioners from the General Assembly of the kirk to sit with their English brethren of a reforming frame of mind at Westminster in 1643.

As the General Assembly sought to uphold the place of the doctoral office in the judicatories of the church, and struggled to maintain it as part of its public ministry, we note that there were employed in the Scottish universities

[71] *Ibid.*, p. 1100.
[72] *B.U.K.*, III:989.
[73] *Ibid.*, p. 994. Brackets indicate lacunae in the text.

seven men of this classification who had not been pastors (1602). To be sure, some of them, like William Forbes, were eventually to be won to an episcopal position, but a number of them were regarded as strong enough Presbyterians that their service to the church (in the school) was continued even following the Presbyterian General Assembly of 1638. In addition to Forbes, we can identify Gilbert Gray, Henry Charteris, Patrick Sands, John Adamson, John Strang, and John Johnston, who with Andrew Melville had been ordered by the king to quit the General Assembly in 1598. In addition to these, we may note the following pastors who had assumed the doctoral function, or who held a pastorate in conjunction with a university position: David Rait, Patrick Sharp, James Martin, and Robert Wilkie.

Presbyter and bishop lived side by side in the Church of Scotland for the next thirty-six years, until in 1638 the kirk rose in revolt against the machinations of Charles I and Archbishop Laud who were, among other things, attempting to enforce a uniformity between the English and the Scottish ecclesiastical establishments. When, in 1638, the General Assembly meeting in Glasgow revolted against royal Anglicization of the kirk, the *Second Book of Discipline* was reinstituted as the standard of government for the kirk and remained in force for seven years, until in February, 1645, the kirk adopted the *Form of Government* of the Westminster Assembly.

The account of the Scottish commissioners as they sat with the Assembly at Westminster and discussed the provisions for the ministry in the debates on the *Form of Government* belong with that section. However, it is necessary to bear in mind the facts as we have presented them in this chapter when we come to the actual proceedings of the London meeting for the references of Baillie, Gillespie, Rutherford, and Henderson are without much substance apart from the background of Scottish practice.

VII

The "Doctor-Teacher" in English Puritanism

THE ENGLISH REFORMATION of 1534 brought with it no radical departure from the medieval hierarchy of ministerial orders. Although Henry VIII entitled himself "head" of the church, the gradations of the clergy were left largely unaffected. With the exception of the suppression of monastic orders, and the impropriation by the crown of much of the lands and goods of the medieval establishment, no great change was wrought on the external framework of the English Church.

Unfortunately, only a small part of the total holdings of the medieval church in England found their way into the hands of those who would use them for the promotion of educational and eleemosynary purposes. Rather, for a complexity of reasons, they were siphoned off by secular powers supporting the new order.[1] With the advent of Edward VI, a more distinctly Reformed tone entered into English religious life and numerous Reformers from the Continent found it expedient to make their headquarters under the protection of the "new Josiah." Among these was the renowned Martin Bucer, who has left us in his *Royaume de Christ* certain reflections on the organiza-

---

[1] Cf. A. F. Leach, *English Schools at the Reformation* (Westminster, 1896), pp. 1–7, 58–73, 114–122, for a very partisan description of the despoilation of endowments for education under Henry VIII and Edward VI.

tion of university, local secondary, and primary education.[2]

REFORM OF SCHOOLS

Appealing to the king to " take in hand immediately your universities and the colleges which are part of them " that an adequate supply of ministers of the gospel might be provided for the church, Bucer outlined an organization for the universities which would have set some colleges apart for medicine and law, and dedicated the remainder " for the reading and interpretation of Holy Scripture, and to exercise themselves in the study of the same." Bucer analyzed part of the difficulty in really reforming the church as stemming from lazy, malingering, and dissident men who had no interest in the doctrine of the gospel of Christ yet who were established in positions of academic preferment. Such men clung to their preferment long after they had finished their course of study. For the universities and their colleges to be " of great and excellent benefit to Christ," Bucer urged the young king to first make it impossible for those who were not sincere holders of the Reformed faith to continue holding academic privileges, and secondly to order that once a man had finished his course he be put to work to make room for others who " will be more faithful." [3]

Bucer constructed his thoughts on the relationship between the church and the Christian school on the basis of Christ's role as " prince, pastor, and doctor of the church." The teaching role of Christ was drawn from the account of

[2] Originally published in 1551 under the title *De Regno Christi* and translated eight years later into French, which text we are using as it has been established by Wendel: *Buceri Martini Opera Latini,* Tome XVbis, " Du Royaume de Jesus-Christ," edit. critique de la traduction française de 1558, texte établi par François Wendel (Paris, 1954).

[3] The question that really motivated Bucer was: Where is one to find the preachers to announce the gospel if the Church of England is to be really reformed? (Bucer, *Opera Latini,* pp. 107–109.)

Jesus' entry into the synagogue at Nazareth where Bucer says " having taken the book which was given him . . . he read some appropriate part of it after which he explicated, adding doctrine and admonition of salvation." This was the proper prototype for the Christian doctor and pastor, who, Bucer says, ought to distribute the gospel to his people by these means: " First by reading and accounting of Holy Scripture, then by interpretation of that which was read, done according to the word of God, then by true doctrine of religion, that is to say clear definition and certain confirmation of the articles of our faith, then as by holy exhortation, admonitions and reprehensions tried by scripture. Subsequently by catechism and instruction . . . eventually by conferences and disputations . . . finally by instruction, exhortation, consolation and correction done face to face." [4]

Bucer drew a distinction between the doctor and pastor, for in one place he identified the " doctor " as concerned with some particular discipline or art.[5] By implication, he associated the schoolmaster in the doctoral office as well as the catechist, but the doctor par excellence for Bucer, was the *professeur des lettres*.[6] Although paying heed to England's episcopal establishment, Bucer's advice to the young king included in some point or other the full fourfold doctrine of the Reformed ministry.[7]

As to education at a level lower than the university or

[4] *Ibid.*, p. 63.
[5] In regard to benefices, he very definitely added *in addition* to faithful pastors, those " who work in the Word and in the Doctrine, to the end also that the schools, that is to say the *docteurs* who teach the arts and the holy letters " may be sustained. (*Ibid.*, p. 139.)
[6] Cf. *ibid.*, p. 64.
[7] E.g., he says that it is not only the office of the bishop to send preachers, but also *docteurs* and *pasteurs* to the churches under their care (*ibid.*, p. 111), and in another place, he counsels that the bishop ought not to try to govern the churches without regard to the realities of the situation, but rather that they should utilize the counsel of the *anciens* and the service of the *diacres* (*ibid.*, p. 122).

college, Bucer advised that each local community be provided with a school, advocating at the same time some kind of compulsory education in the Scriptures and the catechism at this level and attaching the school to the local congregation " in which all the children who have been dedicated and consecrated to the Lord Jesus by baptism would be instructed in the letters and catechisms of our religion." [8] Superior to this rudimentary catechetical training, which included learning to read and write, Bucer would have established local schools to give instruction in languages, arts, and literature. Thus the citizenry would be raised up to the service of the church at the expense both of the church and of the parents. All that he said regarding the teachers in these secondary schools was that they were to be on the lookout for pupils who were fitted for further study in the superior faculties. In view of what he had already said regarding schoolmasters participating in the doctoral office, there is no doubt that he considered this a most necessary and vital function of the church itself.

One additional development must be sketched at this point, before we proceed farther with an account of Puritanism as such. This was the existence during the early part of the sixteenth century of certain sectarian groupings in England, influenced, no doubt, by a touch of the spirit that had characterized Lollardy. As early as 1510, these groups appear to have had a kind of corporate existence, in which their leaders were often referred to as " their Teachers and Instructors in that Doctrine." [9] Doctrinally, the chief

---

[8] *Ibid.*, pp. 233-234. Significantly, Bucer does not disparage learning to read and write, but rather elevates it to a place of importance, and gives as the rationale of the local school that it is a necessary institution " if we wish Christ to reign among us fully."

[9] Cf. John Foxe, *Acts and Monuments of Matters most special and memorable happening in the Church . . .* , seventh printing (London, 1632) ; the continuation and expansion of a work, *Commentarii rerus in ecclesia gestarum,* first printed in Strasbourg, 1554, and then in Basel, 1559. See II:9-10, where Foxe utilized the Register of Richard Fitzjames, Bishop of London, for the years 1509-1517.

points of departure from the established position was a denial of the sacrifice of the Mass and a protest against the efficiency of pilgrimages as a part of the Christian life. Cultically, these groups practiced a pattern of reading or rehearsing the Scriptures in the common tongue, and learning and reciting the Pater Noster and Creed also in English.[10] Foxe recorded that in the congregation at Amersham there were " four principal readers or instructors . . . one was Tilesworth, called then D. Tilesworth. . . . Another was Thomas Chase called amongst them Dr. Chase, . . . the third was . . . Thomas Man, called, also, Dr. Man. . . . The fourth was Robert Coffin, named likewise among them Doctor Coffin." [11] The appellation of " doctor " to the leaders of such sectarian conventicles is interesting. To account for this usage, we must turn to sectarian dissatisfaction with the existing state of affairs in the university,[12] and the fact that the sectarian leaders found themselves in conflict with those holding university doctorates in theology when called to defend themselves before the bishop's courts.[13]

There was also a conventicle in Oxford about 1526 centering around Master John Clark, in which a number of scholars and graduates were involved. Thomas Garret, who narrated the account to Foxe, told how at one time following his reception into this " company " he was deputized by Master Clark to circulate among the members of the group " to resort to every one of them weekly and to know what doubts they had in any place of the scriptures that by

10 *Ibid.*, pp. 26–40.
11 *Ibid.*, p. 29b, lines 47–60.
12 *Ibid.*, pp. 15–16. Richard Hunne had been charged with condemning the University of Oxford and its schools as being " unfit ways of coming to the knowledge of the Gospel."
13 Foxe records that John Stilman, at his trial before the Bishop of London, 22 October 1518, maintained that " the Doctors of the Church have subverted the truth of Holy Scriptures," and that therefore whereas they are in hell, Wycliff is a " saint and in heaven." (*Ibid.*, p. 26.)

me from him that they might have the true understanding of the same." [14]

Following Henry's break with Rome, this kind of activity took on a different aspect. Adam Damlip (George Bucker) while waiting for a ship at Calais was invited by certain religiously interested people of that city to preach to them and agreed to do so if he " might be licensed by such as were in authority." Introduced to the king's deputy, he was given the privilege of preaching until such time as license might be issued and so impressed his peers that he was offered a salary and keep to continue, but refused, asking only maintenance for study,[15] in return for which he would " daily, once in the forenoon and again by one o'clock in the afternoon, preach among them according unto the talents that God had lent him." For some twenty days, he read lectures in the chapter house of the White Friars until the " place was not big enough " and he was asked to read his lectures from the pulpit.[16] This type of teaching ministry is reminiscent of the theological lectures delivered by such as Zwingli, Bucer, and Calvin in their respective cities.

Several things stand out in this brief introduction to Puritan England as far as the teaching office was concerned. Henry's break with Rome had resulted in the effective nationalization of both church and university under royal authority rather than allowing either to remain in an autonomous position. In such a situation the teaching body of the university naturally would look more quickly to a royal authority than to the ecclesiastical for its benefits. The church still retained a vital position of influence and importance at all levels of education, but it was a church subservient to the will of the monarch rather than, as Bucer hoped, a church master in its own house. More-

[14] *Ibid.,* pp. 422–423.

[15] *Ibid.,* pp. 559–560.

[16] *Ibid.,* pp. 557–559; the incident is reported as having occurred in 1544.

over, quite independent of these two streams there was, indigenous to English sectarian life, a conception of religious instruction that operated strictly at the local level and that viewed the university as a source of error and corruption. Both by way of protest and by way of emulation, sectarianism copied the title for the traditional teaching office in the church, the doctor of theology, for the leaders and instructors of its conventicles.

THE MARIAN EXILES

The death, in 1553, of the " new Josiah " brought to the throne Mary Tudor, partisan of the old faith. Within a matter of months, many of those particularly devoted to the Reformation in the English Church found it expedient to take themselves to the Continent in order that they might continue their worship of God according to their own dictates and that they might plan for the restoration of a Reformed religion in the homeland.[17] This group of exiles, numbering all told some eight hundred to a thousand, was made up from all the classes of English society but its chief components were from the educated and the gentry. Zurich, Basel, Strasbourg, and Geneva were all centers for the exiled English Protestants, but the congregation at Frankfort provides the best evidence of the internal relation between church, ministry, and school that Englishmen produced in exile for importation in the day of their return.

We have already discussed the Church Order from the exile congregation in Geneva, but it must be remembered that the Geneva congregation was largely an offshoot of the original Frankfort body. By August of 1554, the English group had edited its own discipline, which established that the congregation would operate with a ministry of four offices: a pastor, " Preachers and such as are learned in the

[17] Cf. Christina H. Garrett, *The Marian Exiles* (Cambridge, 1938).

Church," elders, and deacons.[18]

On the basis of this discipline, John Knox, then at Geneva, James Haddon, then at Strasbourg, and Thomas Lever, among the emigrees at Zurich, were elected and called to the ministry of the church. Haddon refused, and by the end of October, Whitehead had come to Frankfort to take charge temporarily and began preaching on Romans. Knox arrived from Geneva in November of 1554 and Thomas Lever arrived about the same time to be accepted on trial until Easter of 1555.

There was some difference between Knox and Lever as to which service for Holy Communion was to be used: the Second Prayer Book of Edward VI, or the Genevan Order of Calvin. Knox refused to impose the Genevan service without the consent of the " learned men of Strasbourg, Zurich, and Emden," requested to be relieved of the necessity of administering the Sacrament and said that he would be satisfied with preaching only. A compromise order of service was instituted in February, 1555, which lasted just about one month when the whole situation was complicated by the arrival of Richard Cox and another group of English exiles who were committed to the Second Prayer Book. Cox's stay was brief, but resulted in the departure of Knox from the scene, and the election, sometime before 5 April 1554, on the basis of *The Old Discipline* of a pastor, two ministers, four seniors, and two deacons.[19] A part of the Frankfort congregation became increasingly dissatisfied, and by the first part of September were on their way out of the city, the majority of them eventually establishing themselves in Geneva.[20]

[18] [William Whittingham], *A Brief Discourse of the Troubles at Frankfort, 1554–1558 A.D.*, Edward Arber (ed.) (London, 1908), p. 26; cf. pp. 143–149 for text of this Church Order to which we shall refer as *The Old Discipline*.

[19] *Ibid.*, p. 72.

[20] A conference was held 30 August between the "Pastor, Ministers, and Elders" on the one hand and the dissatisfied parishioners on the other. (*Ibid.*, p. 82.)

The pastoral office under *The Old Discipline* was first filled by David Whitehead.[21] However, " the office of Preachers and such as are learned in the Church " is of greater interest to us. As this office had been outlined in 1554, it was " to assist the Pastor in Preaching the Word, Ministering the Sacraments, and in all consultations and meeting with him and the Elders, especially in Causes of Doctrine, and also at other times, when they shall be required." [22] On the very face of it, this is confused. In one breath, it bids those undertaking this office to act with the pastor and elders in everything; in the next, it presumes that these individuals will not ordinarily be on hand, but bids them be in attendance to render their decision on doctrinal matters and at such other times when the need of their presence is felt.

We suggest that a solution to this confusion may lie in the direction of recognizing that this article is actually talking about two separate categories of the ministry: one, a kind of associate pastor; the other, a doctoral office that had been not yet clearly defined. Those who are associate pastors are readily recognizable: Richard Cox and Thomas Becon.[23] These are the men who are expected to preach, administer the sacraments, and hold council with the pastor and the elders. But the identity of those who hold council only under certain conditions escapes us until we take into consideration another factor.

[21] Cf. letter of David Whitehead to Calvin, from Frankfort, 20 Sept. 1955. (*Ibid.*, pp. 87–93.)

[22] Cox's report to Calvin mentioned " two Preachers " in addition to the pastor who had been appointed, but the text of *The Troubles* says that in addition to the pastor, " two Ministers " have been elected (*ibid.*, p. 76).

[23] Their names appear immediately after Whitehead's in the letter to Calvin with the designation " Minister of the Word of God " appended after Becon's signature. Then follow in order the signatures of Richard Alvey, Henry Parry, Bartholomew Traheron, and Thomas Cottisford, who are, without doubt, signing as elders of the congregation, although there was no designation attached to their names.

Thomas Cole, writing to a friend in the early part of 1556, described a unique enterprise of the Frankfort congregation. They had, said Cole, " set up a University, to repair again their estimation by maintenance of Learning (which, surely, is well done), that was fondly brought in decay by willful ignorance, in defending the Ceremonies." Cole then proceeded to identify the men who were responsible for instruction in this educational enterprise: " Master Horne is chosen to be the Reader of the Hebrew Lecture; Master Mullings of the Greek; and Master Traheron, when he is strong, shall take the Divinity Lecture in hand." [24] These, then, are probably the individuals referred to by the phrase "such as are learned in the Church." Their employment is essentially academic, and their involvement in the minutiae of ecclesiastical business was not regarded as obligatory, although their presence was contemplated under a number of circumstances.

Traheron was not well, and Cole indicated that Whitehead, the pastor, had been charged with the Divinity Lecture in addition to his other function. However, he felt overworked and tried to resign the pastorate in order to get out of lecturing, but instead was prevailed upon to continue as pastor and was relieved of the lecture. However, about 6 January 1556, Whitehead did resign his post and Robert Horne, the lecturer in Hebrew was elected to the pastorate.

The year 1556 seems to have passed in comparative peace, but the coming of the new year precipitated a controversy that to all intents and purposes marked the emergence of a congregational type polity, wherein the congregation became the final court of appeal in the decision of ecclesiastical matters and discipline.[25]

[24] *Ibid.*, pp. 94–95, letter of Thomas Cole to a friend of the " Events in the English congregation at Frankfort " in the last quarter of 1555 and January, 1556.

[25] *Ibid.*, pp. 99–112. They " ceased both from Preaching, and also the Ecclesiastical Lectures." Even though Horne seems to have had

As a result of a controversy between Horne and the elders on the one hand and the congregation on the other, *The Old Discipline* was amended sometime between 4 February and 13 February 1557, by a committee of eight men who were particularly at pains to make some provision as to how such a situation should be handled when the governing ministry of the church and the congregation were at loggerheads. With the backing of the Frankfort magistracy, Horne evidently tried to gain admission again to the pastoral office with the stipulation that he be not required to preach, but this was unacceptable to the congregation.[26] The magistracy finally unseated all the officers on the last day of February, 1557, and by the twentieth of March the congregation had edited another new discipline that was ratified by congregational action upon it nine days later.[27]

Essentially, with certain minor exceptions and with some additions, the *Second New Discipline* of 20 March 1557,[28] reiterated the structure of the ministry contained in *The Old Discipline*. In place of the office of pastor were instituted " Two Ministers, or Teachers of the Word " to be elected by the congregation, and to have equal author-

the support of " the most part of them that were appointed Preachers " (p. 118) and " Readers of the Scripture " (p. 119) during the whole controversy, " the Church . . . observed both Public Prayers, Sermons, and Ecclesiastical Lectures, and all other things accustomed " (p. 111).

[26] This took place on 24 February 1557, and the congregation rejected the proposal because Horne was refusing to do " the cheifest part of the Pastor's office, wherein he hath behaved himself well, if in anything well " (*ibid.*, p. 20).

[27] The " Edict of the Magistrates " declared " that congregation might freely, when they would, choose either them [the officers just ejected by city order], or other ministers. Likewise it was permitted and granted that, according to the ability [to remunerate?] of the congregation, they might choose one, or many Ministers of the Word or Doctors." (*Ibid.*, p. 122. Cf. also pp. 124–132.)

[28] The *First New Discipline* would be that of 13 February 1557, but we do not have the complete text for this and it was never really operative in the congregation. The text of the *Second New Discipline* may be found, *ibid.*, pp. 150–205.

ity. Their function was to preach, " ordinary Sermons on Wednesdays, Thursdays, and Sundays before noon; and instruct and hear the examination of the youth on the Catechism on Sunday in the Afternoon, at the hour accustomed; and also to Minister the Sacraments, say the Common Prayers distinctly, visit and comfort the sick, especially at death, bury the dead with orderly observances and rights and direct all their behavior, acts, and life, according to the rule of their Vocation set forth in the Holy Scripture." [29] Even though the term was not used, these two officers were pastors in the Reformed sense of the term, and in this particular instance, copastors.

The next Article spoke of six, " either fewer or more," who were to be appointed by the " Ministers and Seniors " in the name of the whole congregation. Four of these six were to be " well learned, who shall read and expound the Chapters, and shall help the two Ministers of the Word, when needs shall require, in the doctrine of the Word, Catechizing of the Youth, Ministering of the Sacraments, and saying of Common Prayer." [30] The other two were to assist the ministers, seniors, and deacons in visitation of the sick and care of strangers, and in pastoral calling on the congregation.

These six offices were probably patterned on the office of " Preacher " of *The Old Discipline*. The description of the function of four of them makes a good deal of sense when we realize that the *Second New Discipline* included articles recognizing a " Lecture of Divinity and Disputations," and a school as parts of the congregation. The congregation, in turn, not only gave these activities its support but deemed them a necessary function of the church. Indeed, it was stipulated that as an alternative to the Lecture in Divinity " Prophecy be used every fortnight in the Eng-

[29] *Ibid.*, pp. 153, 156; *Second New Discipline*, Arts. 7 and 8.
[30] *Ibid.*, p. 157, Art. 9. We note that *Second New Discipline* did not try to give a specific name to this office.

lish tongue, for the exercise of said Students, and edifying of the Congregation; or both Disputation and Prophecy also; if it so shall seem good unto the Ministers and Seniors." To our knowledge, this was the only mention of " prophesying " in any of the Frankfort Disciplines, and from the tone used it would appear that this was not a primary activity of the congregation, but it is significant that when it was used the usage was directly related to the academic process.[31] Horne and his party objected that " we know not what they mean by the School," to which the answer was given that Horne knew very well that " here are Students, Lectures, and Disputations." [32] The document itself leaves unanswered many questions as to how well organized this school actually was. However, there seemed to be no doubt in the minds of its authors, nor in the minds of those who made answer to Horne's objections in September that not only was this a desirable institution but that it was a functioning enterprise within the life of the congregation.

Only when we hold these facts in mind do we understand the purpose of specifying four of the " six " appointees as " well learned." It was the existence or projection of an academic enterprise that called forth this division of functions. If this were not the case, there would have been no necessity of selecting four from the " six " to be especially qualified for what is obviously a teaching office over against two others who were to function as assistant pastors. Although, we must hasten to add, the four who were to be qualified as " well learned " were charged with additional responsibilities that do not correspond absolutely with the Genevan formulation of the doctoral office, particularly the matter of administering the sacraments.

All ministries, except the copastorate (" teachers and

[31] *Ibid.*, pp. 166, 172, Arts. 12 and 21.
[32] *Ibid.*, p. 173.

ministers of the word ") were to be held for one year only (presumably this included the four " doctoral " appointees and the two " assistant" pastors), but it was most particularly directed at the eldership and the diaconate. No mention was made of the manner of induction into office for the instructors in the school, the associate pastors, or the deaconesses, but it was provided that the copastors, the elders, and the deacons were to be inducted by " imposition of hands with prayer " following their election.[33]

The mention of the school was evidently a real stumbling block, for a group of conciliators tried to get the " Article for exercise of learning " excised as a means of bringing about a reconciliation between Horne and the majority of the congregation.[34] However, this move was rejected by the congregation at large. From March, 1557, until the end of 1558, the troubled congregation in Frankfort operated under a Church Order which spelled out a doctoral office in the public ministry of the church, without actually naming it. This Church Order also specified a relationship to an educational institution based on the idea that this was a necessary and integral part of the church's concern. Interim power in the church's affairs lodged in the hands of the ministers and elders, who together were responsible for the appointment of the individuals designated for the teaching office and as assistant pastors. As had been well pointed out, the Frankfort congregation introduced into this *Second New Discipline* the principle of ultimate congregational supremacy in matters of discipline and affairs over against the will of the assembled ministry.[35]

From their Continental experience, the Marian exiles carried back to England, upon the accession of Elizabeth, two statements on the doctoral office that in spite of very

[33] *Ibid.,* p. 186, Art. 39.
[34] *Ibid.,* pp. 206–208.
[35] Garrett, *op. cit.,* Part I.

close resemblances, exhibited certain differences in detail. The Genevan Order contemplated the doctoral office on a supracongregational level, and did not invest that office with explicitly pastoral functions. The Frankfort Church Order, on the contrary, employing and recognizing the separate function of the academic teacher, overtly invested the doctoral office with pastoral functions — specifically in this case, oversight of people and administration of the sacraments.

THE ATTEMPT TO PRESBYTERIANIZE THE CHURCH OF ENGLAND

Returning to England at Elizabeth's accession to the throne in 1558, the exiles from the Continent looked forward to casting the church of their homeland in a mold more conformable to that which they had experienced during their exile. This struggle was to be carried out on a number of fronts, not the least of which was the one looking toward a restructuring of the form of the church and its ministry in accordance with the Reformed doctrine and practice on the Continent. The Church Order of both the exile congregations at Geneva and at Frankfort was directed toward the ordering of a single congregation. As such, they fell short of providing an adequate pattern for the church of a whole nation; as we have seen in Scotland, that church found it necessary to settle its internal organization on a broader base than was provided by the Genevan Church Order.

However, the return did not work out as the exiles had hoped and prayed. Whatever her prejudices were in regard to the Bishop of Rome, Elizabeth was still a Tudor and, like her father, regarded the crown as the rightful seat of ecclesiastical authority for the English Church. Commencing with the Supremacy Bill and the Act of Uniformity in

1559, she endeavored to work her will on the whole ecclesiastical establishment until finally in March of 1566, the first group of parochial clergy were stripped of their pulpits for refusing to conform to the wishes of the sovereign in matters of ecclesiastical dress.[36]

This kind of treatment only served to convince the stricter sort that nothing short of wholesale reformation would avail in the English Church. Not only were sides being chosen in the parishes, but also in the universities, and especially in Cambridge, where Thomas Cartwright had been made Regius Professor of Theology in 1569.[37] He increasingly contended for an essentially presbyterian position on the organization of the church and the ordering of its ministry. This inflamed the court party, and by 21 September 1572, Cartwright had been deprived both of his professorship and his fellowship in Trinity College.[38] Although only in deacon's orders (used by Whitgift as a lever to oust him from the academic community), Cartwright regarded his tenure as Regius Professor as constituting his induction into the doctoral office, for " he himself being a reader of Divinity is a Doctour exercising the office named . . . and therefore must only read [lecture], and may not preach." [39]

Cartwright's deprivation coincided with the issuance of two documents of English Puritanism which we will now examine. They are the first and second editions of *An Admonition to the Parliament* and *A Second Admonition to the Parliament*, which appeared in October of 1572.[40]

[36] John Brown, *The English Puritans* (Cambridge, 1912), pp. 20–44.

[37] Cf. A. F. S. Pearson, *Thomas Cartwright and Elizabethan Puritanism; 1535–1603* (Cambridge, 1925), especially pp. 25–30.

[38] *Ibid.*, p. 63.

[39] *Ibid.*, p. 31, quoting S. P. Dom. Eliz. LXXI, No. 23, i, and Grindal, *Remains*, p. 323, to the effect that Cartwright expressed this point of view 25 June 1570.

[40] The texts in W. H. Frere and C. E. Douglas (eds.), *Puritan Manifestoes* (London, 1907); " An Admonition . . . ," pp. 5–55,

Right ministry and right government. The basic presupposition of both documents was that " either must we have a right ministry of God and a right government of His Church, according to the scripture set up (both which we lack) or else there can be no right religion." [41] *An Admonition* followed the Reformed pattern of projecting a public ministry of the church to consist of pastors, elders, and deacons.[42] No mention was made of a doctoral office, but it is of interest to note that a significant deletion occurred between the first and second editions of this work which gives some indication that the doctoral office, although not formulated fully in the mind of the author, was of some concern to him. Frequent allusion was made on the pages of *An Admonition* to the various ecclesiastical offices of the English Church: chancellors, archdeacons, commissaries, curators, summoners, churchwardens, archbishops, bishops, suffragans, deans, and archdeans.[43] The first edition uniformly included with these lists of noncanonical office-bearers in the English Church the simple title of " doctors." However, in the second edition of *An Admonition,* the term " Universitie Doctor and Bachelors of Divinity " was substituted for the initial use of the term "doctors." In all the other places, save one,[44] where the term " doctor " had been used by the first edition as an evident term of opprobrium, the use was dropped altogether. Admittedly, this is negative evidence, but it is suggestive that growing within the mind of Puritanism was some recognition of a doctoral office related to the ministry of the Reformed Church.

---

and " A Second Admonition . . . ," pp. 81–133. The first edition of " An Admonition . . ." appeared sometime before 27 June 1572; the second edition had gone through its second printing by 25 August. Hereafter cited as *Admon.* and *2d Admon.*

[41] *Admon.,* p. 6 (the phrase is repeated in *2d Admon.,* p. 97).

[42] *Admon.,* pp. 15–33.

[43] *Ibid.,* pp. 5, 16, 17, 18, 31.

[44] Which is probably a quotation from another work known as " View of Popish Abuses," (*ibid.,* pp. 20–37) ; cf. p. 31.

This suspicion is reinforced when we come to read the text of the *Second Admonition*. Its style is most diffuse and prolix, so that it is hard to say that the document produced a coherent view of a Reformed ministry as it was projected for the English Church. However, in its own way, it did set forth a series of church judicatories and a fourfold doctrine of the ministerial office. In addition to elders and deacons [45] as office-bearers in the church, " there are then in the ministry only two sorts of ministers, namely pastors and teachers." [46]

The pastoral office was to consist of the oversight and charge of the whole parish: in instruction, in admonition, in exhortation, in the correction of doctrine and behavior of everyone in his congregation, and in the administration of the sacraments within the parish. A teacher,[47] on the other hand, although called in the same manner as the pastor, was specifically to concern himself with " lectures, and expositions of the scriptures, to the end that there may be set forth . . . a soundness of doctrine." Every congregation must have a pastor,[48] and if there was some doubt in the mind of the writer as to the necessity of *each* congrega-

[45] *2d Admon.*, pp. 118–122, where the office of ruling elder (*ancien* or *ouderling* of the Continental Reformed) is sometimes called " assistant " and sometimes " elder."

[46] *Ibid.*, p. 98.

[47] The author preferred the title of " teacher," but recognized the claim of Continental usage by frequently using the phrase " teacher or doctor." (*Ibid.*, pp. 98–99.) What he was at some pains to avoid was confusion of the ecclesiastical office with an academic title, for to him " a plaine case it is, that ostentation and outward glory is sought by these names & by the name of Masters of Arte, which is esteemed [by] many beneathe the titles of Doctor, or Bachelor in divinitie, for otherwise they would not offer those title to such as the universities would shewe pleasure unto, as to noble men and others."

[48] *Ibid.*, p. 100; the provision was expressed overtly: the pastor's responsibility for doctrine " whether there be a teacher or doctour or no " (p. 99), and was underscored by implication in the emphasis placed on the necessity of a pastor at the very point where the doctoral office was being discussed.

tion employing a doctor, still, " the use of such an one is most needful, where the frie [youth] of the church (as I might call it) is, to enter them well which after should be employed to the ministry, whether it be in the university or elsewhere, that such be brought up to this turn." [49]

The teacher, or doctor, of the *Second Admonition* was closely related to the business life of the church by being, together with the elders and the pastors, included in all levels of synodical responsibility from the parish consistory to the national assembly.[50] The hierarchical structure of the church was maintained by the projection of a graduated series of judicatories (parish consistory, conference, provincial synod, National Assembly),[51] and it was at the level above the local parish that the *Second Admonition* sought to introduce the practice of the exercise of prophesying. Declared to be about the size of a rural deanery, these conferences were " to confer and exercise themselves in prophesying or interpreting the scriptures, after the which interpretation, they must confer upon that which was done, and judge of it, the whole to judge of those that spake and yet so, as some one be appointed by all, to speak for them, as they shall among themselves agree what shall be spoken, which thing was always used among the Apostles, one to speak for rest, which conference may sometimes be more general than some other time, as occasion of the churches may require." [52] Not only were the pastors

[49] *Ibid.*, p. 98.
[50] *Ibid.*, pp. 97, 107–109.
[51] *Ibid.*, pp. 118 f. — consistory; pp. 107 f. — conference; p. 108 — provincial synod; p. 109 — National Synod or Council.
[52] *Ibid.*, p. 107. Of some significance, we believe, is the fact that although during the period of the early 1570's the Puritan clergy began to meet in regular Exercises or Prophesyings (some with the approval of their bishops — cf. J. Brown, *The English Puritans,* pp. 64–68) this is the only explicit mention of the practice we have found in a presbyterian-type discipline of the period. To fill out the reference, we need to note that the author of the *Second Admonition* was extremely doubtful of the value of the " Exercises of proph-

and teachers to be certified by the conference,[53] but the conference was to exercise an appellate role above the local consistory to which questions beyond the capacity of the parish consistory would be brought for decision.[54] No mention was made about the attendance of elders at the conference, although elders and deacons were specifically ordered to accompany pastors to provincial synods.[55] However, the conference was a meeting of "some certain ministers and other brethren" which may be interpreted out of other contexts to include the teachers, or doctors, as "the other brethren." [56]

  When we gather the evidence from *An Admonition* and the *Second Admonition,* we are forced to conclude that the doctoral office was indeed ambiguous in the minds of both authors. Hopefully, they may have wished to construe it in an academic framework, but the practicalities of their situation prevented them from being too hopeful. Almost in the vein of the English congregation at Geneva, they admit of it as desirable, but do not know just what they are to do about it. The universities, along with the bishops, fell under suspicion of being strongholds of conservatism; institutions not quite to be trusted as fit instruments for the propagation of God's true religion. Because of this distrust, the writers were forced to the expedient of lodging the office of instruction at the parish level, an expedient, incidentally, which corresponded to their basic concern for the pastoral office and the reform of national religious life at the grass-roots level of the parish.

---

esying" allowed under the permission of the bishops, for he considers them "exercises in rote memory" with no order, "except perhaps an order not to speak against any of their proceedings" (pp. 110–111). See also Pearson, *op. cit.,* pp. 155–156.
  [53] *2d Admon.,* p. 97.
  [54] *Ibid.,* p. 108.
  [55] *Ibid.,* p. 121.
  [56] "The teacher (save that in the consistory of the same parishe, and in all conferences of ministers he is to be joined with the ministers)." (*Ibid.,* p. 98.)

The question, of course, obtrudes itself: Why did they not think in terms of the grammar schools and Latin schools of the nation? If they did, they made no mention of such employment being a fit function of the doctoral office. Such an approach was very nearly made by Geffroey Fenton, who, two short years following the publication of the *Admonitions*, published a work called *A Forme of Christian Pollicie Drawn out of French.*[57]

The same year in which Fenton eulogized the schoolmaster, Walter Travers published a presbyterian-type Church Order for the English Church with a preface by Cartwright, who immediately translated the whole work into English.[58] As à Lasco had done, Travers attempted to correlate the ministry of the existing English Church with the Genevan pattern by postulating two orders: that of bishops and that of deacons.[59] Each of these orders he divided into two offices: the episcopal order being made up of pastor and doctors; while the diaconate was made up of elders and deacons. The confusion of this kind of arrangement is readily apparent when we find him defining elders as " deacons, who are appointed to take heed of the offenses which arise in the church " and a few pages later when he says that " under the name of elders . . . mean only Pastor, Doctor, and those who are by proper name called Elders." [60]

The only place Travers had departed from the Lascian

[57] Geffroey Fenton, *A Forme of Christian Pollicie Drawne out of the French* (London, 1574).
[58] *Ecclesiasticae Discipline, et Anglicanae Ecclesiae ab illa aberrationis plena e verbo Dei & dilucida explicatio* (LaRochelle, 1574) ; Cartwright's Preface written at Heidelberg and dated 2 February 1574. Cartwright's English translation entitled *A Full & Plaine Declaration of Ecclesiasticall Discipline out of the Word of God* ([Heidelberg], 1574), to which reference will be made herein. Cf. also, Pearson, *op. cit.,* pp. 135–136; and Thomas Cartwright, *The Second Reply of Thomas Cartwright to Dr. Whitgift Second Answer Touching Church Discipline* ([Zurich], 1574), pp. 296 f.
[59] *A Full & Plaine Declaration,* pp. 73, 123 [132], 153–160.
[60] *Ibid.,* pp. 155, 159.

scheme was in the statement that the doctoral office is separate from the pastorate.[61] Here he revived Calvin's definition: that the doctors of the church are to be correlated
with the prophets of the former dispensation. But in the
correlation he drew on one strand at which Calvin had
only hinted, for he regarded pastors as successors to the
" apostles and after a sort also the priests of the law,
whereas Doctors do rather resemble and are more like unto
the Prophets and the Levites. Therefore Pastors administer
not only the word, but also the Sacraments." [62]

Travers specifically identified the doctoral office with the
scholarly ministry as over against the ministry of shepherding and sacraments, for he said: " Let the Doctor have a
chaire set for him. Let him have schollars appointed him
whom he may teach and instruct in the fear of God and
knowledge of heavenly mysteries; I mean a chair wherein
he may sit to teach and to catechize, not wherein taking his
ease he may be idle and fall asleep." [63] Instructing and
catechizing were the only functions required by the doctoral office. Although Travers would not prohibit their
employment in the schools or the universities, he was as
much, perhaps more, concerned that they function at the
parochial level.[64]

Referring to the " office of preachers " (perhaps a reflection of the sectarians), he identified it as extraordinary,
and pleaded that it be replaced by properly constituted
pastors and doctors in the English Church.[65] Occasionally,

[61] *Ibid.*, pp. 123 [133], 146.
[62] *Ibid.*, pp. 88, 147.
[63] *Ibid.*, p. 141.
[64] *Ibid.*, p. 139; "Let Teachers and Doctors be provided . . . to
teach the Churches and especially the rude and ignorant " (p. 141) ;
" Let these learned Doctors [Elizabethan doctors who lie idle in the
universities] be assigned and appointed to churches to expound the
Scriptures, to Catechize."
[65] This is an interesting passage: " Wherefore we ought to have
Pastors and Doctors appointed in our Churches, and not to retain
still the extra-ordinary office of preachers [in which] . . . many

he joined the term " teacher " with that of " doctor," yet in other contexts used the term " teacher " as though he were speaking of the pastor. Even in this document, where a clear distinction was recognized between the pastoral and doctoral offices, a certain terminological ambiguity was allowed to confuse the issue.[66]

A decade later William Fulke wrote *A Briefe and Plaine Declaration*,[67] which said nothing new about the doctoral office, or about the Puritan doctrine of the ministry. However, for the first time in an English Puritan Church Order the fourfold Calvinian ministry was adopted without equivocation and with little sense of ambiguity. Although Fulke did not consistently use either " doctor " or " pastor " as the primary office, he did consistently speak of a ministry consisting of pastors, doctors, governors (elders) , and deacons.

Initially, he spoke as though the doctoral office was to be located in the congregation, but Fulke regarded the low estate of the church to be in part the result of the fact that qualified candidates for the ministry were in short supply. To remedy this condition, he was convinced that, " we must provide that this office [the doctorate] be restored, both in the universities, and in as many other places as may

---

worthy men have labored with some fruite . . . for the love they had unto the Gospell, thought it lawful for them . . . to take upon them this Apostalic or Evangelical kind of office and embassage: whereas rather they ought to have urged the full and perfect reformation off our church, and to have striven by the word of God, that every Church might have been provided of a fit Pastor." (*Ibid.*, p. 137.) We have suggested one possibility in the text; another is that the reference here may be to the " outed " men who had obtained numerous lectureships.

[66] " The Consistory . . . is the company and Assembly of the Elders of the Church " (*ibid.*, p. 159) ; the consistory consists of " these three orders: Pastors, Doctors, Elders " (p. 160) .

[67] [William Fulke], *A Briefe and Plaine Declaration, concerning the desires of all those faithful Ministers, that have and do seek for Discipline and reformation of the Church of Englande* (London, 1584) .

be as well for the better instruction of all men, which are
desirous to learne, as especially for the information of those,
which should occupy the roomes of Pastours, of which sort
there ought to be a great number always in good toward-
ness to take charge of so many several flocks, as must of
necessity be so great a Church as this is." [68] The need for
properly qualified men to fill the pulpits of the land was
very great, and out of this need the author was brought to
viewing the office from an academic perspective, but we
cannot get away from the feeling that such was not his
primary concern. Rather, he veered away from the idea
quickly to restate in general, but unmistakable, tones that
the office was really for the edification of the church in its
congregational manifestation. In doing so, he may have
contemplated the training of Reformed pastors in an extra-
academic, or at least an extra-university, environment.
However, we do not find in Fulke the extreme disenchant-
ment with the university that we have seen in some other
Puritans.

The need for a coherent expression of the Presbyterian
position in the 1580's brought forth in 1585 (or 1586) a
document entitled *Disciplina Ecclesiastica Sacra: Disciplina Synodica,*[69] which set forth the fourfold ministry,
familiar in other contexts, but using for the second order
the term " teacher." [70] The term " pastor " was used for

[68] *Ibid.,* pp. 18–19.

[69] Cf. Pearson, *op. cit.,* pp. 253–258, for a full discussion of this
work; Pearson concluded that the book in its original form (author,
Walter Travers) was never printed and that aside from those who
may have had a hand in its composition, or may have seen it in
manuscript, it was unknown until it was published in an English
edition in 1644 under the title, *A Directory of Church-government
anciently contended for, and as farre as the Times would suffer prac-
tised by the first Non-conformists in the daies of Queen Elizabeth.
Found in the study of the most accomplished Divine Mr. Thomas
Cartwright, after his decease; and reserved to be published for such
a time as this* (London, 1644).

[70] *A Directory* (1644), p. A2 rect. The teachers are those " which
are occupied in wholesome doctrine."

the office " which doe administer the Word and Sacrament." [71] In some places in the text, the term " preacher "
was used in such a way as to be synonymous with the pastoral office.[72]

Formulation of the teacher's office was very sketchy and
the closest that the work came to an exact definition was
in the section entitled " Of Students of Divinity, and their
Exercises." These exercises were to be organized in such a
way that, hopefully, some kind of academic training of an
advanced stature would be carried on in relation to the local parish church, for it was said that " in every church
where [it is convenient] care is to be had that some poore
schollers studious of Divinity be fit for the theological exercises, and especially for expounding of Holy Scriptures." [73]
The exercises were to be held in the presence of " at least
one Minister," and only by interpretation are we able to
say that he may be regarded as the " Teacher " mentioned
previously.

Three years later Travers published a *Defense of the
Ecclesiastical Discipline.*[74] Although on the initial pages of
this work he used the terms " Pastors and Doctors," he soon
dropped " Doctor " for the more English term of
" Teacher." [75] However, before doing that he also used the

[71] *Ibid.:* " Ministers of the Church " include all four offices; pastors and teachers are " Ministers of the Word."

[72] " Let only a Minister of the Word that is a Preacher minister
the Sacraments, and that [,] after preaching of the Word, and not
in any other place than in the publique assemblies of the Church."
(*Ibid.,* p. B2 ver.)

[73] *Ibid.,* p. B3 rect. The section " Of Schooles," which immediately preceded the article on " Students of Divinity," made no mention of the church's stake in education beyond the general statement
that children were to be instructed in schools " in other learning
and in the Catechism."

[74] [Walter Travers], *A Defense of the Ecclesiastical Discipline
ordayned of God to be used in his Church. Against an Replie of
Maister Bridges, to a Brief and Plain Declaration of it which was
printed An[no] 1584* (London, 1588). Travers was defending the
work by Fulke.

[75] The shift took place at p. 39.

intermediate terms of " Pastours and Ministers " in such a way that the co-ordinate ministries were both charged with the duty of preaching and administration of the sacraments. Having substituted the English word for the Latin derivative, he did not return to the Latin except in one instance. When he discussed Bridges' attack on the doctoral office, based on Bridges' use of the *Scottish Book of Common Prayers,* Travers quoted extensively from the document being cited against him to the effect that at the place in question, " Nothing impugnes the ministry of the Teacher in the Church." [76]

In common with other English Puritans of this period, Travers did not regard the location of the teacher's office to be the university or the academic arena. [77] Rather, he interpreted the doctoral office to be an auxiliary of the pastorate and in a number of places spoke of the " Ministers of the Word, both Pastors and Teachers." He did this so frequently that it is difficult to distinguish when he spoke of " Ministers of the Word " whether he was referring to the ministry of pastors and teachers or just to the pastoral charge. The administration of the sacraments was explicitly given as one of the duties of the pastoral office. [78] At no place in *A Defense* did Travers prohibit the teacher from participating in this part of the parochial ministry, indeed, in the face of no explicit prohibition, his syntax may be said to sanction such an involvement. [79]

It is very hard to say whether the teacher of Travers' *Defense* is anything different in substance, office, or form

[76] The section of the document that Bridges had cited against the Reformed office of " Teachers or Doctors " being not a " necessary function in the Church " was that section of the Genevan Church Order (cf. above, p. 128) which begins, " We are not ignorant that there is a fourth kind of ministers left unto the Church of Church (*sic*) . . . where time and place doeth permit " (Genevan Church Order, pp. 69–70) .

[77] Travers, *A Defense,* p. 109.

[78] *Ibid.,* p. 54.

[79] *Ibid.,* p. 7.

than the pastor for whom Travers was contending. There is no need to labor the point, but it is interesting to point out how the Calvinian doctorate begins to be stripped of its distinctive qualities as soon as the lack of an academic arena or function is either taken away or not mentioned.

The doctor, not " a right ministry." The lack of clarity and the essential ambiguity that persisted in the formulation of the doctoral office in the presbyterian disciplines did not escape notice by the court party within the church. Saravia published, in 1592, a work entitled *Of the Divers Degrees of the Ministers of the Gospel*,[80] and Bancroft published the year following, his *Survay of the Pretended Holy Discipline*.[81]

Saravia was at some pains to demonstrate that the doctoral office as it was held in the Reformed churches was not an office of the ministry in the same way in which the pastoral office was. He interpreted the early doctorate of the apostolic church as being a lay office,[82] and admitted that although " certain Doctours publicly professed in the Church, which were not pastors," such persons fulfilled an extraordinary office of necessity in apostolic times which made it unnecessary to continue this office in the better ordered church of the sixteenth century, " for the ordinary Doctours of the Church are the Bishops themselves." [83]

Bancroft took a slightly different tack. He quoted from Travers' *Defense of the Discipline*,[84] arguing that according to the Puritans, if a church did not have a " Doctour in

[80] Hadrianus Saravia, *Of the Divers Degrees of the Ministers of the Gospel* (London, 1592), ch. xxvi, " Of Doctors," pp. 92–97. Cf. also the original text, *De Diversis Gradibus Ministrorum Evangelii* (London, 1591).

[81] Richard Bancroft, *A Survay of the Pretended Holy Discipline* (London, 1593), Ch. IX, " They disagree verie greatly concerning Doctors," pp. 136–152 (according to the printed pagination, which is in error). See also Bancroft's *Dangerous Positions and Proceedings* (London, 1593), pp. 103–104.

[82] Saravia, *op. cit.*, pp. 93–94.

[83] *Ibid.*, pp. 96–97.

[84] Bancroft, *Survay*, p. 137.

every Parish," then it was not a properly Reformed church.
He then turned to a survey of the Genevan, French,
Dutch, and Scottish Reformed churches and remarked that
none of them " do account of Doctors, as our men do." [85]
Thus far he was on safe ground, for, as we have seen, the
Continental and Scottish practice as of the end of the six-
teenth century associated the doctoral office particularly
and peculiarly with the school and with instruction.

Having made his point, Bancroft continued: " They
reckon them not among those officers, that Christ has appointed for the government of the Church. They have no
place or voice, but of curtesie, in their consistories." Certainly the practice of the Continental and Scottish Reformed was not completely consistent. It was, however,
carrying the argument a good deal too far to say that those
churches did not count the doctoral office as a necessary
part of the ministry or that they allowed their doctors to
maintain a relationship with the consistory only as a matter
of courtesy.[86] Having made this rather gratuitous interpretation of the Reformed orders of the other churches, Bancroft went on to quote, or cite, five Continental authorities
in such a way that it would appear that the doctoral office
was not to be involved in the duty of ecclesiastical government and oversight.[87] Taking advantage of the fact that in
Reformed circles the term " ministers " had come to be
used as a synonym for " pastors," Bancroft wrote in a tone
of mock incredulity, " They are not agreed (for anything I
can find) whether their Doctors, in that they are Doctors,

[85] *Ibid.*, p. 146.

[86] Ambiguity in the use of the term " consistory " could have
misled Bancroft. The only instance he cited, however, was that which
we have discussed (cf. above, p. 74) taken in 1563, which was *not*
a matter of courtesy, but a matter of distinction.

[87] Bancroft, *Survay,* pp. 147–148; Bertrand, Sohnius, Danaeus,
Vezelius, and Junius. Bancroft said that Lambert Daneau's *Christianae Isagoges* (pars 3, cap. 54) " does not mention doctor," but he
failed to note that Book II, ch. 9, of *pars tertia,* was all about the
office.

be Ministers, to take (as we commonly speak) the cure and charge of souls upon them." [88]

The fact that Bancroft had missed, wilfully or not, the whole point of the Calvinian doctorate was, perhaps, quite beside the point. What he had not missed was the basic disorientation of Elizabethan Puritans who copied slavishly the pattern of Genevan, Huguenot, Dutch, and Scots practice without postulating similar working conditions for the fulfillment of their theory which would square with the Continental distinction.

Having abandoned the academic arena as the proper sphere of the doctor's function, the English Puritan had no answer to such criticisms from the pen of Saravia or Bancroft. In very truth, it is difficult to see how it would be possible to separate the pastoral from the doctoral functions on the parochial level.

THE " LECTURER " AS A PURITAN OFFICE

Haller has called our attention to the fact that the early Puritan preachers resemble somewhat an " order of preaching brothers." [89] The practice of supporting lectureships in divinity predated the Reformation period and was not necessarily tied to the parochial system. As early as 1553, the morning and afternoon lectureships at Stepney, and the lectureships at Colchester, at Woodbridge, and at Boston had come into the patronage of the mayor and corporation of the place rather than into the hands of the local clergy.[90] Thus, there already existed an activity of a

[88] Bancroft, *Survay*, p. 151.

[89] William Haller, *The Rise of Puritanism* (New York, 1938), p. 52.

[90] Geoffrey F. Nuttall, *Visible Saints: The Congregational Way, 1640–1660* (Oxford, 1957), p. 24. The background of the local lectureships is quite shrouded in mystery, and no generalizations are safe. We suggest that no solution will be found until there has been a thorough investigation of records of the localities with this end in view.

religious character established in the life of the English community to which "outed" Puritan ministers could turn for sustentation, when it became impossible for them to minister with a clear conscience in a parochial situation according to the dictates of a liturgy that they considered insufficiently reformed. As early as the return of the Marian exiles from the Continent, there were men who found it impossible to square their convictions about the manner of worship with the demands of the Elizabethan Church.[91] Especially following the repressive measures of 1566 and 1571, numbers of these men found themselves deprived of their parish posts and forced to flee the country, go into other occupations, or become involved in lectureships that were not under specific ecclesiastical jurisdiction.

Some men might find employment as tutors in the homes of wealthy, or even noble, Puritan families where they were able to pursue their intellectual interests as well as conduct family devotions and even public worship according to the usages of Geneva.[92] In other instances these men might be employed by the civil corporation of a town to hold a lectureship either for a terminal period or for an indeterminate time. There was no question as to the status of the majority of these men. Most of them had their orders in the Church of England, had served at one time or another as rectors or vicars of parishes, and were only out of employment because of their refusal to conform to propositions of the English hierarchy that they considered to be without warrant of Scripture and against their conscience as Christians. As time went on, it became increasingly difficult for graduates in theology of this frame of mind to

[91] E.g., Thomas Lever; cf. M. M. Knappen, *Tudor Puritanism* (Chicago, 1939), p. 180, who recognized the significance of the "lecturer" at this early stage.

[92] Haller, *op. cit.*, p. 52; Winthrop Hudson, "Ministry in the Puritan Age," Ch. 7, in H. R. Niebuhr and D. D. Williams, eds., *The Ministry in Historical Perspective* (New York, 1956), p. 200.

secure adequate employment, without at the same time
obligating themselves for a kind of service that they regarded as unlawful according to the Word of God. These
young men also often found employment in Puritan families as tutors and took upon themselves the giving of lectures, or employment as lecturers in nonparochial systems.
Those who were employed in families, of course, received
the most of their support from their employer, but those
who were hired in the capacity of lecturers received their
support either from endowments supporting the lectureships or from stipends appropriated by such persons or cor-
porations as called them to the work.[93]

Attempts by the ecclesiastical hierarchy to control the
person or activity of the lecturers were not always very successful, for the lecturers received their support from
sources not directly in the control of the hierarchy. In
many cases the support of the lectureship was on an interim basis, made by the freewill offering or subscription of
the individuals who supported a particular person as their
spiritual director.[94] The license of the bishop to preach was
at first directed to the parochial clergy to insure conforma-
tion to the Church of England's liturgy. But as time went
on the strictures of the license were applied on a progres-
sively wider basis, including in 1604 the schoolmaster,[95]
and finally in 1629, under Archbishop Laud, all lecturers
were ordered to read the service as the *Prayer Book* had it
before commencing to lecture.[96]

[93] Niebuhr and Williams, *op. cit.*, p. 201.

[94] Hudson, *op. cit.*, p. 201, and Knappen, *op. cit.*, p. 221, who
definitely states that lectureships did not involve pastoral duties or
use of the established *Book of Common Prayer.*

[95] *Constitutions and Canons Ecclesiasticall . . . for the Province
of Canterbury* (London, 1604), Art. LXXVII, "None to teach
Schoole without License."

[96] Hudson, *op. cit.*, p. 201. The initial move in this direction had
been undertaken in 1603; cf. *Constitutions and Canons*, Art. LVI,
" Preachers and Lecturers to read divine Service and administer the
Sacraments twice a year at least." However, the provisions of this
article were confined to those who labored "in any Church or

Until a more thorough study has been made of the lectureship and the office of preacher within the structure of Tudor and Stuart society, we can only sketch in some of the similarities that may be noted between this type of ministry and the office of the teacher as it was set forth in the various presbyterian disciplines of the 1570's and 1580's. Haller, Hudson, and Nuttal have made reference to the lectureship as a refuge for Puritan ministers or Puritan candidates who could gain little foothold within the parochial structure of the English Church, as it became increasingly unfriendly to those of a reforming tendency. What none of these authorities have seemed to notice is the very great similarity that seems to have existed between the actual practice of the lecturer's office, as they have painted it, and the parochial dimensions of the doctoral — teaching — office as it was constructed in such documents as we have cited earlier. However, Richard Bancroft was impressed by the similarity. " The most of them, that are but Doctors (as they terme themselves) and readers of Lectures in other mens charges, do seldom or never come to the Service, which is read in the Church according to her Majesties Lawes; but under pretence of studying for their sermons, do absent themselves until service bee done, or at the least almost finished, and then they come in, (gravely I warrant you) and do goe to this their owne forme of service. The rest of the fraternity, that have cures of their own, some of them will have a Parliament Minister, (as they terme him) under them, to say service: and then he himselfe dealeth, as it hath been noted of the Doctor." [97]

One of the questions that begs for an answer is: Why should the Puritan churches of Commonwealth England

Chapel," and thus could be circumvented without too much trouble.

[97] *Dangerous Position,* p. 103; also, *A Survay,* p. 150, says that Cartwright " & some others, might more safely take upon them the office of doctor, than of pastors who are tied more strictly to the observations of divers ceremonies."

and of Puritan New England have constructed within their public ministry the parochial office of teacher? The example and practice of the Reformed churches on the Continent and in Scotland gives no adequate explanation for this type of fourfold ministry at the parochial level. However, the functioning of the lecturer in Elizabethan and Stuart England does give an example of a purely didactic ministerial office at a parochial level. When this example is coupled with the actual exposition of the doctoral office as it had been interpreted in the writings of the Elizabethan Puritan disciplinarians, it becomes apparent that later Puritan practice in this instance drew, not upon the example of the Continent or of Scotland, but upon the actual practice of a *de facto* office at the parochial level essentially uninvolved in pastoral responsibilities.

The fact that this type of activity was regarded as being important enough for a number of influential Puritan leaders to associate to buy up the endowments for such lectureships, in order to control the appointments, is good evidence of the importance this particular type of ministry came to assume in the thinking of English Puritanism.[98] And the fact that Archbishop Laud found it advisable to suppress and limit the holders of these lectureships, subjecting them to ecclesiastical discipline, is one more bit of evidence of the important place this type of ministry played in the over-all structure of the Puritan ministry.

The teacher-doctor in New England churches before 1650. It is possible to identify the Puritan doctorate, or the teacher, as New Englanders were in the habit of calling the office, in at least ten of the most important settlements of the early colonial era. Drawing heavily on the Church Orders of the Elizabethan period, the Puritans when they crossed the waters and were free to establish

[98] Cf. Isabel Calder, *Activities of the Puritan Faction of the Church of England, 1625–1633* (London, 1957).

their internal ecclesiastical discipline as they saw fit, immediately turned to the teaching office as one hallmark of parish life. In each case, the teacher was but one of the church officers which those of the New England Way regarded as the fit and proper office-bearers of the church " well reformed." [99]

The Salem Church at its foundation in 1629 settled over it Samuel Skelton as its pastor and Francis Higginson as its teacher.[100]

Boston's First Church, at its organization in Charlestown in 1630, selected and ordained John Wilson as its teacher.[101] There is no record of it having a pastor until its removal to the present site of Boston two years later, when Wilson was reordained as pastor of the church.[102] A month or so later John Cotton, recently arrived from England, " was then chosen Teacher of the congregation of Boston, and ordained by the imposition of hands of the *presbytery* in this manner: First, he was chosen by all the congregation testifying their consent by erection of hands, then Mr. Wilson, the pastor, demanded of him, if he did accept of the call. . . . Then the pastor, and the two elders laid their hands upon his head, and the pastor prayed, and

[99] I am greatly indebted to an account by the Rev. Samuel Sewall, M.A., pastor of the Church in Burlington, Massachusetts, of a manuscript entitled " A Brief Survey of the Congregational Churches & Ministers in the County of Middlesex, and in Chelsea in the County of Suffolk " from the papers of Judge Samuel Sewall, the pastor's grandfather, in *American Quarterly Register*, Vol. 11 (1839), pp. 45–55, 174–197, 248–279, 376–402; Vol. 12 (1840), pp. 234 f.; Vol. 13 (1841), pp. 37, 237; Vol. 14 (1842), pp. 251 f., 293 f. The account displayed a good deal of insight in a discussion of the lectureship and the teaching office in New England (Vol. 13, pp. 49–50), but no mention was made of the Continental Reformed doctorate, nor of the usage made of the term " doctor-teacher " in the presbyterianizing Church Orders of late sixteenth-century Puritanism. Hereafter cited as Sewall with volume and page.

[100] Cf. Bradford, *History of Plymouth Plantation, 1606–1646* (New York, 1908), pp. 261 f.

[101] Sewall, 12:242.

[102] *Ibid.*, II:48; 22 November 1632.

then, taking off their hands, laid them on again, and speaking to him by name, they did thenceforth design him to the said office, in the name of the Holy Ghost, and did give him charge of the congregation, and did thereby (as by a sign from God) indue him with the gifts fit for his office; and lastly did bless him. Then the neighboring ministers, which were present, did (at the pastor's motion) give him the right hand of fellowship." [103] Cotton, after twenty years,[104] was succeeded, although not immediately, by John Norton, who served concurrently with Pastor Wilson.

The Church of Cambridge (Newtown), gathered by Thomas Hooker and Samuel Stone in 1633, selected Hooker as its pastor and Stone as its teacher,[105] positions which the two men maintained even following the removal of the congregation to Hartford, Connecticut, in 1636.

Zechariah Symmes [106] became the teacher of the Charlestown Church in 1634, during the pastorate of Thomas James, and on his death, Symmes was ordained pastor. He had as his fellow teachers Thomas Allen [107] and Thomas Shepard, Sr.,[108] throughout most of his pastorate.

[103] *Ibid.*, 12:243, quoting *Winthrop's History,* 10 October 1633.

[104] Indication of the confusion about the status of Cotton may be gathered from the fact that in 1642, in the middle of his service to the First Church, at least five works from his pen were published in London. Two of these describe him on the title page as " Pastor," while the other three refer to him as " Teacher " — C. R. Gillett, *The McAlpin Collection of British History and Theology* (New York, 1924) , II:114–115.

[105] Sewall, 11:174–197.

[106] *Ibid.*, p. 49.

[107] *Ibid.*, 13:44.

[108] *Ibid.*, 12:244, quoting the Church Records: " 1659, 2 Moneth 13th day. Mr. Thomas Shepard was ordained with prayer and fasting unto ye office of a Teacher to the Church of Christ in Charles Towne, by me Zechariah Symmes Pastor to the same Churche Mr. John Wilson Pastor to the Churche of Christ in Boston, and Mr. Richard Mather Teacher to the Churche of Christ in Dorchester. . . . Mr. Norton Teacher to the Churche at Boston in the name of the rest of the messengers of 4 Churches, to witt of Boston, Roxbury, Cambridge, Watertown, giving unto him the right hand of fellowship."

In Concord, Massachusetts, Peter Buckley and John Jones shared the ministerial labors of the church from 1636 until the resignation of Pastor Jones in 1644, at which time Buckley remained the only " teaching officer " in the congregation but was not reordained as the pastor, and simply retained the title of teacher until his death in 1659.[109]

Richard Mather's service to the Dorchester Church from 1636 until 1669 was in the office of teacher, during which period he was for the greater bulk of the time the only installed minister. Stephen Bachiller and Timothy Dalton shared the ministry of the Hampton, New Hampshire, Church for a period of two years with Dalton in the teacher's office. However, the two men did not work well together, and in 1641, Bachiller resigned and Dalton was ordained pastor of the church, a position he held until 1661.[110] John Norton was in the teacher's office of Ipswich Church from 1638 until 1655, at which time he was called as teacher of the First Church of Boston as successor to John Cotton. In the church of Roxbury, Massachusetts, John Eliot fulfilled his long ministry from 1632 to 1690 in the office of teacher of the congregation.[111] The structure of the ministry in the Plymouth, Massachusetts, congregation is somewhat confused, yet we are able to say that from 1636 until at least 1639 John Ravner fulfilled the office of teacher in that church, although at a later date he is called its pastor.[112]

[109] *Ibid.*, 11:183. This incident was indicative of the fact that in spite of the *Cambridge Platform* and Thomas Hooker (pp. 192–193 below), the distinctiveness had gone out of the idea of the office of the teacher.

[110] Cf. Albert E. Dunning, *Congregationalists in America* (New York, 1894), p. 159. I am indebted for this reference to the Rev. Prof. John Brush, of Andover Newton Theological School.

[111] Sewall, 12:242.

[112] Bradford, *History*, p. 334. During the controversy with Charles Chauncy over the proper mode of baptism, we are told that Ravner, as teacher, was expected to baptize.

In passing, we may also mention the practice of the Indian churches gathered at Nantucket, Martha's Vineyard, Mashpee, and Natick. Without exception, these congregations enjoyed the labors of one or more teachers in addition to pastors. John Eliot, teacher of the church at Natick, is reported to have instituted lectures in theology and logic on alternate weeks. The result of this activity was that a supply of Biblical interpreters was available to staff the newly evangelized villages farther north and west.[113]

The actual practice of the New England congregations in regard to the teaching office was almost precisely that which we are able to view in the latter disciplines of the presbyterian Puritan period. The activity of the teacher was confined strictly to a parochial ministry, and was not solely occupied in a ministry of instruction, but was equally involved in the government and discipline of the local congregation along with the pastor and ruling elder. As were the pastor, the ruling elder, and the deacons, the teacher was ordained by the laying on of hands, either by other office-bearers or by selected members from the congregation itself. When other teachers or pastors were to be ordained, teachers along with the pastors of neighboring churches were involved either in the laying on of hands of the " presbytery," or the giving of the " right hand of Fellowship."

The Synod begun in Cambridge in 1646 and concluded in 1648 produced the famous *Cambridge Platform*. In its provisions as to the teaching office in the church, this document closely parallels the thinking of Thomas Hooker in his *Survey of the Summe of Church Discipline*,[114] in which

[113] I am indebted to the Rev. Harold Worthley, teaching fellow in church history at Harvard Divinity School, for calling my attention to this Indian practice; cf. Martin Moore, *Memoirs of the Life and Character of the Rev. John Eliot* (Boston, 1822), pp. 93–94.

[114] Thomas Hooker, *A Survey of the Summe of Church-Discipline. Wherein the Way of the Churches of New England is warranted out of the Word* (London, 1648), pp. 20–21.

he holds that "the Teachers office" was "distinct from the Pastors place and imployment," but "I find some difference in the apprehensions of interpreters, touching the nature and work of the Teachers amongst themselves. Many and those of exact judgement, seem to confine him to the School (with whom under favor) I can not so fully agree: I should rather conceive, Doctour may be attended with some distinction.

"There is a Doctor in (*Schôla/eccleâ*) both have special use and imployment: but the second is here meant, for he is given to the Church, and that with this intent and aim, *for the gathering and perfecting of the body,* and that is the *Church* or *congregation* and *ergo* they are to choose him, to imploy and improve him for their special and spiritual edification which the school will not reach so immediately unto, as his place, our Saviours purpose, and the Churches necessity, and spiritual edification will require.

"In this second sense we understand the Officer we now inquire after, and that wherein he shares in common with the Pastor is, that they have both of them Authority and right delegated from Christ to consecrate and administer the Sacraments."

Thus in practice and theory, the teaching office of the New England churches had, by 1648, become indistinguishable from the pastorate. So thoroughly had the teaching office been torn loose from its Calvinian base that Hooker could with perfect composure reject employment in the school as a condition of its function. It is very necessary to understand this development as a prelude to the debates that accompanied the attempts to define the office at Westminster in 1643.

Dr. George H. Williams has demonstrated the use made by the New England ecclesiastical leaders of Calvin's concept of Christ, as prophet, priest, and king, in their foundation and advancement of Harvard College.[115] However,

---

[115] Williams, *op. cit.,* pp. 340–348.

prior to 1650, the material is insufficient to allow us to attempt to show that there was any sense of succession *in the doctoral office* from Geneva to Cambridge on the banks of the Charles. Dr. Williams has served us well in pointing out the underlying affinity between eighteenth-century New England theory in regard to the college, and sixteenth century Genevan practice in respect to the doctoral office.[116]

[116] *Ibid.*, pp. 295–313.

VIII

The Westminster Assembly and "Whether The Doctor Be a Distinct Officer"[1]

DURING THE FIRST PART of the seventeenth century, the religious interests pressing a further reformation of the Church of England gradually coalesced with other interests of a political, social, and economic nature so that the inept policy of Charles I toward these various groups brought about a state of near-revolution. When in 1638 the Church of Scotland finally took matters into its own hands and upset the unpopular English-type ecclesiastical establishment, this was but the prelude for a general uprising of many different sentiments that coalesced into a general discontent, which soon crossed the border and brought the Puritan and parliamentarian factions into open revolt.[2]

The securing of London by the parliamentary party early in 1642 brought about a situation into which religious Puritans leaped with alacrity. Now was the time for

[1] Westminster Assembly of Divines, "Minutes of the Sessions," exist in three folio MS. volumes, which are in the possession of Dr. Williams' Library, London. Prior to 1872 a transcript was made, and two years later the transcript became the basis for the printing of MS. Vol. iii; cf. A. F. Mitchell and John Struthers, eds., *Minutes of the Sessions of the Westminster Assembly of Divines* (Edinburgh, 1874). In all cases, citations from the manuscript will be indicated as WAD *Min.* with the page number of the *transcript*.

[2] Cf. S. A. Burrell, "The Covenant Idea as a Revolutionary Symbol," *Church History.* XXVII (1950), pp. 338–350.

the reformation that had been so long awaited and which had been suppressed with such " brutality." Giving voice to this feeling through its Parliament, the Puritan faction demanded and got an " Assembly of learned, godly, and judicial divines " [3] to be given the duty of translating the reformation so earnestly desired into concrete fact that would allow the Church of England to hold its head up among the other Reformed churches.

Originally convened in July of 1643, the Assembly of Divines turned to business of peculiar interest to us, only at the behest of Parliament, on the twelfth of October following, when they received an order from the Lords and Commons to turn their attention from general theological discussions to the practical work of preparing a " Discipline." [4] Five days later, the motion was made by Dr. William Gouge that a single committee be set up out of the membership of the Assembly to discuss and to bring in the duties incumbent upon the offices of " pastors, doctors, elders," [5] so that the Assembly as a body could discuss a document of some form or another. At the same time, it was decided to proceed on the plan of taking up particular matters (such as the individual offices), discussing them as they came under consideration, rather than attempting to establish a prior rule of interpretation.[6]

Early in the proceedings, it became obvious that there were two ways of thinking among the members of the Assembly as to the kind of evidence that was to be brought forward in support of any particular position. On the one hand, there were those, like Dr. Burgess, who desired that

[3] Cf. S. W. Carruthers, *The Everyday Work of the Westminster Assembly* (Philadelphia, 1943), p. v. The Assembly was established by ordinance of Lords and Commons, dated 12 June 1643, and the objective standard of " the Church of Scotland, and other Reformed Churches abroad " was a part of the ordinance.

[4] WAD *Min.*, I: p. 210, sess. 73.

[5] *Ibid.*, p. 222, sess. 76: " Wether such officers as this church have been governed by long [since] are *jure divini*."

[6] *Ibid.*, p. 215.

what was done be "most agreeable to the best reformed churches." [7] And on the other hand there were those who, like Goodwin and his friends, felt that the only standard which was to be used was that of Scripture itself.[8] Gataker argued that the establishment of a thoroughgoing rule of interpretation right at that point would consume a great deal of time. He was answered by Simpson that, on the contrary, a great deal of time would be saved because after a basic interpretation had been agreed upon, it would not be necessary to argue each point of the proposed Form of Government.

From the eighteenth of October until the thirteenth of November the discussion was almost entirely concerned with the pastoral office.[9] Mention of the " doctor " had intruded itself in the discussion some ten days previously when the discussion had centered around the necessity of the pastoral office being responsible both for the *reading* and *preaching* of the Word. Jean de la March, pastor of the French congregation, gave his opinion that reading of the Scriptures was " a distinct office from the pastor according to the practice in reformed churches, the pastor expounds the word & applys it, doctor expounds & not applyes it, and then a reader yt neither expounds nor applyes." In this exchange, Goodwin stuck to the subject of the teaching function of the pastor's office, but served notice that in the near future " when we come to debate [it]," that he would take the position that " there is a peculiar office of teaching to the teacher." [10] However, at the close of the session on 13 November, it was " ordered to go on in the reports of the first and second reports concerning teachers." [11] This discussion consumed the better part of the subsequent six meeting days: Tuesday, Wednes-

---

7 *Ibid.,* p. 213.
8 " My conscience is settled that there is a rule." (*Ibid.,* p. 216.)
9 *Ibid.,* pp. 230–262.
10 *Ibid.,* p. 319.
11 *Ibid.,* p. 362.

day, Thursday, Friday, Monday, and Tuesday — 14, 15, 16, 17, 20, and 21 November.

When on Tuesday, 14 November, the reports of the first and second committees were given " concerning teachers," the debates on the matter got down to cases in earnest. Almost immediately, the ambiguities that we have noted made their appearance as various points of view were presented on the floor of the Assembly. Most pressing from a strictly pragmatic point of view was the endeavor to determine whether the office of the teacher was indeed distinct from that of the pastor.[12] The difficulty of arguing exclusively from Biblical proof texts soon became apparent; for example, Seaman argued that there were but two distinct orders in the church, that of " presbiters & deacons," and that the difference between the pastor and the teacher was not represented here, but rather that " pastors & teachers are both one." In rejoinder, Goodwin granted that there was far less difference between the teacher and the pastor than there was between the presbyter and the ruling elder. But, he insisted, the distinction was not one of order, but rather of office and the gifts given by God necessary for the exercise of the office.[13] To this, Dr. Hoyle replied that if the ministry of the church were to be based on the talents that were given by God to individuals " then we should make more officers than God made."

In other minds, it was evident that the difference between pastors and teachers was not that of " distinct orders nor offices," but dealt rather with the administration of the gifts with which they were endowed.[14] Repeatedly the assertion was brought forward that there was nothing that " one may do, but the other may do for the substance of the office." [15] A further confusion in terminology was introduced by Walker, who insisted that the term " office " was

[12] *Ibid.*, p. 364.
[13] *Ibid.*, p. 365.
[14] *Ibid.*, p. 366; this was contributed by John White.
[15] *Ibid.*, p. 365.

in rather doubtful connotation in Reformed churches, and that, in fact, the ministry was divided into "several administrations."[16] However, Burgess would not allow the matter to rest thus and insisted that the word "office" was a very definite term and defined it as "a power and designation to some particular act, yt it is lawful for me to do and not another."[17] Ley, one of the Independents, granted that the semantic difficulty was being overworked and appealed to the Assembly to remember that most of its members were agreed that "the pastor may exhort & the exhorter may teach," and that the real problem lay in distinguishing not those things which the two offices had in common but those in which they were different.

Earlier in the day Burgess had acknowledged that the pastor and/or teacher in a "particular congregation are the same: but if in university or where you plant any to read a divinity lecture, then we acknowledge there is use of such an office in the Church." Also when De la March gave his opinion that there was a distinct office and that "one may do what the other cannot," he continued that the "doctor, he only expounds scriptures, exerciseth his charge in universities, but doth not apply the word as the doctor." Furthermore, he contended that "one and the same man may" exercise both charges, "as in the Old Testament." Significantly, perhaps, mention of the university and the reading of divinity lectures by both Burgess and De la March seems to have elicited no response from the Assembly at large because the discussion immediately proceeded to gravitate around the place of the teacher in the local church.

However, in commenting upon the matter of which De la March had spoken, Wilkinson did admit that there had been in the congregations "many that have read lec-

---

[16] *Ibid.*, p. 367. The seating of the Scots Commissioners was minuted just prior to this exchange.
[17] *Ibid.*, p. 368.

tures . . . & yet they never took any charge of souls." [18] This probably is a reference to the Puritan lectureships of the Elizabethan and Jacobean periods and is more evidence that, when discussing the doctoral office, it was natural for the Puritan to think in terms of the institution of the lectureship.

Goodwin continued to argue strongly that, from Scriptural example, a diversity of gifts implied a diversity of administration and that a diversity of administration in turn implied a diversity of office.[19] In this, he was countered by Marshall, who denied specifically " this proposition yt because distinct gifts & peculiar command from [Christ] to attend upon yt gifts [it] is a distinct office." On this note, the debates for the day ended with the order that they be continued on the fifteenth.

The discussion on the fifteenth began and continued largely with debates on the relative merit and meaning of the passages from I Cor., ch. 12, and from Rom., ch. 12. Gataker [20] argued that the distinction in the offices was not maintained by these passages, but Bridges declared that it was.[21] Marshall sought to bring the matter to a head by admitting that there was a difference in the names of the office but that the real question lay in " what is meant by office." He also granted that it would prolong the dispute to define what was meant by " office " and offered the solution that the form of government would say that pastors and teachers are " different administration though they do all of the self-same thing." [22]

[18] *Ibid.*, p. 369.
[19] *Ibid.*, p. 370; the two passages that he used were I Cor. 12:8 (really the argument was based on the whole passage, vs. 4-11) and Rom. 12:3-8.
[20] WAD *Min.*, p. 373.
[21] *Ibid.*, p. 374.
[22] *Ibid.*, p. 375. John Lightfoot in his " Journal of the Assembly " has an interesting comment to make in regard to this exchange. " Mr. Marshall offered, that we should express it thus, ' That pastors and teachers are different administrations, though they do one and the

Once again, the issue of the doctor in the school was raised by Dr. Smith, who said that he found " a doctor in antiquity is rather for the schooles than congregations," [23] and called upon the Independent [24] brethren to lay aside their insistence upon the " necessity of a ' doctor & teacher in every ' particular congregation & we shall easily agree." The position held by Smith in the second day of debate on the doctoral office can be said, in general, to be the position that was characteristic of most of the " presbyterians " of the Assembly.

The debate on the matter continued throughout the remaining part of the Wednesday session, and Goodwin agreed that pastors and teachers were of the same order, that the substance of their work was the same, that they were both prophets and teachers, and that the chief differences between them lay *in modo* of the way they administered their office.[25] Goodwin contended that pastors may teach, although as an adjunct to their exhortation, and that the teachers might exhort, but the chief difference still lay in the fact that Christ, by specific institution, had established these two offices, and from this point Goodwin would not depart very far. The more Goodwin talked, the more obvious it was that he was concerned for a preservation of an existing institution; the only institution we can identify fitting the pattern of his remarks is the congrega-

---

same thing.' This was much urged to be put to the question, but Mr. Ley first, and after him Dr. Temple, opposed it, as proving that this word ' administrations ' would prove as obscure as officers; and this cost some large debate." Cf. *The Whole Works of the Rev. John Lightfoot, D.D.* (London, 1825), 13:53.

[23] WAD *Min.*, p. 376.

[24] Cf. Robert Baillie, *Letters and Journals* (Edinburgh, 1841), II:110: " At our first coming, we found them in a verie sharp debaite, anent the office of Doctors. The Independent men, whereof there are some ten or eleven in the synod, manie of them very able men, as Thomas Goodwin, Nye, Burroughs, Bridge, Carter, Caryll, Philips, Sterry, were for the divine institution of a Doctor in everie congregation as well as a Pastor."

[25] WAD *Min.*, p. 377.

tional teacher of the New England churches and the congregational teachers found in some of the Independent
congregations of Commonwealth England.[26]

Both sides to the argument agreed that there was " an
Identity in the name & work," [27] but the question remained
how to maintain the distinction in any ordinance setting
forth the two offices. Dr. Burgess appealed to the Scots
commissioners to make some comment on this matter.
Alexander Henderson replied that, as far as the practice
of the Church of Scotland was concerned, there was no
" difference between pastor & teacher," yet in the teaching
of the church there was some distinction drawn and the
church did feel the necessity of the catechism being taught
as " necessary to every congregation." [28]

There is some question in our mind just where Henderson was taking his stand. Initially, he seemed to confuse
the Scots *catechist* with the Independent notion of a
teacher, and when the distinction had been made plain con-
fessed that there was no distinction. But he modified this
lack of distinction in a subsequent exchange.[29] As well he
might, in light of the fact that on the fourteenth, when the
debates on the doctoral office began, the Scots commissioners specifically stated the position of the kirk, " 2. That
there are these four permanent officers in the Church,
pastor, teachers, ruling elders, and deacons: this their
Church hath ever retained; and their teachers are readers
in the universities; but which some were added to cate-

26 Nuttall, *op. cit.,* pp. 18–19, 24–25. However, we must observe
against Nuttall's contention, " The distinction between the two
officers [pastor and teacher] was conceived in charismatic terms and
not in terms of status "; that the evidence he cites is all later than
the material with which we are dealing here, and it seems to us that
Goodwin and his colleagues were worried every bit as much about
status as they were about *charisma.* This does not undercut Nuttall's
point that the ground of the distinction was *eventually* worked out
in terms of a charismatic distinction.

27 WAD *Min.,* p. 379.

28 *Ibid.,* p. 380.

29 *Ibid.,* p. 382.

chize." [30] In addition to this, Henderson had written a
book the same year that explained the doctoral office
in rather definite terms: " The Church of Scotland hath
no other Doctors, but Masters and Professors of Divinity
in Universities and Colledges . . . and besides these the
Teachers of more private and particular schools." Furthermore, he said that presbytery was the judge both of their
life and learning, that they " do keep " the presbyterial
meeting taking their turn in the prophesying, or exercise,
and that they were sometimes employed by the pastors in
catechetical instruction, as well as having a primary responsibility for training in " humane literature . . . liberal arts . . . Civil Conversation . . . good manners, but
especially in the Grounds of [the] Christian Religion." [31]
Henderson stressed the primacy of the pastoral office in the
congregation, and while identifying the doctoral office and
the school, he considered it might possibly be worth-while
to discuss whether or not these were ecclesiastical officers,
but that they certainly were not like " teachers of phisicke."
Once again he returned to the fact that the Church of Scotland hoped for " a catechist in every parish." In extension
of this, Ley put the case very well when he pointed out that
the Independents insisted that the ministry of the local
congregation " not only may but must " support the office
of teacher, and in addition the office of a catechist in a
large church, but that the latter was not really necessary
in every parish.[32]

On Thursday, the debate continued unabated, but the
emphasis now shifted to a discussion of the proposition
" that pastors & teachers are both ministers of the word &
have power of administering the sacraments," and secondly
" that the Dr or teacher is not an ordinary or perpetual
officer distinct from the pastor in every perticular congre-

[30] *Ibid.*, p. 362, and Lightfoot, *op. cit.*, 13:51.
[31] [Alexander Henderson], *The Government and Order of the
Church of Scotland* (Edinburgh, 1642), sec. iv, pp. 28–29.
[32] WAD *Min.*, p. 382.

gation." [33] Commencing the debate, Goodwin held that there were two main questions to be decided, " 1. whether the scripture hold out this distinction of office," and " 2. whether proper to a congregation or university." Calamy, hoping to place the discussion on a broader plane, again reminded the Assembly that it was necessary to consider the practice of the other Reformed churches. He also wanted to substitute " that a teacher be an officer allowed or agreeable to the Word of God," in place of the much more specific wording of the second proposition under debate. Gataker contended somewhat ambiguously that there was really no distinction between the pastor and the teacher in the French and the Dutch churches, but it is not clear whether he had reference to the French and Dutch churches in London or whether he was referring to the Huguenot and Netherland churches across the channel.

Arguing in opposition to those who maintained that the doctoral office ought to be included at the parochial level, Dr. Temple maintained that " in primitive times those teachers were rather in the schools than in the Church." [34] This, of course, did not satisfy Goodwin and his cohorts, for they immediately countered with the contention that the offices of the gospel ministry " are given to perticular churches & not to Church in general & first to perticular churches." [35] Calamy stressed that all the texts which had been used to support the doctoral office in the congregation were equally applicable under most circumstances to the pastoral office as well, and that this compounded the difficulty of determining whether one or two offices were called for in the Scripture text. The debates on Thursday ended on this rather inconclusive note.[36]

[33] *Ibid.*, p. 383.
[34] *Ibid.*, p. 384.
[35] *Ibid.*, p. 386.
[36] The MS. *Minutes* reflect some remarks by John Lightfoot, but nothing like the detail he gives in his " Journal " (*op. cit.*, p. 55) where he gives it as his opinion that although two offices are named

Charles Herle commenced the debates on Friday by observing that it would be better for the Assembly to get on with business rather than for any part to gain a victory in detail. Evidently Goodwin was somewhat of this mind, although he kept to his point, only mellowing enough to admit that the " question is when churches are enlarged, increased & able to maintain them then whether the command of Christ do not fall upon them." [37] In the course of the day, Thomas Carter put his finger on one of the problems that was to arise in the exercise of the office in New England, when he pointed out that it would be difficult for the pastor and the teacher actually to function in a co-operative sense within the congregational body.[38] This, however, did not daunt Simpson, who replied that because the office of the teacher was distinct from the pastor in the Scriptures, therefore a well-reformed and properly organized church of Jesus Christ must include both offices. He was quite blunt about it, that " there must be an office because a special gift." The pastor's gift was the word of Knowledge, while to the teacher was given the word of Wisdom.[39]

Philip Nye acknowledged that the debate had been overlong and wished to bring it to a conclusion by reminding the Assembly that there was no discussion as to the " doctor being an elder " and that the offices were of such dependency, one upon another, " as the hand cannot be without the ey, etc." Henderson complimented the two parties on their learning and the calmness with which they debated the matter but reminded them that they were no

in Eph. 4:11, that " a pastor, indeed, is to continue . . . But a doctor is not of such necessity," because that office, along with apostles, prophets, and evangelists, " were those that God appointed for the bringing in of the Gentiles to union with the Jews, *en enotéti pisteos*, and therefore is not institution of full offices for the time to come."

[37] WAD *Min.*, p. 389.

[38] *Ibid.*, p. 397: " For the pastor & teacher their danger lyes in this — the teacher may think possibly he can doe it better than the other."

[39] *Ibid.*, pp. 397–398.

nearer a conclusion than they had been at the start. He also commented that there was a greater agreement between the offices of the pastor and the teacher than any other offices, of which they were taking account, and pleaded with the Assembly that, although there was no doubt a peculiar teaching function, certainly it was the pastoral office that was important in the particular congregation, just as it was necessary that every congregation have a deacon, and that to press the necessity of the doctoral office at the congregational level would probably be fruitless.[40] He also urged the Assembly to appoint a committee to draw up some conclusions on the matter to which all might agree.[41] At this point Herbert Palmer voiced what must have been on everybody's mind, that there were in the Assembly three distinct persuasions regarding the doctoral office, " some in every congregation, some altogether the same, others 2 but not in every congregation." In general terms this described the position of the English Independents, the English Presbyterians, and the Church of Scotland men.

The committee, consisting of Thomas Goodwin, Philip Nye, Charles Herle, Cornelius Burgess, Richard Vines and Thomas Hill, was appointed and brought in its report on Monday morning, 20 November.[42] The report was evidently conceived in five propositions; however, with the reading of the first one, " On the name and office of a doctor or teacher as well as that of a pastor," the whole debate was on again, for Obadiah Sedgwick objected that the inclusion of the pastor in this proposition prejudiced the whole business of the distinction of the offices. The remaining propositions were read at this time and are given by Lightfoot as: " 2. A Teacher may be in a particular church where there is a pastor, though not always in every

---

[40] *Ibid.*, pp. 398–399.
[41] *Ibid.*, p. 400.
[42] *Ibid.*, p. 401.

particular congregation. 3. A doctor is of excellent use in schools and universities, they being either churches or parts of the church. 4. Where but one minister is, he is to do the office of pastor and teacher. 5. The nature of the doctor's office is to expound Scripture, to hold forth sound doctrine, and convince gainsayers." [43]

To maintain the distinctiveness of the office, Goodwin now turned to the " doctrine of reformed churches " as witnesses that " they are distinct offices & necessary offices." [44] It is interesting how Goodwin appealed to the Church Orders of the Continental churches to buttress his own interpretation of the doctoral office, as he sought to locate it in the parish. So far as we have been able to determine, his interpretation was never the Continental practice in relation to the local congregation. When it came to Continental practice in regard to the school and university, such employment of the doctorate was either disregarded or rejected by those who were most adamant in supporting a strict distinction between pastors and teachers in the English context. Once again, Henderson tried to pour oil on troubled waters by suggesting a substitution in the second proposition, which removed the reference to pastors, and an omission from the third, which cut off any mention of a church in relation to the university. [45]

Following the example of Henderson on Friday, Goodwin, on Monday at the close of the debate moved that another committee be set up to consist of three from the Independent faction, three from the English Presbyterians, and " three of Scotland," who would meet to try to draft another compromise set of propositions for further dis-

[43] Lightfoot, op. cit., 13:57: " 1. The Scripture holds forth the name of doctor and teacher, as well as pastor." Vines had objected that " we are not inquiring after Dr. in scooles & yt they are not church officers qua tales, & what they read as an act " (WAD Min., pp. 403–404).
[44] WAD Min., p. 406.
[45] Ibid., p. 409.

cussion.[46] The manuscript record does not list the text of their work, but Lightfoot again supplies us with the missing material:

" 1. That there be different gifts, and different exercises, according to the difference of those gifts in the ministers.

" 2. Those different gifts may be in and exercised by one and the same minister.

" 3. Where there be several ministers in the same congregations, they may be designed to several employments.

" 4. He that doth excell more in exposition, doctrine, and convincing than in application, and accordingly employed therein, may be called a teacher, or doctor.

" 5. A teacher or doctor is of excellent use in schools or universities.

" 6. Where there is but one minister in a particular congregation, he is to perform, so far as he is able, the whole work of the ministry." [47]

In the discussion of the first four propositions, some attention was paid to the matter of prophesying, and Sidrach Simpson expressed the opinion that the gift of prophecy ought not to be " tyed to the ministers of the word but to the people [so that] all of them may exercise [it]." [48] The prospect of all people with a right of vocal spiritual expression in the assemblies of the church was not congenial to the Presbyterians, such as Thomas Wilson, Lazarus Seaman, and William Gouge, and even Goodwin, although he wanted freedom of prophesying, evidently did not feel that this gave license to every individual to exercise the function. Lightfoot tried to interpret prophesying as an activity confined to the primitive church, but Jeremiah Burroughs [49] reiterated Simpson's contention, and Lightfoot

---

[46] *Ibid.,* p. 410.
[47] Lightfoot, *op. cit.,* p. 58.
[48] WAD *Min.,* p. 412.
[49] *Ibid.,* p. 413.

says that "it was voted against us." [50]

Then, for the first time, the discussion centered with some degree of intensity around the question of the employment of the doctor in the school and university. Initially, Acts 13:1 was put forward as being a fitting proof text for the support of such an employment,[51] but Thomas Wilson argued that the text under consideration had nothing to do with " universityes, it speakes of the church." [52] Philip Nye countered that they did not have to split hairs about the distinction " between universityes & churches [for] in Scotland their Achademyes are churches." Nye used Acts 19:9 and the " scoole of Tirannus " and his interpretation of the " established church of the Jewes [which] had schooles & fathers and doctors " as justification for " a moral equity [that] Teachers and Drs are of excellent use." Immediately, Seaman and George Walker sought to adduce from Old Testament example the fact that centers of study were a legitimate part of the religious heritage, and that therefore such institutions were a necessary part of a church that would model its life on a primitive example.[53] However, to this kind of interpretation of the Biblical material, Lightfoot took exception and insisted that the " schools of the prophets " were not universities, but " societies of men inspired." [54]

Such a split in the ranks of the Presbyterians did not

[50] The notation in the MS. *Minutes* would scarcely convey this meaning, but Lightfoot records it unmistakably in his " Journal," *op. cit.*, 13:59.

[51] Introduction of the fifth prop. in the MS. *Min.* is very jumbled (WAD *Min.*, p. 414), but Lightfoot (*op. cit.*, 13:59) tells us that the reference to Acts, ch. 13, was introduced by Dr. Burgess, and also that Seaman and Sedgwick wanted the word " [of] theology " appended to the statement.

[52] WAD *Min.*, p. 414. In answer to this, Joshua Hoyle made some statement about the necessity of schools to " teach teachers," but Wilson would not allow this as the proper use of the office because, he contended, " this teaching others may be in the church."

[53] *Ibid.*, pp. 414–415.

[54] Lightfoot, *op. cit.*

produce the kind of intensity necessary to win through in
the face of Independent disinterest and active antipathy.
Walker, as he sought to shore up, with Scriptural identification, the cause of institutional education, admitted that
" there are divers men amongst us [who] deny the necessity of learning & universityes." [55] We have already taken
some account of the prejudices apparent in the ranks of
the Elizabethan Puritans regarding the possibility of close
ties with the university community. Those days were long
past, but that heritage continued, in the hands of the Independents, to produce an active line of demarkation between church and school, rejecting the possibility that the
gifts of Christ had anything to do with the institutional
school; in the hands of the Presbyterians, to produce an
uncertainty about the nature of the relation that existed
between the church and school, although most of them
hoped for some such arrangement as they conceived to
have existed in Continental Reformed communions.

So uncertain had the whole matter of the relationship
with the school become in the minds of the men assembled
at Westminster in 1643, that they rejected out of hand any
notion of their competence to deal with such an important
matter as education for the Christian ministry. Rather,
they shifted the whole burden of providing for educational
opportunities for the youth upon the Lords and Commons. On Monday, 20 November, a request was read in
the Assembly from some former members of Oxford University who found it impossible to continue their education because the school was in the hands of the Royalists.
Their request was directed toward the formation of " a
college some where about London " so that they could continue their academic work. The request was referred to a
committee, after Burgess had suggested that the Assembly
petition the Houses of Parliament to provide support for
scholars out of the endowments of deaneries and chapters.

[55] WAD *Min.*, p. 415.

The committee brought back its report on 23 November to the effect that the whole matter be left up to the Houses of Parliament. The strongest language used was that the Assembly " recommended " the matter to the consideration of the Parliament.[56] In this they proved themselves apt pupils of Bèze, rather than conscientious followers of Calvin.

The debates on the twenty-first of November exhausted the interest in the doctoral office. Having won their point that the teacher was to be regarded as a part of the parochial ministry, the Independents were not adverse to allowing the office to be located in the school as well. The course of the debates on the office of teacher on Tuesday had never seriously challenged the basic assertion of the Independents that the main function of the teacher was to be carried on within the context of the local church. At the end of the day, having established the principle of the parochial parity of the pastoral and doctoral office, further debate was cut off as to what points of distinctiveness might attend the separate exercise of these functions, by an order: " That the difference betweene pastor & teacher shall be further taken into consideration when we come to the directory of worship [,] to consider what the pastor & what the teacher is to doe if any of the brethren doe desire it." [57]

Because the matter was never really considered in the Directory of Worship,[58] the results of the debates of November, 1643, were the substance of the language of the *Form of Government* adopted by the Westminster Assembly of Divines in 1644.[59] Here the section on the doctoral office read as follows:

[56] *Ibid.*, pp. 402–403; Lightfoot, *op. cit.*, pp. 57, 62, 64.

[57] WAD *Min.*, p. 416.

[58] Cf. *A Directory for the Publique Worship of God throughout the three Kingdoms of England, Scotland & Ireland* (London, 1644), pp. 6, 11, 18.

[59] Cf. *The Form of Presbyterial Church Government and Ordination of Ministers agreed upon by the Assembly of Divines at Westminster with the Assistance of Commissioners from the Church of*

"Teacher or Doctor" [60]

"The Scripture doth hold out the name and title
a of a teacher, as well as of the pastor. *Who is also a
minister of the Word as well as the pastor, and hath
power of administration of the Sacraments.*
The Lord having given different gifts and divers
b exercises according to these gifts in the ministry of
the Word, though these different gifts may meet in,
and accordingly be exercised by one and the same
c minister. Yet where there be several ministers in the
same congregation, they may be designed to several
employments according to the different gifts, in
d which each of them do most excel. And he that doth
most excel in exposition of Scripture, in teaching
sound doctrine, and in convincing gainsayers, than
he doth in application, and is accordingly employed
there, may be called a teacher or doctor, (the places
alleged by the notation of the Word doth prove the
proposition;) nevertheless, where is but one minister
in a particular congregation, he is to perform so far
e as he is able the whole work of the ministry.
"A teacher or doctor is of most excellent use in
schools and universities; as of old in the schools of the
prophets, and at Jerusalem, where Gamaliel and
others taught as doctors."

Thus the Westminster Assembly, under the persuasive
influence of the English Independents, defined the doctoral
office in terms of a relationship to the local and particular
congregation. Only by way of concession to the example of
the other Reformed communions, especially to the Church

Scotland, in Walter Steuart of Pardovan, *Collections and Observations* (Philadelphia, 1813), pp. 476–507.
[60] *Ibid.*, pp. 485–486. The Scriptural proof texts were as follows:
a I Cor. 12:28; Eph. 4:11; b Rom. 12:6-8; I Cor. 12:1-7; c I Cor.
14:3; II Tim. 4:2; d all under a, b, and c, plus I Peter 4:10-11;
e II Tim. 4:2; Titus 1:9; I Tim. 6:2.

of Scotland, was any mention made of the employment of this office in the context of an academic ministry. From the progress of the debates, it is hard to believe that the concept of an academic employment of this office weighed heavily upon more than a very small number of the participants. Heirs of a tradition that was (to say the least) suspicious of the school as an agency of true religion, aware of a growing anti-intellectualism,[61] bound in a situation where the Royalist forces were in effective control of the centers of university learning, faced with well-disciplined protagonists of a theory of the nature of the church that would not permit the structuring of the ministry on anything but a congregational basis, the English Presbyterians were not in a position to present a united front and see the matter through. Because of the indecision on the part of the English Presbyterians, there is grave doubt whether the majority of them really understood what Calvin had meant by the doctorate in the church, and, even more pointed, whether they really cared. At no place in the symbols set forth by the Westminster Assembly was there any attempt to deal with the relationship of church and school. In terms of the Reformed doctorate, this was fatal.

[61] In connection with the development of a militant anti-intellectualism in a part of Puritanism of the time, cf. William Dell, *Works* (Philadelphia, 1816), particularly " The Stumbling-Stone . . . Wherein the University is Reproved by the Word of God," pp. 325–381; " Testimony from the Word against Divinity-Degrees in the University, or any Academical Degrees made use of for the Ministry of the Gospel," pp. 560–571; and " The Right Reformation of Learning, Schools and Universities, according to the state of the Gospel," pp. 586–592.

IX

The Doctoral Ministry in
Later Reformed and
Presbyterian Polity

WITH THE PUBLICATION of the *Form of Government* by the Westminster Assembly in 1644,[1] the die was pretty well cast on the matter of the doctoral office, as far as English Puritanism was concerned. As we have noted, the doctoral office emerging from the Westminster Assembly was not the office Calvin had envisaged for the Church in Geneva, nor was it the office that had functioned in the Huguenot Church, the Church of the Netherlands, nor in the Church of Scotland. It was in effect a special kind of congregational ministry that its proponents found hard to differentiate from the pastoral office. It was a truncated definition of the doctoral office that was forwarded to the Scots General Assembly.

Before the matter was submitted to the kirk, the whole question of ordination was subjected to scrutiny in the spring of 1644. The specific question of doctoral ordination never seems to have been raised.[2] Rather, the matter turned on the definition of ordination, and most particularly on the necessity for ordination by a presbyterial or classical assembly. The Independents kept insisting that the power lay in the local congregation or at the very least

[1] Carruthers, *op. cit.,* pp. 29–30.
[2] Cf. George Gillespie, *Notes of Debates and Proceedings of the Assembly of Divines . . . February 1644 to January 1645* (Edinburgh, 1846), pp. 12–75.

in the congregational " presbytery," whereas the Presbyterians and the Scots were quite as insistent that the act of ordination was to be reserved to the classical " presbytery." A compromise of sorts was reached in May by which it was " by both sides agreed . . . that [ordination] is not to be left to the congregations in England . . . [but] that it is expedient that ordination be an act of an associated Presbytery." The fact that the term " associated Presbytery " never appeared in the Westminster Symbols indicates that this was just another way of burying a bit longer the head-on conflict between the two factions of reform. In the light of everything else we know about the situation at Westminster, it is a safe assumption that at least in the minds of the Independents, anything that was said regarding pastoral ordination would be applied to the doctoral office.

Robert Baillie and George Gillespie left London in January 1644/1645 [3] to report to the General Assembly of the kirk and to carry with them, among other things, the draft of the *Form of Government*. Gillespie has recorded the fact that he and Baillie were present as the Assembly convened on 22 January, and that the following day they presented their reports, the *Directory for Worship* and *Propositions of Church Government*, for the Assembly's consideration.[4] Evidently both matters were submitted to committees for study and report, for on 7 February, Gillespie notes that: " At Committee for examination of the Propositions of Government, after great debate about the article, That the Doctor or Teacher may minister the sacraments as well as the Pastor, which is contrary to the Book of Discipline [1581]. I show the reasons of it, that Eph. iv proves it. Those officers who are appointed for the edifying of the Saints, the work of the ministry, &c may minister the sacraments: But Teachers &c.

[3] Carruthers, *op. cit.*, pp. 30–31.
[4] Gillespie, *Notes*, p. 120.

" 2. I Cor. 12; Rom. 12, make the difference only in the manner of teaching.

" 3. They that preach, ex-officio, may baptize — Matt. 28. It was resolved, to refer this article to further discussion."

It is difficult to know whether Gillespie was presenting his own point of view,[5] or whether he was defending the position taken by the Westminster Divines. But what is not difficult to note is the fact that this was regarded as a real departure by the Scots churchmen, a matter, indeed, which did not find final resolution in the committee. When the Form of Government finally came to the floor of the Assembly on 10 February in the afternoon following the third reading of the document, the Assembly first warned those who had " exceptions against the same " to make their positions known, and then went on to " Agree to, and Approve the Propositions . . . touching Kirk-government and Ordination." [6] However, the matter of doctoral involvement in the administration of the sacraments, which had raised some question in the committee, evidently caused some members to interject enough exceptions so that the adoption was not absolutely wholehearted. The action specifically singled out that provision in the following terms: " Provided alwayes, That this Act shall be no ways prejudiciall to the further discussion and examination of the Article, which hold forth, that the Doctor or Teacher, hath power of the administration of the Sacraments as well as the pastor; . . . But that it shall be free to debate and discuss these points as God shall be pleased to give further light."

This does not say a great deal for a positive point of view

[5] He does not deal with the matter in either his *An Assertion of the Government of the Church of Scotland* (Edinburgh, 1641), or in his *Aaron's Rod Blossoming* (London, 1646).

[6] Church of Scotland, *The Acts of the General Assemblies of the Church of Scotland . . . 1638 to . . . 1649* (Edinburgh, 1691), pp. 259–260.

of the doctoral office in the Scots Church, but it does present a good negative point of view. The doctor qua doctor was not regarded by a significant part of the kirk as being engaged in a sacramental ministry and these wished to reserve the matter for future discussion. The record does not preserve a further debate of the point, if it ever did take place.

In fairness, we must question exactly what the Assembly understood by the term " doctor." Evidence from parish and presbyterial records indicates that, up until this time, the term was a common designation for the undermaster of the parochial grammar school, or the Latin school of the larger towns, and also on occasion was used of the schoolmaster. Furthermore, the masters and undermasters of these schools were expected to perform certain liturgical and catechetical duties. If this usage was what was in the minds of the kirk's commissioners, we can readily understand their hesitancy about admitting such a class to sacramental administration. On the other hand, the reference made in the record to the *Second Book of Discipline* would seem to minimize such a terminological confusion.[7]

We have already indicated how Alexander Henderson viewed the practice of the doctoral office in the kirk at the time of the Westminster Assembly as an extension of the church's ministry into the academic community, and how George Gillespie did not deal with the issue. Samuel Rutherford, another of the Scots Commissioners to Westminster, engaged in a controversy with the Independents on the matter of Presbyterian government,[8] in which he took as

[7] Cf. G. D. Henderson, *The Scottish Ruling Elder* (London, 1935), pp. 150, 157; J. Strong, *A History of Secondary Education in Scotland* (Oxford, 1909), p. 70; A. Wright, *The History of Education and the Old Parish School of Scotland* (Edinburgh, 1893), pp. 90, 98; J. Edgar, *History of Early Scottish Education* (Edinburgh, 1893), pp. 91, 103–104; J. Grant, *History of Burgh Schools of Scotland* (Glasgow, 1876), p. 40.

[8] Samuel Rutherford, *The Due Right of Presbyteries* (London,

his protagonists two works entitled *The Way of the Church of Christ in New England,* and *An Apology for the Church in New England.* Rutherford accused the author of laboring to prove that pastors and doctors were two different offices. Rutherford did not dissent that there were two separate functions and that they might well be two distinct offices, but he took the view that the nature of the functions involved in the offices were such that they might well be lodged " in one man's person." [9] Rutherford said that he made this observation out of his own experience. However, he was quite explicit in stating that he conceived the doctoral function more appropriate to the college and university than to the parish.

James Guthrie, writing a few years later, pointed out that because of the poverty of the individual congregations of Scotland " there be few or no Doctors, or teaching elders, distinct from Pastors or Ministers, who perform the duties of the Preaching Elder, and of Teaching Elder." [10] Guthrie had previously adopted a definition of the doctoral office as part of the eldership of the church, saying there are several kinds of elders, " Preaching Elders or Ministers, Teaching Elders or Doctors, and Ruling or Governing Elders." [11] This subdivision of the eldership had been used by Gillespie, who appealed to Peter Lombard as authority that there were " only two perpetual offices, the order of Deacons and the order of Elders." [12] We have already commented on the fact that Calvin had been less than specific in his use of the term *presbyteroi,* but the probability exists that in this particular case, Gillespie and

---

1644). Rutherford singled out the author, John Robinson, and the two works for special comment (p. 84).

[9] *Ibid.,* p. 140.

[10] [James Guthrie], *A Treatise of Ruling Elders and Deacons* (Edinburgh, 1699), pp. 50–51; originally published 1652.

[11] *Ibid.,* p. 21.

[12] Gillespie, *An Assertion of Government of Church of Scotland,* p. 8.

Guthrie reflected more dependence on à Lasco's attempt to relegate the public ministry to two orders: *de Eltesten, und die Diaken.* Calvin had not put it quite that simply.

Although Guthrie acknowledged that the office of doctor did not exist on a parochial basis in the Church of Scotland, he did say that those who were employed " in the Schools of Divinity " were the doctors of whom the *Form of Government* spoke. He contended that once an individual had been inducted into the eldership, only specific removal from that office could terminate his status, and that occasional or accidental nonfunctioning did not impair basic status. Although he was primarily concerned to safeguard the status of the ruling elder at this particular point,[13] the use he made of the terms would indicate that as strong a case could be made for the doctors of the church.

Contemporary usage in the Church of Scotland is not entirely consistent. The use of the terms " pastors and doctors " is kept at a minimum, but the same idea is maintained by the use of " Ministers and Professors," so that we are quite justified in saying that " minister " has replaced the more Calvinian term of " pastor." [14]

In the case of the " professor," the contemporary Church of Scotland construes the term to mean any " principal, vice-principal, or professor holding office as such in any of the Universities, or in any college in Scotland connected with the Church, and in the case of a professor, one who is admitted to any share of college funds . . . and shall include a colleague and successor or assistant and successor to a principal or professor, but shall not include [women or those not on tenure]." In other cases, the term is further restricted so that it is defined as " Theological Professors," [15] and the presumption is that this is what is gen-

---

[13] Guthrie, *op. cit.,* pp. 31–32.

[14] J. T. Cox, *Practice and Procedure in the Church of Scotland* (Edinburgh, 1935) , pp. 101–102, 115, 331–332, 486.

[15] *Ibid.,* p. 123: Professors of theology are members of the presbytery within whose bounds they labor; p. 160: for purposes of enu-

erally meant by the term. As a professor of a theological
discipline, the individual is expected to " be and continue
to be an ordinand or ordained minister of the Church." [16]

By this, we see that the kirk contemplates that professors
of the theological disciplines in the colleges and divinity
halls perhaps may be drawn from the ranks of the nonpastors, and this impression is further fortified when we
note that provision is made for the ordination to the holy
ministry of a probationer who is appointed to fill a theological chair.[17] In addition, a formula for ordination and
admission of professors into their charge is in print, which
is significantly worded to make a distinction from the constitutional questions required of ministers (pastors) .[18]

Thus the Church of Scotland preserves some strong
traces of its Calvinian heritage of a doctoral office. The
distinguishing marks between it and the pastoral office
have been blurred at many points, especially by the use of
the comprehensive term " minister " for the pastoral office.
However, the basic outlines of a public ministry of the
Word of God in the academic world have been preserved,
and even if it be confined to some particular chairs, or be
practically submerged in the pastoral ministry, nonethe-
less there seems to be a significant sense in which the Scots

---

meration theological professors count as "ministers" in determining presbyterial representation in General Assembly; pp. 233, 332:
the professor's relation to the presbytery, upon demitting a chair,
is (as the minister's demission of a charge) governed by a series of
statutory procedures.

[16] *Ibid.*, p. 337.

[17] By an act of 1919, the terms "licentiate" and "probationer"
are declared to be synonymous in status, and that any distinction is
one of "outlook"; the licentiate being "content with the seal set
upon the completion of his studies and . . . authority to conduct
public worship, . . . may make no effort to enter on the other functions of the ministry"; whereas the probationer "desires and in-
tends to obtain a promotion to a pastoral charge or other office"
(*ibid.*, p. 194) . Neither are counted members of presbytery without
ordination (pp. 123 f. and p. 230) .

[18] *Ibid.*, pp. 520–522.

divinity professor preserves the heritage of a separate ecclesiastical office occupied by Mark Duncan, George Buchanan, James Melville, and a host of others.

As far as the Westminster Symbols were concerned,
American Presbyterianism inherited as much of the doctoral office as did the Church of Scotland. What the American Church did not inherit was the tradition and practice
of the office. To further complicate the matter, it also inherited a strong measure of the Puritan understanding of
the church and its ministry.[19] Moreover, when the Synod
of New York and Philadelphia was in the process of trans-
forming itself into a General Assembly of a national denomination rather than adopting bodily the Westminster
Symbols as the confessional, liturgical, disciplinary, and
political standards of the new national church, the Synod
appointed committees to present drafts of all the pertinent
documents to its meeting in 1787.

The committee charged with the formulation of the
" Plan of Government " presented a very interesting text,
part of which we believe will be worth quoting in full, not
only for what it says about the idea of the doctoral office,
but as to what it does not say about the teaching function
of the pastoral office. In this connection, we must bear in
mind the duties of the pastoral office as they were conceived in the *Form of Government* as it was approved at
Westminster: " [1] to pray for and with his flock . . .
[2] to read the scripture publickly . . . [3] to feed the
flock, by preaching of the word, according to which he is to
teach, convince, reprove, exhort, and comfort, [4] to catechize, which is a plain laying down of the first principles of
the oracles of God . . . [5] to dispense other divine mysteries, [6] to administer the sacraments, [7] to bless the people of God . . . [8] to take care of the poor . . . and

[19] For a detailed analysis of this facet of the American Presbyterian Church, see L. J. Trinterud, *The Forming of an American
Tradition* (The Westminster Press, 1949).

[9] to exercise a ruling power over the flock as a pastor." [20]
Now, see how the New World churchmen handled this
same office and with what hesitancy they ventured to speak
of the doctoral ministry immediately following.

" Of Bishops or Pastors "

" The first office in the Church, both in dignity and usefulness, is the office of Bishop or Pastor, which in Scripture hath obtained different names, expressive of the various duties belonging thereto. As this officer is to preside
and watch over the flock of Christ, and inspect their spiritual interest, he is termed *Bishop;* as he is to feed them with
spiritual food, he is termed *Pastor.* As he is to serve Christ
in his Church, according to the abilities God has endued
him with; to offer up the prayers of the people; and to bless
the congregation in the name of the Lord, he is termed
the *minister* of Christ. As he is to be grave and prudent,
and an example of the flock; and to govern well in the
house and kingdom of Christ, he is termed *presbyter* or
elder. As he is the messenger of God, he is termed the
angel; as he is sent to declare the will of God, and to be-
seech sinners to be reconciled to God, through Christ, he
is termed *ambassador.* And as he is to dispense the mani-
fold grace of God, and all the ordinances of Christ's appointment, he is termed *steward* of the mysteries of God.
" In the primitive Church there seems to have been also,
an order of men stiled *teachers,* and afterwards *catechists,*
distinct from the bishops, or pastors, but assistants to them
in instructing the people. Their office seems to have been
to explain the first elements of religion; and particularly,
to take care of the education of the youth in sound principles of piety. This is an office of great importance. Hith-
erto, it hath been exercised in the American Churches by
the bishops and pastors alone; arising from their poverty,

[20] [Westminster Assembly of Divines] *The Confession of Faith*
. . . (London, 1658) , p. 312.

and imperfect organization; but as so many other weighty and important duties lie upon the ministers of the Gospel, it is earnestly recommended, that distinct and separate officers be instituted for these objects under the title of *catechists,* as soon as the state and circumstances of the Church will admitt.

" *Doctors* and *professors of theology* in schools and colleges, when not invested likewise with the pastoral office, ought to be considered simply in the light of Catechists or of Teachers, and are not entitled by virtue of that office alone to be members of any of the judicatures of the church.

" Under this title likewise are to be included all licentiates, and candidates for the ministry of the gospel, who are not ordained to exercise the government of the Church, or to administer its sacraments." [21]

The antecedents of the statement on the pastoral ministry of the church are not difficult to trace. There is a reminiscence of the Genevan doctorate in paragraph three, but only a reminiscence, for the article denied the doctoral office as a public ministry except in cases where the individual was also a pastor. The second paragraph seems to call for a class of ministers that on the one hand may reflect Puritan practice in New England, and on the other, may be simply a reflection of certain Scots practices about which Alexander Henderson had occasion to make reference over a century previously. What is most interesting, however, is the fact that the first paragraph of the American recension made no mention of the function of catechizing, the fourth duty listed by the Westminster Assembly as the responsibility of the pastoral office. Presumably, if the drafting committee's recommendation had been followed, paragraphs two, three, and four would have been

[21] *A Draught of a Plan of Government and Discipline for the Presbyterian Church of North America.* Proposed by a committee appointed for that purpose (Philadelphia, 1786), p. 7; italics have been added.

amplified into more positive language by the Synod in 1787, when this document was submitted for debate. If such had been the case, the American Presbyterian Church would have retained at least the shell of Calvin's fourfold public ministry.

However, the Synod of 1787 did not proceed in this fashion. It made only unimportant grammatical changes in the first paragraph.[22] But the second, third, and fourth paragraphs were excised completely, so that no hint remained of their ever having existed. In the process, the duty of catechizing was dropped out completely, for the material dealing with that aspect of the ministerial calling was cut, whereas the function was not reintroduced into paragraph one.

We are in the unhappy position of not knowing just why the cut was made by the Synod of 1787, for although submission of the draft was minuted and the existence of a debate was cited, the contents of it are lacking. Not lacking, however, are the obvious attendant results. The American Presbyterian Church ceased to mirror in its ecclesiological Standards any notion that it had a large stake in the educative process of its own constituency, especially its youth.[23] What is more, it cut itself loose from any recollection that a part of its public ministry had a special call to labor in the academic community.

This state of affairs was evidently not quite tenable for the church. One branch of it has gradually reintroduced both catechetical and doctoral offices into its polity under other forms. With the adoption in May of 1958 of *The*

---

[22] *A Draught of the Form of Government and Discipline of the Presbyterian Church in the United States of America*, proposed by the Synod of New York and Philadelphia, for the consideration of the Presbyteries and Churches under their care (New York, 1787), p. 8.

[23] J. D. Smart, *The Teaching Ministry of the Church* (The Westminster Press, 1954), pp. 12–13, notes a current disinterest and lack of a sense of responsibility on the part of the church's pastors for the peculiarly educational ministry.

Constitution of The United Presbyterian Church in the United States of America,[24] we witness the full incorporation of one of these lost offices, and the partial realization of the other. The office of commissioned church worker,[25] although broader than the category of a catechist, is nevertheless particularly designed to provide a measure of status for individuals who wish to exercise a full-time didactic ministry at the parish level, without assuming the obligations of ordination.

In regard to the doctorate, the appropriate section of the *Form of Government* no longer speaks of " bishops or pastors, . . . ruling elders, and deacons " as the " perpetual officers in the Church," [26] but of " bishops or *ministers,* and ruling elders and deacons." [27] Farther along the text repeats in a condensed version the wording of the definition of the pastoral office of 1786, but the section " When a minister is called to labor as a pastor " returns to the language of Westminster on the pastoral office. It is the section " When a minister is appointed to be a teacher in a theological seminary, or to give instruction to youth assembled in a school, college, or university " that most nearly approximates the Calvinian doctorate, but even here, the function is conceived in shepherding (pastoral) and hortatory terms, rather than in a critical (prophetic) and didactic context.[28]

Comment on the eclectic nature of Chapter VIII (" Of Ministers ") was not long in coming from the church. Even

[24] *The Constitution of The United Presbyterian Church in the U.S.A.* (Philadelphia, 1958); ratified and adopted at Pittsburgh, Pennsylvania, May, 1958, by the Presbyterian Church in the U.S.A. (Northern) and the United Presbyterian Church in North America.
[25] *Ibid.,* pp. 153–158, Form of Government, Ch. XXIII.
[26] Cf. *The Constitution of the Presbyterian Church in the U.S.A.* (Philadelphia, 1953), Form of Government, Ch. III, Sec. 2.
[27] *The Constitution of The United Presbyterian Church in the U.S.A.,* p. 122; italics added for contrast.
[28] *Ibid.,* p. 123; an academic chaplaincy is also included under this heading.

before the final adoption of *The Constitution,* the Presbytery of Chicago (Presbyterian Church U.S.A.) submitted an overture to the General Assembly which called upon that body to appoint a commission to " study the nature of the ministry of the Church that the doctrinal basis of our diversified ministries may be clarified." [29] This overture granted that the church had recognized the need of a more diversified ministry, but that it had only " been able to give due recognition, adequate discipline, and economic and ecclesiastical security to these newer ministries . . . by some kind of assimilation to the office of pastor. Thus while the offices of elder and deacon remain clearly defined and their responsibilities distinct, [the pastorate] has become increasingly ambiguous and amorphous." The overture went on to point out that *The Constitution,* still to be formally ratified and adopted, had attempted to meet a very real and pressing need in the comprehensive coverage " Of Ministers," but that to include under that title " not only the pastor but the teacher, missionary, evangelist, administrator, writer, editor, and those engaged in ' any other like needful work ' . . . [represents] . . . only the most recent of a number of piecemeal alterations." [30]

It would be too much to say that the Calvinian doctorate is about to reappear in American Presbyterianism; it is safe to say that the diversity of function that Calvin recog-

[29] *Minutes of the General Assembly of The United Presbyterian Church in the U.S.A.,* Part I, Journal and Supplement (Philadelphia, 1958) , pp. 138, 280.
[30] *Ibid.* Some of the "problems raised by a diversified ministry " are enumerated as: " 1. Our larger presbyteries are no longer made up only of pastors and elders of the congregations of the Church, and an increasing number of persons bear rule in the Church who have no official relationship whatever to a local congregation. 2. The non-pastoral ministers have no adequate relationship to the ongoing life of the Church, for they are neither pastors nor members of local congregations, and there is no substitute for this. 3. While the Church has an excellent tradition of training for pastors, it has developed no adequate program for the other ministries which are vital parts of the contemporary work of the Church."

nized between the pastoral and doctoral office is still food for thought, and perhaps action.

The history of the doctorate in the two major branches of the Continental Reformed family in America is surprisingly consistent. On the one hand, the Church Orders of these denominations persist in formally recognizing the existence of a fourth order of the public ministry of the church which is given specific academic obligations. On the other, they are as uniformly united in spelling out this fourth office as a part of the pastoral office.

The Reformed Church in America traces its independent existence from the organization of the General Synod of the Reformed Dutch Church in the United States in 1792.[31] Although Queen's College (forerunner of Rutgers University) had been founded about 1766 with provisions for a divinity professor, none was appointed as such. Beginning in 1784, with the appointment of J. H. Livingston, associate pastor of the Dutch Reformed Church in New York, as synodical professor of theology, and H. Meyer, also a pastor, as synodical professor of languages, the Dutch churches sought to provide some standardized training for their ministerial candidates, without establishing an institutional campus. The practice of appointing " Lectors in Theology " in various geographical areas of the church to instruct candidates and assure their competence was begun in 1786.[32] Even before the establishment of the General Synod, the Dutch churches were conscious of a special function attached to those who instructed candidates for the ministry.

The General Synod of 1792 adopted as part of its constitution the " Rules of Church Government Established

[31] C. E. Corwin, *A Manual of the Reformed Church in America, 1628–1922*, 5th edition revised (New York, 1922), p. 77.
[32] *Ibid.*, pp. 109, 121–123.

in the National Synod, in the years 1618 and 1619," [33] which in Art. II declared, " The *Officers* in the Church of Christ are fourfold, viz. 1. The office of *Ministers of the Word.* 2. The office of *Teachers of Theology.* 3. The office of *Elders.* 4. The office of *Deacons.*" Subsequently, the only mention of the second office was to be found in Article XVIII, " The *office of the TEACHERS or PROFESSORS of Theology* is to explain the holy scriptures, and vindicate the pure doctrines of the gospel against heresy and error." However, the Netherland standards in translation were not regarded as sufficient for the new church, so a number of " Explanatory Articles " were appended that illustrated much more clearly what the General Synod really had in mind. [34]

These " Explanatory Articles " are filled with ambiguities when they come to discuss the professors of theology. [35] For example, hope was expressed that the Synod would be able to provide sufficient monetary reward, so that the professors " may not be dependent upon any particular congregation, while they are employed for the common benefit of all the churches." Yet a few pages before it was decreed that " Professors of Theology have as such, no power, jurisdiction or government whatever in the Church; but as they are Ministers [of the Word] who preach occasionally, they are entitled, when they stand in connection with any Congregation, equally with other Ministers [of the Word], to administer the sacraments, and to a seat and voice in ecclesiastical assemblies." The questions implicit in this statement alone are legion, but when it is followed by an expressed desire to decrease the congregational dependence of the professors, one can only confess that the section must have been spun out of the rarest kind of

---

[33] *The Constitution of the Reformed Dutch Church in the United States of America* (New York, 1793), pp. 260 ff.
[34] *Ibid.,* pp. 298 ff.
[35] *Ibid.,* pp. 312–318.

theorizing. At the time when the " Explanatory Articles " were adopted, all the individuals holding title as synodical professors were active pastors in the church, and at least in Livingston's case, this fact had caused some trouble with the consistory.[36] This can account for the fact that hope of sufficient remuneration for an independent professor would be expressed. However, the rather severe restrictions put upon the professor, in case he be not a minister of the word [pastor] also, can only be accounted for by reference to the restrictions already noted in the account we have given of the Netherlands Church commencing with the *Kerkenordening* of the Dort Synod of 1578.

But by far the most interesting thing about the " Explanatory Articles " was the rationale of the office of the professor of theology. Scripture was not the ground of appeal, except that Bèze was cited using Eph. 4:11, but rather " the nature of the respective offices " (i.e., ministers vs. teachers), the primitive church and the fathers (Ambrose, Jerome, Augustine, and Origen), and the fact that it was not a good idea to leave the preparation of candidates " for the service of the sanctuary . . . indiscriminately to every Minister, or any individual who may choose to assume that office." In this last, we probably witness not a derogation of Livingston and the synodical professors, but a slap at other pastors who undertook to train young men for the ministry by the apprentice system, and at those churches which hung back in rendering financial support for the founding of a theological seminary proper.[37]

Selection of the professors of theology was to be by majority vote in the General Synod at least one day following the submission of a nomination or nominations.[38] Also, the professors were required to sign, upon election, in the presence of the synod, a long " formula " or oath of

[36] Corwin, *op. cit.*, p. 123.
[37] Corwin, *op. cit.*, pp. 110–111, 122–124.
[38] " Explanatory Articles," *op. cit.*, p. 314, Art. XXI.

loyalty to the provisions of the Synod of Dort.

The provisions of 1792 left in doubt the ecclesiastical status of a professor who was not at his election already a pastor of the church. The Dutch Reformed have since solved that problem by categorically defining professors of theology as " ministers in good standing." [39]

At the same time, although the office " Of Ministers of the Word " is initially defined in purely pastoral terms,[40] an omnibus provision, similar to what we have already described in relation to the United Presbyterian Church, makes it possible for " a licensed candidate [to] be entitled to an examination for ordination when he has purposed to accept a call to a church, or when he is to be assigned to *educational,* missionary, *or other ministerial work,* including service as chaplain in the Armed Forces or any other career chaplain, either under the direction of a Consistory or of a Classis or in foreign lands." [41] Thus, in effect, although ordination as a minister of the word is required, it is entirely possible that an individual may be ordained *as* a professor of theology, without ever intending to undertake any pastoral vocation. As a professor, he is prohibited from taking " pastoral charge of any congregation," although it is stated that " he may preach and administer or assist in administering the Sacraments in any church as a minister of the Gospel on request of the minister or Consistory of said Church." [42]

In regard to the professor's ecclesiastical duties and obligations, he is required upon election to transfer his ecclesiastical membership from the classis of previous connection to the General Synod. Then, so as not to disenfranchise him, and reminiscent of the Netherland *Kerkenordening,* the professors of theology in each of the theological schools

[39] *The Constitution of the Reformed Church in America* (New York, Grand Rapids, 1957) , p. 11, Art. III, Sec. 30.

[40] *Ibid.,* p. 6, Art. II.

[41] *Ibid.,* p. 8, Art. II, Sec. 16 (italics added) .

[42] *Ibid.,* p. 13, Art. II, Sec. 34.

of the church are entitled " to appoint one of their number as a delegate to the General Synod." [43]

The Evangelical and Reformed Church traces its history as an independent body from the Synod of the German Reformed Church that convened in Lancaster, Pennsylvania, in April of 1793.[44] This meeting adopted a *Synodalordnung* which was revised in 1800 to include catechists and licentiates, as well as ordained ministers, elders, and deacons as part of the public ministry of the church. Licentiates were authorized to administer the sacraments by virtue of a license renewable yearly and could withdraw from the ministry without incurring censure; catechists were denied the authority of sacramental administration; both were literally required to take back seats at synodical assemblies.[45] No mention was made of a doctorate or professorate as part of the church's ministry.

However, by 1882, the office of professor of theology had been introduced into the Constitution of the Reformed Church in the United States (German), in language that suggests that the inspiration for this had come from the Dutch Reformed " Explanatory Articles " of 1792.[46] Verbal correlations are exact in some instances; the major point of difference being that the German Reformed did not include a rationale for the inclusion of the teacher of theology as part of the public ministry. Unlike the Dutch, however, the Germans did not hedge the exercise of the doctorate around with postscriptions or prescriptions as to relationships with congregations and administration of the sacraments. Under none of the provisions was there any attempt to describe the office of professor in terms that

[43] *Ibid.*, p. 13, Art. II, Sec. 35.
[44] E. T. Corwin, J. H. Dubbs, and J. T. Hamilton, *A History of the Reformed Church, Dutch; the Reformed Church, German; and the Moravian Church in the United States* (New York, 1894), p. 324.
[45] *Ibid.*, pp. 330–332.
[46] Cf. text in *The Church Member's Hand-book* (Tiffin, Ohio, 1882), pp. 113–152.

were basically drawn from the pastoral office; rather, aside from the opening admonition that " it is the duty of Teachers of Theology to explain the Holy Scriptures and to defend the pure doctrine of the Gospel against errors," [47] the office was defined almost exclusively in terms of the duty to instruct " theological students and to prepare them suitable for the office of teachers in the Church." The range of this instruction was stipulated to be " Ecclesiastical History, Didactic Theology, Church Government, and the duties of the Pastoral office, as well as . . . the interpretation of the Scriptures." With minor variations, the remainder of the provisions were all reminiscent of the Dutch " Explanatory Articles."

With the merger of the Reformed Church in the United States and the Evangelical Synod of North America to form the Evangelical and Reformed Church in 1934, the constitutional provisions regarding the teacher, or professor, of theology were drastically curtailed.[48] Under this merger, the teacher of theology was simply " a minister who is chosen to be a professor in a theological seminary of the Church."

The situation at mid-twentieth century seems to be rather consistent for all traditions of Presbyterian and Reformed polity. On the one hand, the shadow of the doctoral office has been preserved, in some cases more clearly, in some cases less so. In some cases it has faded almost to the point of extinction. In all cases the rationale has been consistently eliminated, and for all practical purposes as to training, induction, and participation, it has been either completely subsumed in the pastoral office or at most is regarded as a subspecies of the pastorate. On the other hand, the eradication of memory has not been complete, for on a number of fronts we see the church struggling

[47] *Church Mem. Hand-book*, p. 118, Art. 15.
[48] *The Constitution and By-Laws of the Evangelical and Reformed Church*, as amended to June, 1950 (n.p., n.d.), p. 8.

with its educational task, and partly as a result of this, we are aware of movements toward a rethinking of the structure of the public ministry because of the obvious needs of a diversified responsibility.

It remains to trace the situation in American Congregationalism, heir of the Independent insistence that the " doctor, not only may, but must be " in the congregation. In so far as American Congregationalism has a common source for its polity, we may turn with assurance to the *Cambridge Platform* of 1648 for the evidence.[49] However, the authority of this document for individual congregations within the denomination was of a different kind from the authority the *Form of Government* bore toward American Presbyterianism. The *Platform* witnessed to the thinking and practice of a particular generation that was only willing, even in its own time, to commend its provisions " to the churches of Christ amongst us . . . as worthy of their due consideration and acceptance," rather than establishing an authoritative statement of ecclesiastical polity that a congregation was bound to accept if it desired to remain in connection with the wider fellowship.

The *Platform* exhibits all the confusion we have already encountered in regard to the use of the simple term " elder " as a designation for an order of the church's ministry.[50] On the one hand, the ruling elder was first mentioned with pastors and teachers; on the other, the duties of the ruling elder and deacon are discussed under a single heading.

The only mention of the office of teacher was in the immediate context of the congregational pastoral office:

" 5. The office of *Pastor & Teacher,* appears to be dis-

[49] Text in Williston Walker, *The Creeds and Platform of Congregationalism* (New York, 1893), pp. 194–237.
[50] *Ibid.,* pp. 211–213; Ch. VI:4.

tinct. The Pastors special work is, to attend to *exhortation:* & therein to Administer a word of *Wisdom:* the *Teacher* is to attend to *Doctrine,* & therein to Administer a word of *Knowledge:* & either of them to administer the *Seales* of that Covenant, unto the dispensation whereof the[y] are alike called: as also to execute the *Censures,* being but a kind of application of the word, the preaching of which, together with the application thereof they are alike charged withall.

" 6. And for as much as both *Pastors & Teachers* are given by Christ for the perfecting of the Saints, & edifying of his body, which Saints, & body of Christ is his church; Therefore wee account *Pastors & Teachers* to be both of them church-officers; and not the Pastor for the church: & the *Teacher* only for the Schools, Though this wee gladly acknowledge, that Schools are both lawfull, profitable, & necessary for the trayning up of such in good *Litrature,* or learning, as may afterwards be called forth unto office of *Pastor* or *Teacher* in the church."

No other mention of the office of teacher appeared in the whole of the *Platform,* and in the section where the congregational presbytery was outlined and its duties enumerated, the only office mentioned was that of the " elders " in a general way.

The significant thing about all of this is that for all their intense insistence that the teacher's office was separate from the pastor's, an issue that their brethren in Old England had made abundantly evident only five years previously at Westminster, and for all their insistence that the nature of this separation was patterned on the New Testament Church based on Scripture analysis, the New England divines at Cambridge did not adduce a single Scripture proof text from the New Testament that had not already been discussed at length at Westminster.[51] When they re-

[51] *Ibid.,* p. 211, Eph. 4:11; Rom. 12:7-8; I Cor. 12:8; II Tim. 4:12; Titus 1:9.

jected the location of the teacher's function in the school, they appealed, not to the New Testament, but to the record of the Old Covenant, particularly to those places in the historical material which give evidence that the prophetic office in the early Hebrew community was exercised in community groups of an ecstatic character.[52] In the light of the traditional usage of this material among the Reformed, as a ground for the doctoral office *in the school*,[53] and the theological foundation of the school,[54] we must conclude that the New England divines were unable to find any sanction for a divorce of the doctoral office from the school, apart from their congregational doctrine of the church and ministry that was so well expressed in the *Cambridge Platform*.

Toward the end of the seventeenth century, Isaac Chauncy attempted to say something about the polity and ministry of Congregationalism, but terminologically, at least, succeeded only in further confusing the understanding of the teacher's office. He very specifically classed the teachers and prophets of the New Testament along with the apostles and evangelists as extraordinary ministers whose function had terminated with the foundation of self-propagating churches.[55] He was most certain that such prophets and teachers did not have " any office or governing Power in the Church," and that they did not actually differ greatly in their function.

However, when he dealt with the ordinary continuing ministry of the church, he followed the scheme already

[52] *Ibid.* Two of the proof texts are from I Sam. 12:2; 19:20 and two from II Kings 2:3, 15.

[53] Cf. Bèze, " Inaugural Address," above pp. 62–64.

[54] Cf. Williams, " Excursus," *op. cit.*, pp. 298–302, 340–342, 350, for the evidence that the New England theologians as well as the Continental Reformed looked to the idea of the anointed prophet or the prophetic band of the Old Covenant to establish the theological sanction of the church's involvement in the institutional school.

[55] Isaac Chauncy, *The Divine Institution of Congregational Churches, Ministry and Ordinances* (London, 1697), pp. 54–55.

established in Congregational usage of dividing the whole
public ministry into two orders: the elders and deacons.[56]
The eldership was subdivided on the traditional pattern
into pastors, teachers, and ruling elders. Nothing about
this was new, but a new construction was to be found in
the detailed analysis of " the Ministerial Charge " where
Chauncy allowed, " in the case of bodily infirmity, or great-
ness of the congregation, if he [pastor] is not able to go
through the governing Work, Christ hath provided helps
and assistance for him: a Teacher in his Teaching Work,
and a ruling Elder to aid and assist in Ruling (I Tim.
5:17).

" He that is called and ordained of Christ by the Church
to concur with the Pastor in the Teaching Work . . . is
called a Teacher. . . .

" He that is called and ordained of Christ by the Church
to concur with the Pastor in diligently ruling, is required
to wait on the Work especially . . . and is called a Ruling
Elder, and is Ordained in the same manner with a Teaching Elder." [57]

This statement of the matter effectively cuts out the
office of teacher as a co-ordinate ministry of the church,
for the whole emphasis is put on the pastoral office and in
reality the teacher and ruling elder become associate
pastors. Furthermore, according to Chauncy, it was no
longer a point of principle to maintain *both* a pastor and
a teacher in the local church. Whatever may be the justification of Burrage's comment that " it was probably the
difficulty of properly supporting more than one principal
Church officer that in time led to the abolition of Doctors
or Teachers among the Congregational Puritan Churches
both in England and in America," [58] the fact of the case
would seem to be that the Congregational Churches had

[56] *Ibid.*, p. 58.
[57] *Ibid.*, pp. 61–62.
[58] C. Burrage, *Early English Dissenters* (Cambridge, 1912), I:37.

begun the abandonment of the doctoral office the moment
that ministry had been cut loose from the arena of academic involvement. Also, Chauncy's explanation points
up a further development, one which so far has received
no attention. Put very simply: separate functions for pastors *and* doctors (teachers) are no longer distinguishable
in the congregations. Worship for the great bulk of those
who followed the New England way had become synonymous with the sermon; in effect, the pastor, although re-
taining that title, had become the teacher and the sermon
had become a lecture. In short, there was no more need for
a distinct teaching office in the congregation, and if this
analysis is true, the New Englander would not be likely to
pay for that which he did not need. The fact that something drastic had happened to the idea of the pastoral office
in this assimilation is also obvious, but this is not the place
to press it further.

A century and a half later, the Congregational Churches
had occasion to speak of the academic labor of certain of
their ministers. But the formula that developed out of the
Albany Convention of 1852, and the National Council of
Congregational Churches at Boston in 1865 was certainly
not a clear-cut statement of a doctoral ministry.[59] Rather,
within the context of Congregationalism, it raised some
interesting questions when it dealt with those who were
to be responsible for ministerial training. " Those who are
to teach and train men for the ministry must needs be
ministers, recognized as such among the churches, and
esteemed for their zeal and power in holding forth the
word of life; and yet they cannot ordinarily be at the same
time officers in churches." [60] The rationale of this statement would seem to be that individuals vocationally in-

[59] Walker, *op. cit.*, pp. 553–569, gives an account of the development and proceedings.

[60] *Ecclesiastical Polity, the Government and Communion Practiced by the Congregational Churches in the United States,* 2d edition (Boston, 1879) , p. 66.

volved in certain types of academic community should be closely related to the church, but the precise nature of that relationship, and its articulation, was allowed to remain ambiguous with the attendant development that no distinction was made between it and the pastoral office.

X

Conclusion

THE PRACTICAL CHURCHMAN says: " You were right; it was dead! Why do you insist on beating it yet another time? " In answer, we insist that we are being eminently practical, and that really it is not a case of death vs. life, but rather a situation of confusion and atrophication vs. clarity and full vigor. This study has been made within the boundaries of certain presuppositions, one of which is that the public ministry of the church is collegiate in structure. Furthermore, this collegiate ministry is the overt expression of a still larger and more profound ministry: that of the whole church of Jesus Christ.[1]

In a time when the church is being challenged as irrelevant, in an era when one of the pressing practical questions before many people has to do with the purpose of life, and thus with the values to be expounded in the contemporary situation and transmitted to coming generations, we do not think that a reassessment of the teaching office of the church is of exclusively " academic " concern. Rather, we think that the church must take a hard look at the instruments by which it seeks to accomplish its God-given task of reconciliation. But reconciliation is neither cheap nor is it something to be fashioned out of thin air. Rather, it has its beginning and its end in a right understanding of

[1] Cf. W. A. Visser 't Hooft, *The Pressure of Our Common Calling* (Garden City, New York, 1959).

God who, according to Calvin, makes himself known both as Creator and Redeemer. Thus there is a place within the church's public ministry for an office dedicated to a sound knowledge of the many-faceted manner in which God has accommodated himself to the finite understanding of men, and more particularly to a constant critique of the institutional tendency of the church (and of society at large) to absolutize any partial apprehension of this revelation.

As to the factual results of our study, there are a number of issues that appear to be clarified. Initially, the appearance of the doctorate as a second order of the church's ministry in the ecclesiology that Calvin shared with other Reformers was based on at least two considerations quite apart from a desire to mirror New Testament practice in contemporary guise. Significantly, Calvin did not labor a detailed analysis of the New Testament prophet or doctor in a particular situation, nor did he appeal explicitly to New Testament practice, as such, in his definitive statement in the *Institutes*.[2] The first of these was a desire to establish a contemporary avenue for the exercise of the prophetic office of Christ in his church analogous to the ruler's exercise of the kingly office and the pastor's exercise of the priestly. The prophetic office was conceived by Calvin as didactic rather than predictive, which made it very easy for him to appropriate the form of the university doctorate as a proper channel by which to introduce the prophetic function into the ecclesiastical structure. This adaptation was made the easier because of the relation of the university to the institutional church that had already been asserted by example during the movements toward conciliarism.

The second consideration was allied to the first, but differed in its immediate objective. It had to do with the very practical problem of the source of authority for education, both university and secondary. In spite of the fact that lay

[2] *Inst.*, IV. iii. 4.

initiative had developed greatly in the Netherlands, the Rhineland, and Switzerland, the temporal community, especially in the latter two, had not yet developed sufficient independent stamina to manage the complex affair of public education completely on its own initiative. The promptness with which both Bucer and Calvin turned their attention to public instruction, and the repeated efforts they made to deal with its administration, as well as their participation in its conduct, witness to an existing dislocation in community concern and authority. Into this breach stepped the Reformed Church, with its early recognition of the necessity of an educated constituency as well as an informed citizenry, as the motivating force for the foundation, continuation, and expansion of the educative enterprise that was a distinct heritage from the medieval church. Not only was the Reformed Church a motivator, but equally important, it served as an organ of administration. In these areas, the Reformed Church and its leadership were but carrying out a function that was already regarded as a vital and necessary part of the medieval and Renaissance concern.

To project the ministry of the church to include the offices of the most important positions in the educative system was but an acknowledgment of the extremely sensitive nature of the enterprise for all concerned. The fact that the magistrates of Strasbourg resisted the clericalization of the teaching office more quickly than did the Genevan council can be attributed, in part, to the fact that community initiative was more advanced in educational matters in the Rhineland than it was in Switzerland. The fact that the idea of the doctoral office took a greater hold on the Huguenot and Scots Churches than it did in Germany may be attributed to the same condition. In both France and Scotland, the whole process of education, right up to the onset of the Reformation, had been more closely identified with the medieval church than was true elsewhere. In the case of the Dutch, we believe that there was some of the same influence at work. Although the Netherlands was liberally supplied with elementary and secondary institutions,[3] and was the scene of an early break with ecclesiastical control, there was not established among the Dutch an institution of university caliber until after the Reformed Church had become identified with national self-realization. Thus, in effect, the Dutch university foundation was tied up with the Calvinian ecclesiology that was adopted for the ordering of the church.

Quite apart from theory or sociological conditioning, there remains the unquestioned fact that international Calvinism, for well over a century, regarded a distinct doctoral office as one of the hallmarks of its public ministry. What is more, specific individuals can be identified within the body of the church who sustained this office as an office co-ordinate with the ministries of pastors, elders, and deacons, but dependent on none of them, and distinct from all. On the Continent, this office was regarded as being almost exclusively involved in the instruction of students in an academic setting (apart from the elementary-secondary level). Only in England was there a consistent attempt to establish this office at the parochial level, a movement that had its roots in some peculiar English conditions.

Eventually, this forced Puritanism to maintain the distinction between the pastoral office and the doctoral office on the basis of a distinction in *charisma* rather than on the basis of vocation, function, and office. Such a distinction was hard to maintain in the face of (1) Calvin's argument that the pastoral office included the doctor's functions in relation to the parish, and (2) the reinterpretation of the pastoral office in New England. Although the Puritan argu-

[3] Cf. R. R. Post, *Scholen en Onderwijs in Nederland gedurnende de Middeleeuwen* (Utrecht, 1954).

ments were among those most resolutely buttressed by
Scripture, the difficulty they experienced in a practical
demonstration of the distinction between the two offices at
a parochial level, and their denial of a doctoral ministry in
the school, eventuated in the absorption of the doctoral
office in the pastoral to such an extent that the memory of
the former has been all but obliterated among their descendants. But in passing, we may point out that the memory is not quite dead. Numerous congregations, particularly of New England Congregationalists, still identify the
chief parochial office as that of " pastor and teacher." I remember particularly an Installation Council held in a sub-
urb of Boston during which the pastor-elect was asked what
he considered to be the meaning of the title " teacher " in
his call to be " pastor and teacher " of that particular
church. His answer, couched in terms that would have
fitted exactly Calvin's definition of the pastoral office, completely satisfied his interrogator.

To assess the attrition in the scope of doctoral involvement in the Reformed Church, which took place during
the first century of its separate existence, we suggest that
at least a partial solution may be found for a narrowed
perspective in two developments. First, we recall mounting
signs of concern in the early decades of the seventeenth
century within the French Reformed Church as to the nature of the subject matter to be dealt with by those instructing the youth of the community. Particularly was
this concern directed to two areas of study: Greek and philosophy. In the case of Greek, the objections were based on
a moralistic concern to shield the future ministry, in its
youth, from too intimate association with a stratum of literature that was deemed morally inferior or even degrad-
ing. The problem that philosophy presented to the mind
of the church was doctrinal. Speculative philosophical
thought was viewed as a positive danger, and the church

considered that it was necessary to guard certain doctrinal presuppositions, even to the extent of prohibiting the raising of " certain curious questions." The interaction of these two concerns as they contributed to the amalgamation of the doctoral office into the pastoral, a process already under way prior to the termination of our discussion in the mid-seventeenth century, will bear further intensive investigation.

Secondly, the experience of the Dutch Church demonstrates another facet of the narrowing of the doctoral perspective of the church. We have come across no evidence that the issue of moralistic censorship was a major problem in this quarter. However, like the Huguenots, the Dutch Reformed became involved in the problem of how far the doctrinal commitments of the church were to be used as standards of classroom performance. In addition, the issue of lay initiative rose on the Dutch scene to complicate the problem for the church. This was not an unnatural development in view of the long-standing history of nonecclesiastical control of the educative process in the Low Countries. That it should finally make itself felt in the realm of higher education was perhaps inevitable. But in terms of the church's control over one section of its ministry, such a development was critical, for it posed a problem that few of the Reformed had worked through in any detail. With the exception of the *Second Book of Discipline* of the Church of Scotland, the Reformed Church never worked out a theoretical basis for the doctoral office that took into account its distinctive qualifications as a ministerial order co-ordinate with the pastor, elder, and deacon, yet separate from them. Such deliverances as dealt with the doctoral office in its distinctiveness were of an *ad hoc* variety.

Originally, in the life of the Reformed churches, the distinction between pastor and doctor was the distinction between an office specifically called and set apart to be the vehicle of the word of God in preaching, teaching, shepherding, and sacramental administration within the context of a parish, and a ministry, which by vocation was regarded as the vehicle of the same word of God in the academic community. Even here a distinction was operative, for the doctoral status was confined in almost every instance to those who were involved in instruction at the university or academy level in theology, Old and New Testament, Hebrew, Greek, and the arts. Gradually, under the press of a number of circumstances — confessional concern with orthodox doctrinal conformity, moralistic interpretation of the Christian life, revived political initiative as to both motivation and authority for the education process — the Reformed churches limited their doctoral concern to an increasingly narrowing list of so-called " sacred " subjects, and at the same time began to subsume the doctoral office in the pastoral, meanwhile compounding the confusion by an increased usage of the term " minister " to designate full-time officers of the church from those who functioned in special and representative capacities only as an adjunct to their normal occupation.

Furthermore, we should be attentive to a still more basic shift that was taking place. This is in the area of interpretation of the nature of the function of the Biblical prophet. Calvin had been at considerable pains to minimize the predictive and nonrational interpretation, stressing rather the didactic role. This was as true of his estimate of Christ's prophetic office as it was of his understanding of the position of the Old Testament prophet. In the tumult of Commonwealth England, and again in the upheaval that characterized pietistic reaction on the Continent, the prophetic function came increasingly to be understood along nonrational lines. In some quarters, it was equated with visionary experience. Thus, immediate experience became the desired goal and the highest criterion of the Christian life, together with a de-emphasis on faith mediated and informed by sound learning and clear doctrine. Professor

Dowey reminds us that Calvin's doctor was not an infallible teacher, but rather a fellow believer whose ministry was based upon his competence as a scholar and instructor.[4]

There is perhaps some evidence that much of what goes by the term " prophetic " on the current scene could profit by a re-examination of this basic Reformation position. The church in its prophetic stance far too frequently embarrasses and compromises the gospel it proclaims by ignorance and rootless relativism. On the one hand, there is a naïve assumption that a knowledge of God, both as Creator and Redeemer, comes cheaply. On the other, there is a fierce unwillingness to accept the seriousness of the struggle that is necessary if the believer and the believing community will come to terms with God's revelation of himself in the material, historical, and redemptive order.

Perhaps this is the place to continue on and suggest a course of action for the church in revivifying a special doctoral office, giving place and function to a particular ministry that the church cannot seem to forget, yet which it has so far not been able to articulate successfully. Such a projection would, of necessity, carry the author into several areas he has not yet had the opportunity to prospect. However, there is a deeper reason for reticence.

This is the church's problem, and it is the people of God, in faith and under the guidance of the Spirit, who must wrestle with the question of structure in the ministry. That the wrestling has begun seems quite evident, and so far it is not confined to any particular confession nor to any particular linguistic tradition. It is our hope that this study will provide sinews in this struggle, that it will be an arsenal from which serious and believing men may draw ammunition, not to aim at one another, but to use in the constant feud against too simple and thus insufficient solu-

[4] E. A. Dowey, Jr., *The Knowledge of God in Calvin's Theology* (New York, 1952), p. 36.

tions. As we see it, solutions that do not cope with the teaching ministry of the whole church, the relation of the church to all forms of instruction, and the exercise of teaching authority within the church will be too simple. We say this because it is the one prognostication that seems to be justified; it would appear that the church has not struggled hard enough with these in the past.

Bibliography

A selective list of the most important sources and books relating to this study.

REFERENCE WORKS

van der Aa, A. J., *Biographisch Woordenboek der Neder-landen*, 21 dln. Van Brederode, Haarlem, 1852–1878.

Allgemeine deutsche Biographie, 56 Bde. Drucker & Humblot, Leipzig, 1875–1912.

Univ. van Amsterdam, *Album academicum van het Athenaeum Illustre en van de Universiteit van Amsterdam*. R. W. P. De Vries, Amsterdam, 1913.

Catholic Encyclopedia, 15 vols. Robert Appleton Co., New York, 1909.

Cross, F. L., ed., *The Oxford Dictionary of the Christian Church*. Oxford University Press, London, 1957.

De Bie, J. P., en Loosjes, J., eds., *Biographisch Woordenboek van Protestantsche Godgeleerden in Nederland*, 5 dln. Matinus Nijhoff, 'sGravenhage, n.d. — 1943.

van Epen, D. G., *Album studiosorum academiae gelro-zutphanicae, MDCXLVIII–MDCCCXVIII*. Jacobum Hoekstra, Hagae Comitis, MCMIV.

Hist. Genootschap te Groningen (ed.), *Album studiosorum academiae Groninganae*. J. B. Wolters' U.M., Groningen, 1915.

Gillett, C. R., *The McAlpin Collection of British History and Theology*. Published by Union Theological Seminary, New York, 1924.

Haag, Eugène et Émil, *La France protestante ou vies des protestants français*, 10 tomes. Joël Cherbuliez, Paris, 1846–1858.

—— 2d edition, par Henri Bordier, 6 tomes. Librairie Sandoz et Fischbacher, Paris, 1877–1888.

Hauck, Albert, und Herzog, Johann Jacob, eds., *Realencyklopädie für protestantische Theologie und Kirche*, begründet von J. J. Herzog, hrsg. von d. Albert Hauck, 21 Bde. J. H. Hinrichs, Leipzig, 1896–1913.

Leslie, Stephen, ed., *Dictionary of National Biography*, 63 vols. Smith, Elden & Co., London, 1885–1912.

Univ. van Leyden, *Album studiosorum academiae Lugduno-Batavae, MDLXXV–MDCCCLXXV;* accedunt nomine Curatorum et Professorum, Martinum Nijhoff, Hagae Comitum, MDCCLXXV.

Matthews, A. G., ed., *Calamy Revised, being a revision of Edmund Calamy's Account of the Ministers and Others Ejected and Silenced 1660–1662*. Clarendon Press, Oxford, 1934.

Molhuysen, P. C., en Blok, P. J., eds., *Nieuw Nederlandsch Biografisch Woordenboek*, 10 dln. A. W. Sijthoff, Leiden, 1911–1937.

Scott, Hew, ed., *Fasti Ecclesiae Scoticanae: The Succession of Ministers in the Church of Scotland from the Reformation*, new edition, revised and continued . . . under the superintendence of a committee of the General Assembly, 8 vols. Oliver & Boyd, Ltd., Edinburgh, 1915–1950.

PRIMARY SOURCES, DOCUMENTS, AND RECORDS

Aymon, Jean, ed., *Tous les synodes nationaux des églises réformées de France*, 2 tomes. La Haye, 1710.

Baillie, Robert, *The Letters and Journals of Robert Baillie, A.M., Principal of the University of Glasgow*, D. Laing (ed.), 3 vols. Robert Ogle, Edinburgh, 1841–1842.

Bancroft, Richard, *Dangerous Positions and Proceedings published and practiced within this Iland of Brytaine, under the pretense to Reformation, and for the Presbyteriall Discipline.* Imprinted by John Wolfe, London, 1593.

—— *A Survay of the Pretended Holy Discipline.* Imprinted by John Wolfe, London, 1593.

[de Bèze, Théodore], *Histoire ecclésiastique des églises réformées au royaume de France*, edition nouvelle avec commentaire, notice bibliographique et tables des faits et des noms propres, par G. Baum et Ed. Cunitz, 3 tomes. Fischbacher, Paris, 1883–1889.

Bradford, William, *History of Plymouth Plantation, 1606–1646*, Wm. T. Davis (ed.). Charles Scribner's Sons, 1908.

Bucer, Martin, *Enarrationum in Evangelia, Matthaei, Marci & Lucae*, libri duo. Argentorati, Anno. MDXXVII.

—— *Praelectiones Doctiss. in Epistolam D. P. ad Ephesios*, . . . *Cantabrigiae in Anglia, Anno MD.L. & LI.* Basileae [1562].

—— *Opera Latini*, Tome XVbis, " Du Royaume de Jesus-Christ," édit critique de la traduction française de 1558, texte établi par François Wendel. Presses Universitaires de France, Paris, 1954.

Calderwood, David, *The True History of the Church of Scotland from the beginning of the Reformation.* . . . [Edinburgh] Printed in the Yeare 1680.

Calvin, John, *Joannis Calvini opera quae supersunt omnia*, edited by W. Baum, E. Cunitz, E. Reuss, 59 vols. Schwetschke et Filium, Brunswigae, 1863–1900

(Corpus Reformatorum).

—— *Institution de la Religion Chrestienne*, text établi et présenté par Jacques Pannier, 4 tomes. Société des Belles Lettres, Paris, 1936.

—— *Calvin: Institutes of the Christian Religion*, John T. McNeill (ed.), Ford Lewis Battles (tr.), 2 vols. The Westminster Press, 1960.

—— *The Commentaries of John Calvin*, various translators, 45 vols. Printed for the Calvin Translation Society, Edinburgh, 1844–1856.

—— *Calvin: Theological Treatises*, J. K. S. Reid (ed. and tr.). The Westminster Press, 1954.

Cartwright, Thomas, *The Second Reply of Thomas Cartwright to Dr. Whitgift Second Answer Touching Church Discipline.* [Zurich], 1574.

Chauncy, Isaac, *The Divine Institution of Congregational Churches, Ministry and Ordinances. . . .* Printed for Nathanael Hillis, London, 1697.

Christ on His Throne, or Christ's Church-Government briefly laid downe. Printed in the yeare 1640.

Church of Scotland, General Assembly, *Acts and Proceedings of the General Assemblies of the Kirk of Scotland from the year M.D.LX*, in 3 parts and Appendix with continuous pagination. Maitland Club and Bannantyne Society, Edinburgh, 1839–1845 (" The Universal Buik of the Kirk of Scotland ").

—— *The Acts of the General Assemblies of the Church of Scotland, for the Year 1638 to the Year 1649. . . .* George Mosman, printer to the Assembly [Edinburgh, 1691].

—— Synod of Aberdeen, *Selections from the Records.* Spaulding Club, Aberdeen, 1846.

—— Synod of Fife, *Ecclesiastical Records, 1611–87*, Abbotsford Club, Edinburgh, 1837.

Church of Scotland, St. Andrews Kirk-session, *Records of*

the *Kirk-session and Court of the Superintendent, 1559–1600,* 2 vols. Scottish Text Society, Edinburgh, 1889–1890.

Commission de l'histoire des églises wallonnes, *Livre synodal contenant les articles résolus dans les synodes des églises wallonnes des Pays-Bas,* Tome I (1563–1685), Leiden, 1896.

Constitutions and Canons Ecclesiasticall, Treated upon by the Bishop of London, . . . for the Province of Canterbury, and the rest of the Bishops and Clergy . . . in their Synod begun . . . 1603. Robert Barker, London, 1604.

Daneau, Lambert, *Isagoges Christianae, pars tertia, quae est, De Ecclesia . . . ,* editio secunda, apud Eustathium Vignon, M.D.LXXXVII.

Dell, William, *The Works of William Dell, Minister of the Gospel and Master of Gonvill and Caius College in Cambridge.* Joseph Sharpless, Philadelphia, 1816.

A Directory for the Publique Worship of God throughout the three Kingdoms of England, Scotland & Ireland; Ordered by the Lords and Commons assembled in Parliament, Dei Jovis 13 Marti 1644. Printed for Evan Taylor, Alexander Fifield, Ralph Smith, and John Field, London, 1644.

The Ecclesiastical Discipline of the Reformed Churches in France, . . . the Order whereby they are Ruled and Governed. Printed by N. Bourne, London, 1642.

Fenton, Geffroey, *A Forme of Christian Pollicie Drawne out of the French. . . .* H. Middelton for Rafe Newbery, London, 1574.

Fournier, M., et Engel, Ch., eds., *Gymnase, Académie et Université de Strasbourg, 1525–1621,* Fasc. I, " Les Statuts." Larose et Farcel, Paris/Strasbourg, 1894.

Foxe, John, *Acts and Monuments of Matters most special and memorable happening in the Church . . . ,* 3 vols. Seventh printing by Adam Islip, Foelix Kingston, and

Robert Young, London, 1632.

Frere, W. H., and Douglas, C. E., eds., *Puritan Manifestos: A Study of the Origin of the Puritan Revolt*. S.P.C.K., London, 1907.

[Fulke, William], *A Briefe and Plaine Declaration, . . . A Learned Discourse of Ecclesiastical Government*. Robert Waldegrave, London, 1584.

Gillespie, George, *An Assertion of the Government of the Church of Scotland*. Printed for James Bryson, Edinburgh, 1641.

—— *Aaron's Rod Blossoming: or the Divine Ordinance of Church-government Vindicated*. Printed by E. G. for Richard Whitacker, London, 1646.

—— *Notes of Debates and Proceedings of the Assembly of Divines and Other Commissioners at Westminster, February 1644 to January 1645*, David Meek (ed.). Ogle, Edinburgh, 1846.

[Guthrie, James], *A Treatise of Ruling Elders and Deacons*. Printed by George Mosman, Edinburgh, 1699 [original printing, 1652].

Henderson, Alexander, *The Unlawfulness and Danger of Limited Prelacie*. Printed [London] in the yeare 1641.

[Henderson, Alexander], *The Government and Order of the Church of Scotland*. Printed for James Bryson, Edinburgh, MDCXLII.

Herminjard, A. L., ed., *Correspondance des réformateurs dans les pays de langue française*, 9 tomes. Fischbacher, Paris, 1878–1897.

Heylyn, Peter, *A Full Relation of Two Journeys. . . .* Printed by E. Cotes for Henry Seile, London, MDCLVI.

Hooker, Thomas, *A Survey of the Summe of Church-Discipline. . . .* Printed by A. M. for John Bellamy, London, MDCXLVIII.

Husband, E., ed., *A Collection of all the Publicke Orders, Ordinances and Declarations of Both Houses of Par-*

liament, from the Ninth of March, 1642, until December, 1646. Printed by T. W. for Ed: Husband, London, 1646.

Knox, John, The Works of John Knox, David Laing (ed.), 6 vols. Johnstone & Hunter, Edinburgh, 1846–1864.

Knuttel, W. P. D., ed., Acta der Particuliere Synoden van Zuid-Holland, 1621–1700, 6 dln. Nijhoff, 's Gravenhage, 1908–1916.

Kuyper, H. H., De Post-Acta of Nahandelingen van de Nationale Synode van Dordrecht in 1618 en 1619 gehouden . . . een historische studie. Hövejer & Wormser, Amsterdam, 1899.

À Lasco, John, Opera tam edita quam inedita, A. Kuyper (ed.), 2 vols. Vol. I, Muller, Amsterdam, 1866; Vol. II, Nijhoff, Hage, 1866.

Lightfoot, John, The Whole Works of the Rev. John Lightfoot, D. D. . . ., John Rogers Pitman (ed.), 13 vols. J. F. Dove, London, MDCCCXXV.

L'Ordre du Collège et Leges Academiae Genevensis (Robert Estienne, Genève, 1559), Prof. Charles Le Fast (ed.) Reprint by J.-G. Fick, Genève, 1859.

Luther, Martin, Luthers Werke in Auswahl, Otto Clemen (ed.), Bde. 1 und 2. Walter de Gruyter & Co., Berlin, 1950 (Unter Mitwirkung von Albert Leitzmann).

Melville, James, The Autobiography and Diary of Mr. James Melville . . ., Robert Pitcairn (ed.), 2 vols. Published for the Wodrow Society, Edinburgh, 1842.

Miller, Alexander F., and Struthers, John, eds., The Minutes of the Sessions of the Westminster Assembly of Divines: from transcripts of the Originals. William Blackwood & Sons, Edinburgh and London, 1874.

Müller, Johannes, ed., Vor- und frühreformatische Schulordnungen und Schulverträge, 2 Abt. in 1 Bd. Raschke, Zschopau, 1885–1886.

De Nerec, Richard Jean, tr., Actes du Synode National, tenu a Dortrecht, l'An MDCXIIX & XIX, Mis en

François par Richard Jean de Nerec, Ministre de la parole de Dieu, 2 tomes, Chez Issac Elsevir. Imprimeur juré de l'Academie, Leyden, MDCXXIV.

Paget, John, *A Defense of Church-Government Exercised in Presbyteriall, Classicall, & Synodall Assemblies.* Printed by H. A. for Thomas Underhill, London, 1642.

Peel, Albert, ed., *Second Parte of a Register* (1593), 2 vols. Cambridge University Press, Cambridge, 1915.

—— and Carlson, Leland H., eds., *Cartwrightiana.* George Allen & Unwin, Ltd., London, 1951.

Peterkin, Alexander, *A Compendium of the Laws of the Church of Scotland,* 2 vols., 2d edition. Edinburgh Printing and Publishing Co., Edinburgh, 1837, 1840.

The Platforme of the Presbyterian Government with the forme of Church Worship . . . according to the Word of God, and the practice of our brethren of the Church of Scotland. Printed by R. Austin, London, 1644.

Quick, John, tr. and ed., *Synodicon in Gallia Reformata,* . . . 2 vols. Printed for T. Parkhurst and J. Robinson, London, 1692.

Records of the Presbyterian Church in the United States of America, 1706–1788. Presbyterian Board of Publications, Philadelphia, 1841.

Reitsma, Joh., en van Veen, S. D., eds., *Acta der Provinciale en Particuliere Synoden, gehouden in de Noordelijke Nederlanden gedurende de jaren 1572–1620,* 8 dln. J. B. Wolters, Groningen, 1892–1899.

Richter, Aemilius Ludwig, ed., *Die evangelischen Kirchenordnungen des sechszehnten Jahrhunderts,* 2 Bde. in 1. Landes-Industiecomptoires, Weimar, 1846.

Robinson, Hastings, *The Zurich Letters . . . during the reign of Queen Elizabeth,* translated and edited for the Parker Society, 1st and 2d series. Cambridge University Press, Cambridge, 1842, 1845.

—— *Original Letters, relative to the English Reforma-*

tion . . . *from the Archives of Zurich,* translated and edited for the Parker Society, 2 vols. Cambridge University Press, Cambridge, 1846, 1847.

Rollock, Robert, *In Epistolam S. Pauli Apostoli ad Ephesios . . . Commentarius.* Jacobum Stoer, Genevae, MDCVI.

Rutgers, F. L., ed., *Acta van de Nederlandsche Synoden der zestiende eeuw,* serie III, dl. V, in *Werken der Marnix Vereeniging.* Utrecht, 1870–1889.

Rutherford, Samuel, *The Due Right of Presbyteries. . . .* Printed by E. Griffin, for Richard Whitaker and Andrew Crook, London, 1644.

Saravia, Hadrianus, *Of the Diverse Degrees of the Ministers of the Gospel.* Printed by John Wolfe, London, 1592.

Schaff, Philip, *The Creeds of Christendom,* 3 vols., 4th edition, revised and enlarged. Harper & Brothers, 1919.

Steuart, Walter, of Pardovan, ed., *Collections and Observations Concerning the Worship, Discipline, and Government of the Church of Scotland,* 4 books. J. Findlay for A. Brown, Aberdeen, 1830.

[Travers, Walter], *Ecclesiasticae Disciplinae, et Anglicanae Ecclesiae . . . explicatio.* La Rochelle, 1574.

—— *A Full & Plaine Declaration,* Thomas Cartwright (tr.). [Heidelberg], 1574.

—— *A Defense of the Ecclesiastical Discipline ordayned of God to be used in his Church. Against an Replie of Maister Bridges, to a Brief and Plain Declaration of it. . . .* [London], 1588.

—— *A Directory of Church Government, Anciently contended for, and . . . practiced by the first non-conformists in the daies of Queen Elizabeth. Found in the study of . . . Thomas Cartwright, after his decease. . . .* Printed for John Wright, London, 1644.

A True Relation of the Forme and Government of the Kirk of Scotland. [London], 1640.

Walker, Williston, *The Creeds and Platforms of Congregationalism*. Charles Scribner's Sons, 1893.

[Westminster Assembly of Divines], "Minutes of the Sessions," microfilm of the original manuscripts and of a transcript made in 1872; original in the possession of Dr. Williams' Library, London; transcript in the possession of the Church of Scotland Library, Edinburgh.

[Whittingham, William], *A Brief Discourse of the Troubles at Frankfort, 1554–1558, A.D.*, Edward Arber (ed.). Privately printed, London, 1908.

Secondary Sources

Books

Ainslie, James L., *The Doctrine of Ministerial Order in the Reformed Churches of the Sixteenth and Seventeenth Centuries*. T. & T. Clark, Edinburgh, 1940.

Bacon, Benjamin W., *The Teaching Ministry for Tomorrow*. Yale University Press, 1923.

Bartels, Petrus, *Johannes à Lasco*. Fridericks, Elberfeld, 1860.

Bavinck, Herman, *Het Doctorenambt*. J. H. Kok, Kampen, 1899.

—— *Gereformeerde Dogmatiek*, 4 dln., 3d edition. J. H. Kok, Kampen, 1918.

Becker, Bruno, ed., *Autour de Michel Servet et de Sebastien Castellion*. H. D. Tjeenk Willink & Zoon, N.V., Haarlem, 1953.

Bellardi, Werner, *Geschichte der " Christlichen Gemeinschaft " in Strassburg (1546/1550)*. . . . M. Heinsius, Leipzig, 1934.

Berthault, E.-A., *Marthurin Cordier et l'ensiegnement chez les premiers calvinistes*. J. Bonhoure et Cie., Paris, 1876.

Bétant, E.-A., *Notice sur le collège de Rive*. J.-G. Fick, Genève, 1866.

Boeles, W. B. S., *Frieslands Hoogeschool en het Rijks Athenaeum te Franeker*, 2 dln.; dl. I, H. Kuipers, Leeuwarden, 1878; dl. II, A. Meijer, Leeuwarden, 1889.

Borgeaud, Charles, *Histoire de l'Université de Genève:* Tome I, " L'Academie de Calvin, 1559–1798." Georg & Cie., Genève, 1900.

Bourchenin, P.-Daniel, *Étude sur les académies protestantes en France au XVIᵉ et au XVIIᵉ siècle.* Grassart, Paris, 1882.

Bouvier, Augustus, *La Compagnie de Pasteurs de Genève.* J. Carey, Genève, 1878.

Brown, John, *The English Puritans.* Cambridge University Press, Cambridge, 1912.

Brown, P. Hume, *George Buchanan, Humanist and Reformer.* David Douglas, Edinburgh, 1890.

Burrage, Champlin, *Early English Dissenters in the Light of Recent Research (1550–1641)*, 2 vols. Cambridge University Press, Cambridge, 1912.

Calder, Isabel, *Activities of the Puritan Faction of the Church of England, 1625–1633.* S.P.C.K., London, 1957.

Carruthers, S. W., *The Everyday Work of the Westminster Assembly.* Published jointly by the Presbyterian Historical Society (American) and the Presbyterian Historical Society of England, Philadelphia, 1943.

Choisy, Eugène, *L'état chrétien calviniste à Genève; au temps de Théodore de Bèze.* Ch. Eggimann & Cie., Genève, 1902.

Congar, Yves M. J., O. P., *Lay People in the Church: A Study for a Theology of the Laity*, Donald Attwater (tr.). The Newman Press, 1957.

Courvoisier, Jacques, *La notion d'église chez Bucer.* Librairie Felix Alcan, Paris, 1933.

Corwin, E. T., Dubbs, J. H., and Hamilton, J. T., *A His-*

tory of the Reformed Church, Dutch; the Reformed
Church, German; and the Moravian Church in the
United States. Christian Literature Co., New York,
MDCCCXCV.

Cunningham, John, The Church History of Scotland, 2
vols., 2d edition. Jas. Thin, Edinburgh, 1882.

Dabin, Paul, S. J., Le sacerdoce royal de fidéles dans la tradition ancienne et moderne. Descelee, DeBrouwer &
Cie., Paris, 1950.

Dalton, Herman, John à Lasco, Life and Labors, M. J.
Evans (tr.) . Hodder, London, 1886.

Doekes, G., Het kerkelijk Doctorenambt. J. H. Kok,
Kampen, 1917.

Doumergue, Émile, Jean Calvin: les hommes et les choses
de son temps, 7 tomes. Tomes 1–5, Georges Bridel &
Cie., Lausanne, 1899–1917; Tomes 6–7, editions de
" La Cause." Neuilly sur Seine, 1929, 1927.

Dowey, E. A., Jr., The Knowledge of God in Calvin's Theology. Columbia University Press, 1952.

Ebrard, Fried. Clem., Die französisch-reformierte Gemeinde
in Frankfort a/M. 1554–1904. Richard Ecklin, Frankfort a/M., 1906.

Eby, Fred., and Arrowood, Chas. F., The Development of
Modern Education. Prentice-Hall, Inc., 1934.

Edgar, John, History of Early Scottish Education. Jas.
Thin, Edinburgh, 1893.

Eells, Hastings, Martin Bucer. Yale University Press, 1931.

Erichson, Alfred, L'église française de Strasbourg au seiz-
ième siècle. Fischbacher, Paris, 1886.

Fallaw, Wesner, Church Education for Tomorrow. The
Westminster Press, 1960.

Fazy, Henri, L'Instruction primaire à Genève. W. Kündig
& Fils, Genève, 1896.

Forsthoff, H., Die Reformation am Niederrhein. Evangel.
Presverbandes f. Rheinland, Essen, 1929.

Gabarel, Jean Pierre, Histoire de l'église de Genève, 3

tomes. Joël Cherbuliez, Genève, 1858.

Galama, S. H. M., *Het Wijsgerig Onderwijs aan de Hoge-school te Franeker 1585–1811*. T. Wever, Franeker, 1954.

Garrett, Christina H., *The Marian Exiles*. Cambridge University Press, Cambridge, 1938.

Geisendorf, P.-F., *Théodore de Bèze*. Labor et Fides, Genève, 1949.

Grant, James, *History of the Burgh Schools of Scotland*. William Collins Sons & Co., Ltd., Glasgow, 1876.

Graves, Frank P., *Peter Ramus and the Educational Reformation of the Sixteenth Century*. The Macmillan Company, 1912.

Haller, William, *The Rise of Puritanism*. Columbia University Press, 1938.

Harbison, E. H., *The Christian Scholar in the Age of the Reformation*. Charles Scribner's Sons, 1956.

Harnack, A., *Sources of the Apostolic Canons*, L. A. Wheatly (tr.). A. & C. Black, Ltd., London, 1895.

Henderson, G. D., *The Burning Bush*. St. Andrew Press, Edinburgh, 1957.

Heppe, Heinrich, *Geschichte der hessischen Generalsynoden von 1568–1582*, 2 Bde. in 1. Cassel, 1847.

——— *Reformed Dogmatics,* rev. and ed. by E. Bizer, G. T. Thomason (tr.). George Allen & Unwin, Ltd., London, 1950.

Herminjard, Louis, *Jean de Lasco et son ecclésiologie*. Georges Bridel & Cie., Lausanne, 1901.

Hetherington, W. M., *History of the Westminster Assembly of Divines*. Mark H. Newman, New York, 1843.

A History of the Westminster Assembly of Divines. . . . James Russell, publishing agent, Presbyterian Board of Publication, 1841.

Jansen, J. F., *Calvin's Doctrine of the Work of Christ*. James Clarke & Company, Ltd., Publishers, London, 1956.

Jenkins, Daniel, *The Gift of Ministry*. Faber & Faber, Ltd., London, 1947.

De Jong, Jan, *De Voorbereiding en Constitueering van het Kerkverband der Nederlandsche Gereformeerde Kerken in de zestiende eeuw*. Firma Jan Haan, Groningen, 1911.

Kaajan, H., *De Groote Synode van Dordrecht in 1618–1619*. N. V. de Standaard, Amsterdam, n.d.

Kingdon, Robert M., *Geneva and the Coming of the Wars of Religion in France, 1555–1563*. Librairie E. Droz, Genève, 1956.

Knappen, Marshall M., *Tudor Puritanism*. University of Chicago Press, Chicago, 1939.

Kuyper, A., Jr., *Johannes Maccovius*. D. Donner, Kampen, 1899.

Laas, Ernst, *Die Pädagogik J. Sturms*. Weidmann, Berlin, 1872.

Leach, A. F., *English Schools at the Reformation*. Archibald Constable, Westminster, 1896.

Lechler, G. V., *Geschichte der presbyterial-und synodalverfassung seit der Reformation*. D. Nootheven van Goor, Leiden, 1854.

Le Coultre, Jules, *Mathurin Cordier: et les origines de la pédagogie protestantes. . . .* Secretariat de l'Université. Neuchâtel, 1926.

Leishman, Thomas, *The Westminster Directory*. William Blackwood & Sons, Ltd., Edinburgh, 1901.

McCrie, Thomas, *Life of Andrew Melville*, 2 vols. William Blackwood & Sons, Ltd., Edinburgh, 1824.

MacGregor, Janet, *Scottish Presbyterian Polity*. Oliver & Boyd, Ltd., Edinburgh, 1926.

McNeill, John T., *The History and Character of Calvinism*. Oxford University Press, 1954.

Maxwell, W. D., *The Liturgical Portions of the Genevan Service Book*. Oliver & Boyd, Ltd., Edinburgh, 1931.

Moens, Wm. J. C., *The Walloons and Their Church at*

Norwich, 1565–1832. Huguenot Society of London, Lymington, 1888.

Moore, Martin, *Memoirs of the Life and Character of the Rev. John Eliot.* Boston, 1822.

Morison, Samuel Eliot, *The Puritan Pronaos.* New York University Press, 1936.

Morris, Edward D., *Theology of the Westminster Symbols.* Champlin Press, Columbus, Ohio, 1900.

Mylonis, G. E., and Raymond, Doris, eds., *Studies Presented to David M. Robinson,* 2 vols. Washington University Press, 1953.

Niebuhr, H. Richard, and Williams, Daniel D., eds., *The Ministry in Historical Perspectives.* Harper & Brothers, 1956.

Nobbs, Douglas, *Theocracy and Toleration.* Cambridge University Press, Cambridge, 1938.

Nuttall, Geoffrey F., *Visible Saints: The Congregational Way 1640–1660.* Basil Blackwell & Mott, Ltd., Oxford, 1957.

Pannier, Jacques, *Calvin à Strasbourg.* Librairie Istra, Strasbourg/Paris, 1925.

——— *Calvin et l'espiscopat.* Librairie Istra, Strasbourg, 1927.

——— *Les origines de la Confession de Foi et la Discipline des églises réformées de France.* Librairie Felix Alcan, Paris, 1936.

Pearson, A. F. S., *Thomas Cartwright and Elizabethan Puritanism, 1535–1603.* Cambridge University Press, Cambridge, 1925.

Post, Regnerus R., *Scholen en Onderwijs in Nederland gedurende de Middeleeuwen.* Het Spectrum, Utrecht, 1954.

Rashdall, Hastings, *The Universities of Europe in the Middle Ages,* 3 vols., new edition, F. M. Powicke and A. B. Emden (eds.). Oxford University Press, London, 1936.

von Raumer, Karl, *Geschichte der Pädagogik,* 3 Bde. Gottlieb, Stuttgart, 1857.

Reicke, Emil, *Der Lehrer.* E. Deiderichs, Leipzig, 1901.

Reid, H. M. B., *The Divinity Principals in the University of Glasgow, 1545–1654.* Jas. Maclehose and Sons, Glasgow, 1917.

Reid, J. K. S., *The Biblical Doctrine of the Ministry.* Oliver & Boyd, Ltd., Edinburgh, 1955.

Robbins, C. L., *Teachers in Germany in the Sixteenth Century.* Teachers College, Columbia University, 1912.

De Schickler, Baron Ferdinand, *Les églises du refuge en angleterre,* 3 tomes. Fischbacher, Paris, 1892.

Schmidt, Karl, *La Vie et les traveaux de Jean Sturm.* C. F. Schmidt, Strasbourg, 1855.

Schokking, H., *De Leertucht in de Gereformeerde Kerk van Nederland tusschen 1570 en 1620.* J. Clausen, Amsterdam, 1902.

Seitz, Charles, *Joseph-Juste Scaliger et Genève.* Wyss et Duchêne, Genève, 1895.

Smart, James D., *The Teaching Ministry of the Church.* The Westminster Press, 1954.

Strobel, A. G., *Histoire du gymnase protestant de Strasbourg.* Heitz, Strasbourg, 1838.

Strohl, Henri, *Le protestantisme en Alsace.* Éditions Oberlin, Strasbourg, 1950.

Strong, John, *A History of Secondary Education in Scotland.* Clarendon Press, Oxford, 1909.

Strype, John, *Annals of the Reformation and Establishment of Religion . . .,* 2d edition. Tho. Edlin, London, MDCCXXV.

——— *Ecclesiastical Memorials . . .,* 3 vols. in 6. Clarendon Press, Oxford, MDCCCXXII.

Tanner, Joseph R., *English Constitutional Conflicts of the Seventeenth Century, 1603–1689.* Cambridge University Press, Cambridge, 1948.

Torrance, T. F., *Royal Priesthood*. Oliver & Boyd, Ltd., Edinburgh, 1955.

Trinterud, L. J., *The Forming of an American Tradition*. The Westminster Press, 1949.

Usher, R. G., ed., *The Presbyterian Movement in the Reign of Queen Elizabeth*. Camden Society, London, 1905.

Vallet de Viriville, Auguste, *Histoire de l'instruction publique en Europe*, Tome I, " Administration du moyenâge et la renaissance." Paris, 1849.

Visser 't Hooft, W. A., *The Pressure of Our Common Calling*. Doubleday & Co., Inc., 1959.

De Vries, Herman, *Genève pépinière du Calvinisme hollandais*. Fragniere Frères, Fribourg (Suisse), 1918.

Vuilleumier, Henri, *Histoire de l'église réformée du Pays de Vaud*, 4 tomes. Éditions la Concorde, Lausanne, 1927–1940.

Warfield, Benj. B., *The Westminster Assembly and Its Work*. Oxford University Press, 1931.

Watson, Foster, *The Old Grammar School*. Cambridge University Press, Cambridge, 1916.

Wedgwood, C. V., *The King's Peace, 1637–1641*. The Macmillan Company, 1955.

Weis, Fred. Lewis, *Colonial Clergy and Colonial Churches of New England*. Lancaster, Mass., 1936.

Wendel, François, *Calvin: sources et évolution de sa pensée religieuse*. Presses Universitaires de France, Paris, 1950.

——— *L'Église de Strasbourg: sa constitution et son organisation, 1532–1535*. Presses Universitaires de France, Paris, 1942.

Williams, George H., ed., *The Harvard Divinity School*. The Beacon Press, Inc., 1954.

Wright, Alexander, *The History of Education and the Old Parish School of Scotland*. J. Menzies & Co., Edinburgh, 1898.

Articles

Aubert, H.-V., " Nicolas Colladon et les registres de la Compagnie des Pasteurs et Professeurs," *Bulletin* (Société d'histoire et d'archéologies de Genève), II (1898).

Bonet-Maury, Gaston, " John à Lasco and the Reformation in Poland, 1499–1560," *American Journal of Theology*, 4 (1900), pp. 314–327.

Bouttier, Michel, et Roux, Hébert, " Les diverses formes du ministère de docteur," *Foi et Vie*, Paris (April, 1957), pp. 419–429.

Burrell, S. A., " The Covenant Idea as a Revolutionary Symbol," *Church History*, XXVII:4 (1958), pp. 338–350.

D'Espine, Henri, " Ministères ecclésiastiques divers et consecration," *Revue d'histoire et de philosophie religieuses*, Ann. 36ᵉ:3 (1956), pp. 179–185.

Duley, John S., " The Work of the Church in the University," *The Christian Scholar*, XLII:3 (1959), pp. 201–214.

Fletcher, R. J., " The Reformation and the Inns of Court," *St. Paul's Ecclesiological Society Transactions*, V (1905), pp. 149–157.

Fredericq, Paul, " L'Université calviniste de Gand, 1578–1584," *Revue de l'instruction publique de Belgique*, XXI (1878), pp. 245–262.

—— " L'enseignement public des calvinistes à Gand," *Travaux du cours practique d'histoire nationale*, 1ᵉ fasc. (1883), pp. 51–121.

Green, Theodore A., " Ecclesiastical Organization of Geneva in the Time of Calvin," *Journal of the Presbyterian Historical Society*, XI:8 (1923), pp. 305–367.

Horn, Henry E., " Communication," *The Christian Scholar*, XLIII:1 (1960), pp. 8–10.

Kist, N. C., "De onderteekening der Formulieren door Hoogleeraren en Doctoren," *Archief voor Kerk. Geschiednes,* IX (1837), p. 473.

McNeill, John T., "The Doctrine of the Ministry in Reformed Theology," *Church History,* XII (1943), pp. 77–97.

——— "Thirty Years of Calvin Study," *Church History,* XVII (1948), pp. 207–240; XVIII (1949), p. 241.

Panchaud, Georges, "Les écoles vaudoises à la fin du régime bernois," *Bibliothèque historique vaudoise,* XII (1952).

Pauck, Wilhelm, "Calvin and Butzer," *Journal of Religion,* IX (1929), pp. 237–256.

Reymond, Maxime, "Les écoles dans le Pays du Vaud avant 1536," *Bibliothèque universelle et revue suisse,* LXX:208 (April, 1913), pp. 155–164.

Sewall, Samuel, "A Brief Survey of the Congregational Churches and Ministers in the County of Middlesex, and in Chelsea in the County of Suffolk, Ms.," *American Quarterly Register,* 11 (1838), pp. 45–55, 174–197, 248–299; 12 (1839), pp. 234 f.; 14 (1841), pp. 251 f., 393 f.

Solt, Leo F., "Anti-intellectualism in the Puritan Revolution," *Church History,* XXV:4 (December, 1956), pp. 306–316.

Strohl, Henri, "La théorie et practique des quatre ministères à Strasbourg avant l'arrivée de Calvin," *Bulletin, Société de l'histoire du protestantisme française,* LXXXIV (1935), pp. 123 ff.

Torrance, T. F., "Kingdom and Church in the Thought of Bucer," *Journal of Ecclesiastical History,* VI:1 (April, 1955), pp. 48–59.

Trinterud, L. J., "The Ministry in the Thought of John Calvin," *McCormick Speaking,* IV (April Supplement, 1951).

Vuy, Jules, "Notes historiques sur le collège de Versonnex

et documents inédits relatifs à l'instruction public, à Genève, avant 1535," *Mémoires de l'Institut National Genevois*, XII (1869).

OFFICIAL PUBLICATIONS

Corwin, Charles E., *A Manual of the Reformed Church in America, 1628–1922*, 5th edition revised. Board of Publications and Bible-school Work of the Reformed Church in America, 1922.

Cox, Jas. T., *Practice and Procedure in the Church of Scotland*, 2d imp. William Blackwood & Sons, Ltd., Edinburgh/London, 1935.

Ecclesiastical Polity, the Government and Communion Practiced by the Congregational Churches in the United States, Which were Represented . . . in a National Council at Boston, 1865, 2d edition. Congregational Publ. Soc., Boston, 1879.

Evangelical and Reformed Church, *The Constitution and By-Laws of the Evangelical and Reformed Church*, Adopted by the General Synod, June 16, 1936, Declared in effect by the General Synod, June 30, 1940, and as Amended to June, 1950, n.p., n.d.

Reformed Church in America, *The Constitution of the Reformed Dutch Church in the United States of America*. Wm. Durell, New York, 1793.

——— *The Constitution of the Reformed Church in America*, revised to June 30, 1957. Board of Education, Dept. of Publication, Reformed Church in America, New York/Grand Rapids, Michigan, 1957.

Reformed Church in the United States, *The Church Member's Hand-book*, Containing the Doctrines, Government, Discipline, Customs, and Constitution of the Reformed Church in the U.S. E. R. Good & Bros., Tiffin, Ohio, 1882.

Synod of New York and Philadelphia, *A Draught of a Plan*

of Government and Discipline for the Presbyterian Church of North America. Proposed by a committee appointed for that purpose; 300 copies printed. Francis Bailey, Philadelphia, MDCCLXXXVI.

—— *A Draught of the Form of Government and Discipline of the Presbyterian Church in the United States of America,* proposed by the Synod of New York and Philadelphia for the consideration of the Presbyteries and Churches under their care; 1,000 copies printed. S. & J. Loudon, New York, MDCCLXXXVII.

The United Presbyterian Church in the United States of America, *The Constitution.* The Office of the General Assembly, Philadelphia, 1958.

—— General Assembly, *Minutes:* Part I, Journal and Supplement. The Office of the General Assembly, Philadelphia, 1958.

UNPUBLISHED DISSERTATIONS

Harris, Carl Vernon, " Origen of Alexandria's Interpretation of the Teacher's Function in the Early Christian Hierarchy and Community." Unpublished Ph.D. dissertation, Graduate School of Arts and Sciences, Duke University, 1952.

Henderson, Robert W., " The Doctoral Ministry in the Reformed Tradition: A Study of the History of the Second of the Four Ministries Recognized by John Calvin." Unpublished Ph.D. dissertation, Graduate School of Arts and Sciences, Harvard Divinity School, Harvard University, 1959.

Taylor, George Aiken, " John Calvin, the Teacher: The Correlation Between Instruction and Nurture Within Calvin's Concept of Communion." Unpublished Ph.D. dissertation, Graduate School of Arts and Sciences, Duke University, 1953.

Index

Aberdeen, University of, 134, 139, 143
Abernathy, Adam, 97
Academic regulations, 94
Adamson, John, 155
Adamson, Archbishop Patrick, 143 f.
Admonition to the Parliament, An, 171 f.
Agabus, 30
Ainslie, James L., 11 n. 10
À Lasco, John, 99 ff., 103, 105, 134 n. 14, 176, 218
Albany Convention, 237
Allen, Thomas, 190
Alting, Hendirck, 114
Alvey, Richard, 164 n. 23
American Association of Theological Education, 7
American Congregationalism, 233–238
American Presbyterianism, 221–227
Amsterdam, University of, 113 ff.
Ancien, 32, 58, 72 nn. 2–3. *See also* Elder
Andreae, Tobias, 124

Anjou, Synod of, 85, 92, 96
Anti-intellectualism, 86, 213
Apostle, 59
Arbuthnet, Alexander, 143, 146
Arcerius, Sixtinus, 124
Arminius, Jacob, 117
Articles . . . de l'Église . . . à Genève (1537), 32, 45
D'Aubus, Charles, 97

Baduel, Claude, 66
Baillie, Robert, 155, 215
Bancroft, Richard, 182 ff., 187
Baptist, John the, 28
Barlaeus, Caspar, 117
Basle, 162
Bavinck, Herman, 11, 16, 19
Becon, Thomas, 164
Bédrot, Jacques, 38
Benoist, Jean, 85 n. 40, 86, 89, 96 f.
Benoist, Samuel, 97
Berauld, François, 67
Berchet, Toussaint, 97
Berne, 49–51
Beroalde, Mattieu, 66